Freemasonry in Mexico: A Secret Heritage

FREEMASONRY IN MEXICO: A SECRET HERITAGE

The Impact of Freemasonry on the Secular and Liberal Discourse in Mexico

Guillermo De Los Reyes

Translated from the Spanish by Bradley L. Drew

Westphalia Press
An Imprint of the Policy Studies Organization
Washington, DC

Westphalia Press
An imprint of Policy Studies Organization
1367 Connecticut Avenue NW
Washington, D.C. 20036
info@ipsonet.org

ISBN: 978-1-63723-534-8

Daniel Gutierrez-Sandoval, Executive Director
PSO and Westphalia Press

Updated material and comments on this edition
can be found at the Westphalia Press website:
www.westphaliapress.org

To José Antonio de los Reyes González (†)
and
Magdalena Heredia Alvarez (†),
for showing me the path of life

To Dr. Paul J. Rich,
*for guiding me toward the study
of Freemasonry*

To Stephen,
for walking beside me

ACKNOWLEDGMENTS

This project was made possible thanks to the support and encouragement of many individuals and institutions. I am grateful to the University of Houston for financial assistance through research grants and to the Policy Studies Organization for funding archival visits in Europe, Mexico, and the United States. I also wish to thank the staff of the numerous libraries and archives I consulted, including the Archivo General de la Nación in Mexico City; the Library of Congress and the Scottish Rite House of the Temple in Washington, D.C.; the Masonic Library at the Grand Lodge of Pennsylvania in Philadelphia; the Library at the Grand Orient de France in Paris; and several university and Masonic libraries.

My gratitude goes to colleagues and students from the University of Houston, as well as to friends who offered constructive feedback, guidance, and encouragement throughout this project. I am equally thankful to those who engaged in rich discussions at conferences and symposia where I presented portions of this work. Special thanks to my mentor and collaborator, Dr. Paul J. Rich, and to my dear family of scholars of Freemasonry—*masonólogos*—who have inspired and supported me throughout the years. I am especially grateful to Bradley L. Drew for his skillful translation work and for being a generous colleague throughout this process. Thank you also to Rahima Schwenkbeck, Ph.D. and Daniel Gutiérrez of Westphalia Press for believing in this project.

Finally, I dedicate this book to the memory of my mother, Magdalena (*Chatita*) Heredia, whose love and example continue to inspire me. I am also deeply grateful to *mi querida familia por su apoyo y amor incondicional*, to the Johnson family for always showing interest in my research, and especially to Stephen for his unwavering support and love, *¡Sí se pudo!*

TABLE OF CONTENTS

PROLOGUE

INITIATION

My research into Freemasonry began in response to the academic need for a more thorough examination and better understanding of this controversial and enigmatic organization. I was inspired to immerse myself deeply into the study of Masonic lodges by the excellent works of Paul J. Rich, José Antonio Ferrer Benimeli, and Margaret Jacob, among other scholars, who explore Freemasonry in various parts of the world in an objective and scholarly way.

Jacob, for example, proposes that Freemasonry was one of the first organizations to promote civil society in Continental Europe and that it later extended throughout the world, influencing the political decisions of various European nations as well as both the political and cultural discourses of the Enlightenment. Rich argues that during the period of British control in the Persian Gulf, Masonic lodges contributed to the education of the elite, promoting the establishment and maintenance of imperial control in the region. On the other hand, Ferrer Benimeli proposes that Freemasonry in Europe, particularly in Spain, broke with seemingly inalterable traditions in society (family, the Church, trade unions, corporations, holidays, religious processions, etc.), broadening democratic accessibility and promoting plurality in religious, political, ideological, and social terms.[1]

Although these authors were not writing specifically about Mexico, the ideas they propose may be applied to that country by substituting the appropriate elements and nuance peculiar and exclusive to the region, along with the theoretical-methodological proposals that would contribute to a serious analysis of Freemasonry in Mexico.

The Masons have been present in Mexico since before it won its independence from Spain. The organization has witnessed the transformations Mexico has undergone over the centuries; such transformations have, in turn, served to influence the organization's development. This role

---

1   See Margaret Jacob, *Living the Enlightenment: Freemasonry and Politics in Eighteenth-Century Europe*, Oxford, Oxford University Press, 1991; Paul Rich, *Elixir of Empire*, London, Regency Press, 1993; José Antonio Ferrer Benimeli, coord., *Masonería, política y sociedad, III Simposium de metodología aplicada a la historia de la masonería española*, Zaragoza, Centro de Estudios Históricos de la Masonería Española, 1987.

played by the Masonic lodges—at times as leading characters, at other times in a supporting role—piqued my interest to know specifically what kind of impact this international organization had, and continues to have, in the construction of the Mexican secular discourse. The Masonic lodges served a function as political parties – not only in Mexico (the *yorkinos*—York Rite—and the *escoceses*—Scottish Rite) but also in the United States (the "Anti-Masonic Party" was the first political party in the U.S.) and in other parts of the world.[2] Freemasonry's secretive nature and its involvement in political and social events in various countries have earned them many enemies, who oppose its ideas and proposals. This has engendered even greater secrecy on the part of the association and an impassioned stance on the part of its sympathizers. Both its detractors and its defenders write that Masonry played a key role in the French Revolution, the American Revolution, and the Mexican War for Independence, as well as similar wars in many other Latin American countries. Some of these claims will be discussed and analyzed throughout this book, with the purpose of debunking some narratives that cannot be supported with evidence and exploring the effect they have had on the organization.

Freemasonry in Mexico is a very controversial topic and, more often than not, tendentious. For this reason, I should state that I do not belong to any Masonic or co-Masonic lodge, nor am I a member of any organization that historically has been either an enemy or a critic of Masonry. Although I was baptized in the Catholic faith, I am not a practicing Catholic, so in no way did this circumstance affect my research. When I was a student in junior high and high school, I participated in cultural events sponsored by the Masons, specifically contests of speech and recitation, most of which were held in Tampico, Ciudad Madero, and Ciudad Victoria, Tamaulipas, in the 1980s. I competed in these events as my school's representative in regional, zonal, and statewide competitions; as such, I was sent to other events of that type. Then, as now, I was invited several times to join the Masons. In those years, I declined to join out of fear of the unknown and ignorance; nor have I joined to this date, since after spending over 20 years studying this organization, I have preferred to

---

2   Jean-Pierre Bastian argues that Masonic lodges were the first forms of "pre-politics of association, and that [they] preceded the formation of political parties in the modern sense of the word." Jean-Pierre Bastian, (comp)., *Protestantes, liberales y francomasones. Sociedades de ideas y modernidad en América Latina, siglo XIX*, México, Fondo de Cultura Económica, 1993, 8.

study it as a "profane."[3] Let me repeat: Neither my affiliations nor beliefs abetted any sort of prejudgment concerning the topic. My main goal in writing this book is to present the reader with a perspective on Freemasonry in the most objective manner possible.

Another key element that has awakened my interest in studying this topic is that, in Mexico, discussion of Freemasonry's role in the nation's history is normally limited to the fact that the Scottish Rite Masons and the York Rite Masons fought with each other during the early years of the new republic. Beyond that, there is little mention of it; there is no serious reconsideration of the topic within the works of general history of Mexico; nothing that encompasses the long-term effects of the fraternity in that country; nothing that equates to similar investigations of Freemasonry's influence on the history of other countries, such as the United States, Spain, the United Kingdom, and France, among others.[4] If a survey were carried out to discover how many people know about these groups, it would surely reveal that the prevalent level of knowledge is next to nothing.

By the same token, one should not overlook the fact that many other countries also manifest great ignorance about this organization, and much of what is believed about it is scarcely reliable. Due to the fact that so many of the world's rulers either were or are Masons (George Washington, Simón Bolívar, Emilio Castelar, Benito Juárez, Porfirio Díaz, Francisco I. Madero, Lázaro Cárdenas, and a multitude of others), it is widely held that in order to become a country's president or prime minister one must be a member of this institution. This is an unfounded conjecture that has taken shape over the years.

---

3   Term used by Masons to refer to non-Masons.

4   See Mark C. Carnes, *Secret Ritual and Manhood in Victorian America*, New Haven, Yale University Press, 1989; Mary Ann Clawson, *Constructing Brotherhood: Class, Gender, and Fraternalism*, Princeton, Princeton University Press, 1989; Anthony D. Fels, "*The Square and Compass: San Francisco's Freemasons and American Religion, 1870-1900,*" Doctoral Dissertation, Stanford University, 1985; Allen E. Roberts, *Freemasonry in American History*, Richmond, Macoy, 1985; José A. Ferrer Benimeli, *La masonería española en el siglo XVIII*, Madrid, Siglo XXI, 1974; José A. Ferrer Benimeli, *Masonería española contemporánea, vol. I, 1800–1868*, Madrid, Siglo XXI, 1980. "The level of research into the organization is low, and it deals mainly with lodges' local history or with the recollections of popular heroes or other famous persons who were Freemasons." Michel Brodsky, "Breaking the Ring," Brochure circulated privately at a conference of the lodge Quatuor Coronati, *Ars Quatuor Coronatorum*, num. 2076, November 10, 1994, 3.

Some historical texts note that in the nineteenth century, Freemasonry's involvement in the forming of new nations was of great relevance. They refer to various Masonic groups and their involvement as certain events unfolded, but these texts do not say precisely what these groups' roles were in Mexico's independence, in the Mexican Revolution, in the War of *Reforma*, nor their exact part in the separation of Church and State or in the country's secularization. Seldom is there a detailed explanation of these groups' activities. Similarly, it is never clearly explained exactly what Freemasonry is, nor what its functions, objectives, and purposes are. It is for these reasons that this book is an attempt to study Freemasonry's development in Mexico, from the group's inception to 2010, with the objective of understanding its different periods and cycles in Mexico. This book does not attempt to cover every single aspect of Masonic history in Mexico; rather, it is an analysis and exploration of key passages in which the Masons played a key role vis-à-vis the impact the Masonic organization has had on the secularization of the Mexican Republic. In like fashion, this is an attempt to study Freemasonry's development in relation to other historical events important to the construction of the Mexican nation, as well as to assess the influence of this formative process on the Mexican Masonic organization, and vice versa.

Given the great degree of interest in Freemasonry and secret societies generally in recent years, thanks to such publications as *The Da Vinci Code* and Hollywood productions like *National Treasure*, other works that go beyond fiction must be brought to light. Although it may be important to have a corpus of books with the purpose of fictionalizing Freemasonry, it is necessary to study it from another perspective. Consequently, despite being an academic work on Freemasonry in Mexico, this book aims to contribute to any work on Mexican history and/or Masonic studies. I hope that historical scholars in Mexico and Latin America, as well as experts in the national and post-national cultural movements, will find information in this book that is of value and that complements their own research. It may be of similar interest to scholars in the fields of ritual, political ritual, and religion. In general, I hope that those interested in this topic, whether friend or foe of this organization, will gain a new perspective on it that will provide them with information meaningful to their continued interest in this association.

Note on the Translation

Freemasonry in Mexico: A Secret Heritage was first published in Spanish under the title of *Herencias secretas: Masonería, política y Sociedad en México* in 2009 by the Benemérita Universidad Autónoma de Puebla University Press. A few years ago, inspired by the need to have more English-language works on Mexico's Freemasonry, I contacted Bradley L. Drew, an outstanding translator with whom I have worked on several prior projects. During the years working with Mr. Drew on this new cycle, we had numerous meetings and innumerable productive discussions to ensure the final product conveys the nuances of this complex topic. It is important to note that I have updated and added new information to this new edition. The additions have been either translated and/or edited by Mr. Drew. Thus, the English version does not represent a literal translation of *Herencias secretas*; it is indeed a new version, corrected and augmented from its previous life.

INTRODUCTION

SECRET HERITAGE

"Not even the vertigo of incessant transformation fully
makes fundamental tradition anachronistic, upheld as
it is in writings, in the quest for knowledge, in liberty's
tolerance and customs."[5]

C arlos Monsiváis, in his book *Las herencias ocultas de la Reforma liber-al del siglo XIX* (The Hidden Heritage of the 19ᵗʰ Century's Liberal Reform), revisits a group of liberal writers of the nineteenth century in Mexico in order that their legacy not pass unnoticed. He states:

> Among the truths of forgetful modernity, ubiquitous functional illiteracy, and the inaccessibility of books and periodical collaborations from another time, too many of the seminal works of the 20ᵗʰ century's great writers have fallen by the wayside.[6]

Monsiváis's main argument in *Las herencias ocultas* has inspired me to carefully consider not only the great number of writers but also individuals, political, social, and cultural organizations, and movements, that have played vital roles in the formative process of the Mexican nation, particularly those that have focused on creating a secular state and have been promoters of laicism. Of these, many have been relegated to obscurity or, if they have been studied, have not received the attention they deserve. In some cases, this is due to their not forming part of Mexico's official history; in others, it is because they have not attracted the interest of consecrated intellectuals or scholars.

Such is the case of Freemasonry, an organization that, early in the twentieth century, had a great impact on the liberal movement that began before the turn of that century. Despite this group having contributed significantly to the formation of secular discourses and having had great political prominence, it is one that has not been studied in depth. It is, therefore, this book's objective to provide a closer study of the impact the

---

5   Carlos Monsiváis, *Herencias ocultas de la Reforma liberal del siglo XIX*, Mexico, Random House Mondori, 2006 [2000], 12.

6   Ibid., 11.

Masonic lodges have had in the development of formative and post-na-
tionalist discourses of the nineteenth century and the post-revolutionary
discourses of the twentieth. In addition, I will attempt to bring Freemasonry into the light without considering it a forbidden topic, as has been
conceived by the Spanish/Mexican Inquisition and the Catholic Church,
among others, and to study this organization's impact on the political history of Mexico. As opposed to customary approaches to this topic, this
book asserts that Freemasonry, in its countless aspects, has been a transcendental force in Mexico since the end of the eighteenth century, in
the time of Mexico's War for Independence from Spain, and through the
nineteenth and twentieth centuries.

In this work I argue that Masonry, by means of its lodges, played a key role
in defining the canon of national thought which, in turn, was vital to the
creation of the liberal and secular State, as well as to the development of
rather anticlerical sentiments (among the laity) that promoted secularization, and which endured until the end of the twentieth century. This participation manifested itself in the direct or indirect formation of political
and lettered officials who influenced the national discourses.

Masonry's participation in Mexico unfolded privately, transgressively,
subversively, and/or secretly—and, at times, publicly. Their strategy:
Since its membership was largely secret, this proved of great advantage
to the organization's impact on the national discourses of the nineteenth
century. In like fashion, Freemasonry's participation in Mexico was due
in large part to its forerunners in Europe; as Margaret C. Jacob accurately points out, and as this book corroborates, these Masonic lodges were
the first forms of modern civil society,[7] and in the case of Mexico they
became the first political forces or proto-political parties (*yorkinos y escoceses*), as is explained in Chapter 2.

One possibility that has been largely ignored that is posited here is that
in a Mexican society where opportunities for education were restricted
for economic and social reasons, Masonic lodges provided a secure space
in which political and philosophical topics could be discussed, oratory
practiced, and networks of political influence forged. Likewise, they provided a place for young members with political aspirations to improve
their rhetorical and organizational skills and to have access to the arena of

---

7   Margaret Jacob, *Living the Enlightenment: Freemasonry and Politics in Eighteenth-Century Europe*, Oxford, Oxford University Press, 1991, 4.

government. The close relationship of many Mexican presidents—Guadalupe Victoria, Vicente Guerrero, Valentín Gómez Farías, Benito Juárez, Porfirio Díaz, Francisco I. Madero, Lázaro Cárdenas, and Miguel Alemán, among others—with the Masons illustrates this idea.

On the other hand, the Masons served to counterbalance the influence of the Catholic Church, which constructed a clerical discourse that it used over centuries to maintain the status quo, especially when this institution felt threatened. Since the Masonic lodges served a function as political parties, they promoted the development of a secular-anticlerical discourse that contributed enormously to liberal and lay thought in Mexico. The Church's clerical influence and the anticlerical aspect of Freemasonry, particularly with regard to their constant confrontation, censure, and subversive criticism, gave rise to a mixed lay/religious discourse that combined the conservative traditions, ideas, and morality imposed by the Church with the liberal ideas of Freemasonry. In other words, the Masons contributed to the formation of a hybrid discourse that bore influence upon the national imaginary. This discourse manifests itself as secular in the political realm but with hybrid nuances owing to religious influence culturally.

This book's principal focus is the analysis of the origins of the secular liberal discourse and how that continues to develop. Nevertheless, while it is not the primary purpose of this work, I will emphasize the conservative-religious narrative as well as the mixed type of secular-religious, mixed discourse that has so marked Mexican political culture.[8]

UNVEILING THE SECRETS

When we take up the topic of Freemasonry, it is important to note one's sources, due to the secretive, discreet, or hermetic nature that characterizes this organization. One reason Freemasonry has been so little investigated is the difficulty encountered in compiling the materials necessary to reconstruct and interpret its history. This, in fact, was one of the greatest obstacles at the beginning of this project. In Mexico, neither national ar-

---

8   See Guillermo de los Reyes, "The Cross and the Compass: The Influence of the Catholic Religion and Masonry in the Formation of the Mexican Political Thought," in: Nicolás Kanellos, ed., *Recovering Hispanic Religious Thought and Practice of the United States*, Cambridge, Cambridge Scholars Publishing, 2007, 8-24; Paul Rich and Guillermo de los Reyes, "Freemasonry's Educational Role," *American Behavioral Scientist*, no. 40, June-July, 1997, 957-967.

chives nor private records preserve much of the historical material relating to the Masonic lodges. As a consequence, the researcher's work soon becomes primordial, since in order to be able to create a narrative that allows a better telling of this organization's history, every piece of data must be hunted down and collected like a piece of a puzzle.

Despite this limitation, it ultimately proved possible to assemble reliable information by visiting a great many Masonic lodges within Mexico and in other countries. In Mexico: Tampico, Ciudad Madero, Mexico City, Puebla, Mérida, Zacatecas, Colima, Oaxaca, and Monterrey; in the United States: San Diego, San Francisco, New York, Philadelphia, Albuquerque, Santa Fe, Houston, El Paso, San Antonio, and Washington, D.C.; in Spain: Barcelona, Madrid, and Seville; in France: Paris; and in the United Kingdom: London and Edinburgh. In these lodges it was possible to consult a diversity of primary sources such as documents, letters, and essays. In the archives of lodges in countries outside of Mexico, documents issued from within Mexico were reviewed, the majority of which contained valuable information about the circumstances surrounding Freemasonry in that country across various historical periods. Also, secondary sources such as books, magazines, and monographs were consulted, and a number of Masons were interviewed. It should also be mentioned that the lodges that best preserve their history are those of the United States and Europe.

The lodges in Mexico have not sufficiently preserved their history, particularly their early history, from the end of the eighteenth century through the nineteenth. This was due in large part to the persecution brought by the Inquisition and the prohibition of Masonic practices. Later, the political chaos of the times contributed further to the difficulty of lodges' keeping records and thus preserving their history. During the regime of Porfirio Díaz, a few lodges attempted to safeguard their stories, but the struggles and chaos of the Mexican Revolution prevented such projects from crystallizing. This does not mean that there were no lodges concerned with the preservation of their historical memory, and which have, in fact, saved part of that heritage; however, these efforts are not sufficient sources from which to reconstruct Freemasonry's past in Mexico. For a more complete investigation, it was necessary to search among other archives and to collect information from a wider range of sources. Particularly, this work was richly informed by Inquisitorial documents and by numerous publications put forth by the enemies of Freemasonry, which came to comprise a fund of sources that helped bring about this cultural and historical analysis.

In short, the lodges' lack of resources aimed at preserving their memories, together with the similar lack of the custom of doing so, have resulted in an absence of significant Masonic records within Mexico. Therefore, one purpose I have undertaken with this book is the assembly of a Masonic record, be it private or public, which will enable researchers to consult it as a source and permit the study of an organization that has played a key role in Mexico's history.

For this project, primary sources were consulted: From legal and Inquisitorial documents, the latter of which is in the *Archivo de la Nación in Mexico* (National Archive of Mexico); to political essays, pamphlets, and other written works of the time, both those sympathetic with the Masonic institution as well as those of its enemies. Only a small part of the material collected is presented, since space does not permit me to include it all. Also, it is worthwhile pointing out that when we deal with topics as controversial as Freemasonry, it is important that one be very cautious with the sources one compiles. One should maintain one's distance from the documents and books found within the Masonic institutions, as well as from the sources consulted in the "profane" world, to use Masonic jargon. I recommend that those interested in this topic endeavor to carry out field studies and visit libraries and archives so that they may see up close the inner workings of this institution and gain a better understanding of, among other things, its history, its rituals, and its behavior.

SETTING THE STAGE: A THEORETICAL, HISTORICAL AND CONCEPTUAL APPROACH

The contributions of Margaret Jacob and Paul Rich in the field of Masonry and civil society,[9] and those of Victor Turner,[10] with his theory of ritual-

---

9   Especially their thesis concerning Masonic lodges as promoters of modern society during the 18th century. See Margaret Jacob, *The Radical Enlightenment: Pantheists, Freemasons and Republicans*, Lafayette, Cornerstone, 1981; *Living the Enlightenment: Freemasonry and Politics in Eighteenth-Century Europe*, op. cit,; *The Origins of Freemason: Facts and Fiction*, Philadelphia, University of Pennsylvania Press, 2006. For more on their proposal of Masonry as a model of secular organization and promoter of political ritualism and formers of political patterns, see Paul J. Rich, *Elixir of Empire*, London, Regency Press, 1993; *Chains of Empire*, Regency Press, London and New York, 1991; "Researching Grandfather's Secrets," *Journal of American Culture*, vol. 20, no. 2, Summer 1997, 139-146; see also Paul Rich and Guillermo de los Reyes, "Ritual in the Service of the State," *Papers in International Studies*, Hoover Institution, Stanford University, I-98.

10   Of particular interest is his thesis on ritual and liminality. See Victor Turner, *The Ritual*

ism and liminality; together with the works of Benedict Anderson, Homi Bhabha, and Eric Hobsbawm on national discourse, imagined communities and the invention of traditions,[11] and those of Antonio Gramsci and Ángel Rama on the role of the intellectual and the learned[12] have allowed me to study Freemasonry with an interdisciplinary focus that combines historiography and ethnology with cultural and studies' perspective and, in so doing, to analyze in a more wholistic manner this institution's contributions to and impact on the national discourse.

"Discourse" is defined here according to the French philosopher Michel Foucault's approach, which I conceive as "the general domain of all statements, sometimes as an individualizable group of statements, and sometimes as a regulated practice that accounts for a number of statements."[13] Foucault utilized the term "discourse" to describe a social system tied to specific historical contexts responsible for generating knowledge and significance. He highlights the idea that discourse has tangible consequences, molding what he refers to as practices that consistently shape the subjects they discuss. According to Foucault, subjects come to define themselves through the regulating practice of the official and alternative discourses (by means of knowledge). Consequently, it is through the formation of these discourses that identities and subjectivities already established are reinforced.

Based on the abovementioned critical approaches, combined with archival and ethnographic work, I propose a definition of Freemasonry (particularly for the Mexican context). I define Freemasonry as a ritualistic

Process: Structure and Anti-Structure, Aldine Transaction [1969] 1995; From Ritual to Theatre: The Human Seriousness of Play, PAJ Publications, 1982; Liminality, Kabbalah, and the Media, Academic Press, 1985.

11   In particular, see the works on imagined communities and nationalism, in Benedict Anderson, *Imagined Communities*, New York, Verso, 1991. For his study of nationalism and post nationalism, in addition to his thesis opposing the binarism imposed by Western cultures, see Homi Bhabha, ed., *Nation and Narration*, New York, Routledge, 1990; *The Location of Culture*, New York, Routledge, 1994. See also Eric Hobsbawm, *Nations and Nationalism Since 1780*: Programme, Myth, Reality, Cambridge, Cambridge University Press, 1990.

12   See Antonio Gramsci, Prison Notebooks, New York, International Publishers, 1971. Of particular interest also is Ángel Rama's signal work, *La ciudad letrada* [The Lettered City], Hanover, Ediciones del Norte, 1984.

13   Michel Foucault, *Archaeology of Knowledge and the Discourse on Language* (1969) (trans. AM Sheridan Smith, 1972), 135-140. See also M. Foucault "The Order of Discourse" in R Young (ed) *Untying the Text: A Post-Structuralist Reader* (1981).

organization with rites of initiation; it is philanthropic and transnational, formed by intellectuals and educated people—mostly male—who convene for common interests, with the essential outcome of developing and defending these interests. Entry into the organization requires passage through a special ceremony of initiation; rituals are practiced that give Freemasonry the feel of a secular religion, and its members follow the precepts of its constitution. The organization's meetings are held in a venue called a "lodge." The meetings are conducted according to a certain ritual, according to the rite and the degree, which is itself a collection of symbols and traditions taken from a mythological past to which members feel closely bound. Some interpret this past literally and believe in this interpretation; others see it as a founding myth. Masonic meetings have a bureaucratic and hierarchical structure, which bestows certain titles and offices, such as Grand Master or Grand Potentate.

Throughout the organization's history, the Masons have been responsible for promoting modern civil society in various countries of Europe and Latin America, as well as in the United States.[14] As Margaret Jacob and María Eugenia Vázquez Semadeni have argued, "[t]he masonic vision of improvement was so compelling by the 1780s that some masonic reformers wanted to use the lodges as ways of gaining access to state authority, as places where masonic membership could translate into political power and at reform."[15] In Mexico, the Masons have recruited a great number of the educated class and intellectuals into their ranks. In this way, Freemasonry, from its very beginnings, succeeded in appropriating the images of national heroes, in practicing certain rituals, and in safeguarding its secrecy. These achievements imbued the organization with the mysterious and powerful character that has contributed to its success over the years.

---

14   It is important to note that in each country there are similarities and differences in this process, depending on the region and the time period in which it takes place. See Margaret Jacob, Living.. op. cit.; Antonio Ferrer Benimeli, *Los Archivos secretos vaticanos y la masonería* [The Vatican's Secret Archives and Masonry], Caracas, Universidad Católica, 1976; *La masonería española: la historia en sus textos* [Spanish Masonry: The History in its Texts], Madrid, Istmo, 1996; David Stevenson, *The Origins of Freemasonry: Scotland's Century 1590–1710*, Cambridge, Cambridge University Press, 1988; Steven C. Bullock, *Revolutionary Brotherhood: Freemasonry and the Transformation of the American Social Order*, 1730–1840, Chapel Hill, University of North Carolina Press, 1996.

15   Margaret Jacob and María Eugenia Vázquez Semadeni, *Freemasonry and Civil Society: Europe and the Americas (North and South)*, New York: Peter Lange, 2023, 3.

As stated above, the Masons meet periodically in groupings known as lodges in appropriate locations, also termed lodges, and with the understanding that that they meet to accomplish certain tasks. Even in present-day meetings, the vocabulary of working masonry is used. Some sources suggest that Freemasonry's forebears were the builders of medieval cathedrals. Though that may be, from the seventeenth century to modern times, the organization's main work has been of an intellectual and ritual nature. Today, there is at least one Masonic lodge in every modest-sized town in Mexico, each of which imparts the three basic degrees of symbolism, or Blue Lodge Freemasonry, namely: Entered Apprentice, Fellow Craft, and Master Mason.[16] All of these lodges are incorporated into a Grand Lodge, the limits of whose jurisdiction usually reaches to the border of the state in which it is located.

The Grand Lodges' leaders are elected by the Master Masons of all the symbolic lodges within their jurisdiction, and it is these leaders' duty to oversee the particular aspects of the meetings. Within every country, there is a body or confederation of Grand Lodges. Internationally there are other bodies that prepare and convene regional and global meetings for the study and resolution of problems among the order. These bodies are strictly for the purpose of making recommendations; in other words, they may only make suggestions to the Grand Lodges and lack the authority to impose policy.

The symbolic lodge is the fundamental organic unit of the Masonic institution. These are grouped into Grand Lodges, which in turn belong to one of the recognized rites, which exist above these divisions in an administrative role. Among their objectives is the preservation of the complete unity of Freemasonry's members around the world, whom, in accordance with the organization's rules, are recognized as brothers and supported, and with whom they work in harmony toward a common goal: the pursuit of progress and the wellbeing of humanity. This is the everyday duty of every Mason, one that he takes on voluntarily.[17] This does not mean

---

16   Contrary to what is commonly believed, even so-called profanes can obtain the books of rituals from either Masonic or non-Masonic libraries, as well as on the Internet. Nevertheless, the practice of all the rituals and the dynamic inside the lodge is something that only the initiated know in its entirety.

17   *La masonería es... [Masonry is...]*, Mexico, Herbasa, monograph published by the Coordinación de estudios especiales de la Gran Logia del Valle de México [Coordination of Special Studies of the Grand Lodge of the Valley of Mexico], 1990, 20-22.

to imply that there have not been personal interests served, nor that everything has always proceeded harmoniously and peacefully within the Masonic organization. As with any group there have been difficulties, rivalries and quarrels among Freemasonry's membership, particularly over power and control, as was the case in the struggle between the York Rite and the Scottish Rite.

Historically, as I have previously discussed, Masonry in Mexico has been involved in controversies and struggles; this has contributed to its tight secrecy and, in turn, has helped to create the disinformation one finds about the organization. My purpose here is not to promote Freemasonry nor to create fantastical histories in which it is the cause, either justly or unjustly, of revolutions, independence movements, or attempts at solving humankind's ills. The objective of this discussion is simply to recognize this organization's role within Mexico's historical evolution and its impact on the secular and political discourse in various periods of that country's national history.[18]

The foundational myths and the creation of a literary and philosophical canon have contributed to the expansion and maintenance of Freemasonry.[19] This formative process began with the association's members initially strategically communicating passwords and other various verbal signs of brotherhood. These forms of expansion were similar to those employed by the romantic nationalists during the nineteenth century in some European countries and the Americas. In this regard, Jacob and Vázquez Semadeni argue that in the regions mentioned previously, both "north and south reveal similar nationalistic tendencies, but with vastly different outcomes."[20] In this way, the Masonic precepts could be exchanged and applied with a degree of self-awareness to a wide range of social situations, merging with a variety of ideological and political elements that would

18 For the Masonic view on this topic, see Eulalio Morales Zepeda, "La masonería mexicana en defensa de nuestra independencia política y nacionalismo" ["Mexican Masonry in Defense of our Political Independence and Nationalism"], *Supremo Consejo* 1, Mexico, D.F., Spring 1993, 13.

19 Guillermo de los Reyes, Heredia, "La rehabilitación del mito en las masonerías mexicana y estadounidense," *Cultura masónica: Revista temática de francmasonería*, Vol. XIV, Issue 49, April 2022: 190-200. The production, distribution and translation of Freemasonry's books, as with the creation of regulatory institutions and the writing of a constitution and other documents are examples of this.

20 Jacob and Vázquez, *op cit*, 41.

influence the ways in which Masons perceive themselves and the world.[21]

The main questions I have posed throughout this book are: What has been Freemasonry's influence in the various secularization movements over the course of Mexico's history? And what influence did these efforts have on the development of Freemasonry in that country vis-à-vis the creation of a secular and anticlerical discourse? To answer these questions, it is important to define the concept of influence and how it is treated in this investigation. I understand influence as the process of either imposing policy and/or political practices (one's own) or accepting policy (that of others), aided by the threat of severe deprivations (either real or imagined) in the case such policy is not followed. In other words, "the power to make other persons act, think, or feel."[22] Thus, thinking about the way in which policy has been implemented around the world, one can safely propose that influence is always in play among those holding government office, either within or outside their political party or affiliations. Sometimes this influence is invisible; the influence that groups not occupying positions of power exercise over those in power can be very discreet. The degree of influence can vary, depending on the parties in power and on those who would impose influence. So many organic political groups differ from political parties in that they bring influence to bear instead of directly wielding power. The Masons in Mexico had directly held power, as when they served as proto-political parties (*yorkinos* and *escoceses*) and thus had direct access to it. On other occasions, in fact the majority of the time historically, Freemasonry's power has been attained through its exercise of influence. This does not mean that the Freemasons control Mexico or the world; however, as an organization, through their lodges, they have exercised influence in different realms, particularly in the political realm during certain periods of Mexican history.

Consequently, it is necessary to inscribe Freemasonry's evolution in Mexico in accordance with the influence that it has exerted. To that end, I have developed a framework that permits an understanding of the process of this evolution, based on Gramsci's thesis on hegemonic and subaltern blocs, influence theory, and Foucault's constructivist model, in which a subject or a group is influenced by historical, social, political and cultural

---

21   B. Anderson, *Imagined Communities*, 4.

22   Edward C. Banfield, *Political Influence*, The Free Press of Glencoe, 1971; José F. Gómez Hinojosa, *Intelectuales y pueblo*, San José, DEI, 75.

context. The framework is divided into four phases:

1. The formative years and persecution (1790–1820). In this phase, the Masonic lodges in New Spain took very cautious first steps due to Inquisitorial persecution. During this time, the Freemasons formed part of what Gramsci calls the subaltern bloc, which kept a low profile; but gradually, both within and outside New Spain, those interested in the organization were secretly preparing and promoting Masonic ideas, cautiously so as to avoid being discovered by the Mexican Inquisition.

2. Political prominence, secularization, and anticlericalism (1820–1876). This was the most political and successful phase of Masonic society, which consolidated the organization as part of the hegemonic bloc. Some of the lodges served and/or became proto-political parties and were made up of the intellectual and scholarly class of the time, who influenced decision making and the creation of laws. Often, they were involved in the development of political discourses of the epoch. It should be mentioned that this was also a violent period for Freemasonry.

3. The reign of Porfirio Díaz (the *porfiriato*), Masonic unification, and the Mexican Revolution (1876–1917). During this period, Porfirio Díaz held indisputable hegemonic power, taking advantage of Freemasonry's power, making the organization his ally and, at the same time, controlling it. During this time, the Masons had very little influence as an institution; only a few Masons, such as Bernardo Reyes, achieved any prominence. At the beginning of the Mexican Revolution, the Masonic organization tried to retake hegemonic power, but due to the chaos of the time it was unable to regain the strength it had during the nineteenth century.

4. The post-revolutionary period, decline, re-growth, and transformation (1917–2010). In the 1920s and 1930s, Freemasonry again achieved a certain prominence in the efforts to promote a secular state and in the anticlerical struggle. Later, the Masonic lodges once again began to decline due in great part to the way political institutions develop in Mexico; that is, the institutionalization of political organizations since executive power and the political party of the majority for more than seventeen years (PRI) became the hegemonic bloc. In this way, the Masonic lodges comprised the loyal instrument of the official party and of the State, as well as being a

group that could exert pressure in the question of safeguarding the secular State, which, according to the organization's members, has been threatened in recent decades.

In summary, the purpose of the proposed phases of Freemasonry in Mexico is to provide the reader with a methodological tool to study a given stage of Freemasonry in Mexico. The classification was done considering the impact that the various historical stages in Mexican history have had on the Masonic institution, as well as their own history, both within and outside of Mexico. It is important to place Freemasonry as a transnational organization, and one that should be studied as such because it is part of an international network. Ever since its formation, the Mexican Masonic organization has maintained contact with international Freemasonry, which has been influential in the actions and political tendencies of its members.

As an example, the anticlericalism that has characterized Mexican Freemasonry arose from continental Europe. This point is set forth and illustrated by Antonio Gramsci in his *Prison Notebooks*, where he asserts that religion and Freemasonry have served as a source of political-ideological fugue, both nationally and internationally, have generated various political expedients of historical origin, and that these have contributed to the development and expansion of Freemasonry in some countries, including in Mexico. Gramsci states that the function of Freemasonry and religion, as well as that of other volunteer organizations, "is to mediate between the extremes, to socialize technical discoveries that permit the function of leadership activities, to arbitrate agreements and ways out of tough situations."[23] Such mediation has been exercised by the various Masonic lodges in Mexico over the years, particularly in the discourses of secularization of that country that began in the second half of the nineteenth century. In short, Freemasonry has influenced politics within Mexico— and continues to do so today, although to a lesser extent. This last point will also be explored in this work.

THE SECRETS OF MEXICAN FREEMASONRY

Both within and outside present-day academia, there has emerged a marked interest in the study of Freemasonry, secularization, laicism, and

---

23   A. Gramsci, *Prison Notebooks, op. cit.,* 415-416.

liberalism—all key terms in the cultural, social, and political discourses of Mexico and other parts of Latin America. Up to now, those publications concerned with these topics have been limited to academic articles that only analyzed these questions in part. Among these, the works of Virginia Guedea, Jean-Pierre Bastian, Juan-Jürgen Prien, Christopher Domínguez Michael, Beatriz Urías, Marco A. Zavala, María E. Vázquez, Paul Rich, and the author of this book could be mentioned.[24]

24　On the Mexican case, see Jean-Pierre Bastian, Protestantes, liberales y francmasones (op. cit.); Virginia Guedea, "Las sociedades secretas durante el movimiento de independencia," in *The Independence of Mexico and the Creation of the New Nation*, ed. Jaime Rodríguez (Los Ángeles:UCLA Latin American Center Publications, 1989); Christopher Domínguez Michael, Vida de Fray Servando (México: Era, 2004); idem, "Fray Servando y los francmasones en Cádiz," LetrasLibres, March 2005; Paul Rich and Guillermo de los Reyes, "Reappraising Scottish RiteFreemasonry in Latin America," *Heredom* 4 (1995); idem, "Freemasonry's Educational Role" (op. cit.); idem, "Policy Making and the Control of the Nongovernmental Sector: Porfirio Díaz and the Grand Diet," *Review of Policy Research* 22, no. 5 (September 2005): 721–25; Guillermo de los Reyes, "Freemasonry and Folklore in Mexican Presidentialism," *Journal of American Culture* 20, no. 2 (Summer 1997); idem, "The Cross and the Compass," in Recovering Hispanic Religious Thought and Practice of the United States, ed. Nicolás Kanellos (Cambridge: Cambridge Scholars Publishing, 2007), 8–24; idem, "Translating, Smuggling, and Recovering Books in Nineteenth-Century Mexico," in The Critical Importance of Region, ed. Antonia Castañeda and Gabriel Meléndez (Houston: Arte Público Press, 2006), 143–58; Jesús E. Vázquez Leos, Liberalismo y masonería en San Luis Potosí (s/e, 1996); Marco Antonio Flores Zavala, El grupo masón en la política zacatecana, 1880–1914 (AIF "Francisco García Salinas," 2002); idem, "La masonería en la República Federal," in Raíces del federalismo mexicano, ed. Manuel Miño Grijalva et al. (Zacatecas: UAZ/SECZ, 2005), 125–36; idem, "Los ciclos de la masonería mexicana. Siglos XVIII–XIX," in La masonería en Madrid y en España del siglo XVII al XXI, ed. José Ferrer Benimeli (Zaragoza: Gobierno de Aragón, 2004), 1:489–501; María Eugenia Vázquez Semadeni, "La interacción entre el debate público sobre la masonería y la cultura política, 1761–1830" (PhD diss., El Colegio de Michoacán, 2008); idem, "La masonería mexicana en el debate público, 1808–1830," in La masonería española en la época de Sagasta, ed. José Antonio Ferrer Benimeli (Zaragoza: Gobierno de Aragón, CEHME, 2007), 2:861–82; Beatriz Urías Horcasitas, "De moral y regeneración," Cuicuilco 11 (September–December 2004): 87–119; Alejandro Gutiérrez Hernández, "La masonería mexicana, un caso de estudio pendiente," in El anticlericalismo en México, ed. Francisco Savarino and Andrea Mutolo (México: Miguel A. Porrúa/ITESM, 2008); Ruth Solís Vicarte, Las sociedades secretas en el primer gobierno republicano (1824–1828) (México: ASBE, 1997); María del Carmen Vázquez Mantecón, La palabra del poder (México: UNAM, IIH, 1997); Iris M. Zavala, Masones, comuneros y carbonarios (Madrid: Siglo XXI, 1971), 196–97; José A. Ferrer Benimeli, La masonería española en el siglo XVIII (Madrid: Siglo XXI, 1974); idem, Masonería española contemporánea, vol. 1 (Madrid: Siglo XXI, 1980); idem, Masonería e inquisición en Latinoamérica durante el siglo XVIII (Caracas: Universidad Católica Andrés Bello, 1973); Gabriel Torres Puga, "Centinela mexicano

In 2007, *Masones en México: historia del poder oculto* [*Masons in Mexico: History of Hidden Power*], by José Luis Trueba Lara, was published in Mexico. This work attempts to present a comprehensive history of Freemasonry in that country, focusing on various moments of Mexican history that the Masons impacted. As the author notes, his book's objective is "to cover Freemasonry's history [...] not to claim in any way to be a book for experts in the field; in fact, the opposite is true. The book seeks an audience of readers who are not specialists but who are interested in Freemasonry."[25] As a consequence, Trueba's work, in spite of its limitations, brings the controversial subject of Freemasonry into the light, proposing various viewpoints that will be discussed later in this book. But there has never been a book or monograph of an academic nature published in English that provides an exhaustive discussion of the admixture of Freemasonry, politics, and society within Mexico. Therefore, this work intends to provide a dialogue with the most recent research into the Mexican intellectuals of the nineteenth and twentieth centuries and, in turn, achieve a fresh approach to the study of Freemasonry that has grown in Mexico during the last ten years.

Few publications (those of Domínguez, Rich, and De los Reyes, among others) examine the degree of influence of the works done by the Masons and other co-Masonic organizations. Part of the reason for this is that many scholars believe there not to be adequate material available on Freemasonry. It is, therefore, important that these works be studied with their Masonic influence firmly in mind—works that were instrumental in the development and promotion of political thought within the Republic of Mexico during the periods of independence and post-independence (at the beginning and middle of the nineteenth century).

There are other publications that should be mentioned: The compilation by Jean-Pierre Bastian, *Protestantes, liberales y francmasones: sociedades de ideas y modernidad en América Latina, siglo XIX,* [*Protestants, Liberals and Freemasons: Societies of Ideas and Modernity in Latin America, Twentieth Century*] (1993),[26] and various works by Virginia Guedea, an outstanding example of which is "Las sociedades secretas durante el movimiento

---

contra francmasones," Estudios de Historia Moderna y Contemporánea 33 (2005): 57–94.

25 José Luis Trueba Lara, *Masones en México: historia del poder oculto* [Masons in Mexico: History of Hidden Power], Mexico, Grijalbo, 2007, 18-19.

26 J.-P. Bastian, comp., *op. cit.*, 7.

de independencia" ["Secret Societies During the Independence Movement"] (1989).[27] In the introduction to his compilation, Bastian notes that the study of Masonic lodges, Protestant societies, and liberal clubs is a relatively new field in the historical study of nineteenth-century Latin America. Even so, rarely has their relationship with each other been taken up as a topic of study as societies connected to form informal networks and, at times, political fronts.[28]

As Bastian states, the various organizations that have influenced the political development of Mexico have been given little importance; and on the occasions when these are taken into account, as with the case of the York Rite and the Scottish Rite at the beginning of the nineteenth century, they are not studied thoroughly, their evolution and context not analyzed, nor the wide range of their development and impact over the years examined. Only the fact of these groups' participation in certain events is discussed, without consideration of either the causes or effects of such participation in various episodes in Mexico's history, and with scant consideration of the anti-Catholic front they would become, particularly since this was one of the pillars of the Mexican secular State that, in the nineteenth century, began the process of secularization. As mentioned previously, the Masons' anti-Catholic stance derived from the organization's European influence. Like Gramsci, Virginia Guedea—among other scholars, such as Ferrer Benimeli—argues that from its European beginnings, Freemasonry was regarded jealously by the Catholic Church. In Spain in particular, Fernando VII outlawed the organization because it was "suspicious to Religion and to the State."[29] As we will see further on, Freemasonry's role in Mexico's evolution shows it to be a multifaceted organization, one that cannot be viewed as apolitical and with simply ritualistic aims.[30]

Throughout history, Freemasonry has had a close relationship with politics in Mexico, some of the institution's philosophies influencing certain political actions in that country, as with the separation of Church and

---

27 V. Guedea, "Las sociedades secretas durante el movimiento de independencia" [Secret Societies During the Independence Movement], *op. cit.*

28 J.-P. Bastian, *op. cit.,* 7.

29 V. Guedea, *op. cit.,* 46. See also Iris M. Zavala, *op. cit.,* 196-197.

30 The members of what seem to be secret societies, including the Masonic organizations, maintain that the Freemasonry is not a secret organization but rather a "discreet" one. Allen E. Roberts, *Freemasonry in American History*, Richmond, Macoy Publishing, 1985, 1; "Secrecy," *Royal Arch Mason*, vol. 18, num. 4, winter 1994, 118.

State. In this book, I will specifically undertake a discussion of the impact this organization has had—and continues to have, although on a smaller scale than in the past—on Mexican politics and its participation in efforts to maintain a secular State. By this means I will present an analysis of the ways in which Freemasonry has affected the principal historical episodes through which Mexico's history has moved.

Despite the Masonic lodges' prominence in Mexico's history, few academic works have been published on the topic, as I will mention throughout this book. Only recently has an interest in the study of this subject been revived, in large part because of the important work done at Spain's Universidad de Zaragoza under the direction of Professor José A. Ferrer Benimeli, who has been the chief promoter of Masonry in the Hispanic world. In addition, a group of Latin American scholars led by Ricardo Martínez Esquivel created an academic journal dedicated to the study of Freemasonry: *REHMLAC: Revista de Estudios Históricos de la Masonería Latinomaericana y Caribeña plus.* The most remarkable achievement in the study of Freemasonry in Mexico has been the founding of the "Cátedra Internacional Historia de la Masonería Latinomaericana y del Caribe José A. Ferrer Benimeli (Endowed Chair – José A. Ferrer Benimeli) at the Universidad Autónoma de Zacatecas in Zacatecas, Mexico, led by Professor Marco Flores Zavala and Dr. Marco Antonio Garcia Robles. Its objective is to promote research and academic exchange related to Freemasonry. This is perhaps one of the most impactful initiatives in the serious study of Freemasonry in Mexico. Both the University of Costa Rica and the Universidad de Zaragoza, and other universities in México, have worked together with the "Centro de Estudios Históricos de la Masonería Española" [Center for the Historical Study of Spanish Freemasonry] to organize symposia, colloquia, and various publications about Freemasonry in Spain and Latin America.

It is necessary also to note the work of scholars such as María Eugenia Vázquez Semadeni, who created an updated and precise overview of the historiography of Mexican Freemasonry titled "Historiografía sobre la Masonería en México. Breve revision," published by *REHMLAC* in 2010,[31] where she expertly outlines the current state of Masonic literature in and about Mexico. She categorizes the literature into two main

---

31   María Eugenia Vázquez Semadeni, "Historiografía sobre la Masonería en México. Breve revision," published by *REHMLAC* 2, no. 1 (May–November 2010): 16-29. https://revistas. ucr.ac.cr/index.php/rehmlac/article/ view/6608/6297

sections: non-academic historiography, generally comprising works by Masons and anti-Masonics; and academic historiography, which is further divided into traditional and recent history, with the latter tailored to specific historical periods. To avoid redundancy, I direct readers to her work for discussions on sources that I do not comment on due to the overlap in critical criteria. Meanwhile, María Eugenia Vázquez Semadeni is one of the most prominent scholars of Freemasonry in Mexico during the 1820s. She has published key works on the York Rite and other lodges during that period, among them being, "La Gran Legión del Águila Negra" (Zamora, 2007), "Las Obediencias masónicas del rito de York como centro de acción política. México 1825–1830" (Chiapas, 2009), and "Masonería, Papeles públicos y cultura política" (Mexico City, 2009). However, her most significant and decisive contribution to the history of Freemasonry during the years after Mexico's independence is *La formación de una cultura política republicana. El debate público sobre la masonería. México 1821–1830*, published by UNAM in 2010.[32]

Another important scholar of the history of Freemasonry is Marco Antonio Flores Zavala, whose work on the topic has been of important influence on my own. Among them, *El grupo masón en la política zacatecana, 1880–1914* (Zacatecas, 2002) offers a methodologically focused and promising perspective on the changes that Mexico's new Masonic historiography should pursue regarding regional history. This approach serves as a preliminary step toward creating a demythologized national historical account in the future. Other significant works by Flores Zavala along these lines include "Los ciclos de la masonería mexicana. Siglos XVIII–XIX" (Zaragoza, 2004) and "La masonería en la República Federal." Apuntes sobre las logias mexicanas (1821–1840) (Zacatecas, 2005).[33]

---

32 See María Eugenia Vázquez Semadeni, *La formación de una cultura política republicana. El debate público sobre la masonería en México, 1821–1830*. Mexico City: Universidad Nacional Autónoma de México y Colegio de Michoacán, 2010; _____ "Masonería, Papeles públicos y cultura política." Estudios de Historia Moderna y Contemporánea de México 30 (July–December 2009): 35–83; "Las Obediencias masónicas del rito de York como centro de acción política, México 1825–1830 (Chiapas, México, 2009)

33 See Marco Antonio Flores Zavala. "Los ciclos de la masonería mexicana. Siglos XVIII–XIX." In La Masonería en Madrid y en España del siglo XVIII al XXI, edited by José Antonio Ferrer Benimeli, 1: 489–501. Zaragoza: Gobierno de Aragón, 2004; _____. El grupo masón en la política zacatecana, 1880–1914. Zacatecas, Mexico: Asociación de Investigaciones Filosófcas "Francisco García Sabina," 2002; _____. "La masonería en la República Federal. Apuntes sobre las logias mexicanas (1825–1840)." In Raíces del federalismo mexicano, edited by Manuel Miño Grijalva, 125–136. Zacatecas, Mexico: Universidad Autónoma de Zacatecas, 2005.

Nevertheless, even until very recently, some Mexican historians of the period in which Freemasonry played an important role in Mexican history took it as a given that since the Masons no longer had the power that they had in the nineteenth century, there was no reason to study the organization. In fact, I posed this question to various intellectuals in Mexico whom I know, many of them historians, and their answer was: Why should it be studied? Or even: That seems a question for fanatics. I do not know if these views were due to ignorance of or bias toward the topic, or perhaps simply that they believed it to be irrelevant. Such views may be partly credited, as was pointed out earlier, to both the pro- and anti-Masonic propaganda that is so plentiful that it deflects interest from the topic and to cause scholars to keep away from it because of the many conspiracy theories surrounding it.

Fortunately, in the last few years, as mentioned earlier, a group of scholars from different parts of the world, particularly from Latin America, Spain, and France, have contributed to *REHMLAC* and have published academic works that have had a big impact on the study of Mexican (and Latin American) Freemasonry. A pivotal work I must not omit is, *Historia mínima de la masonería en México*, edited by Ricardo Martínez Esquivel, which includes works from scholars such as Yvan Pozuelo Andrés, Marco Antonio García Robles, Rogelio Aragón, María Eugenia Vázquez Semadeni, Marco A. Flores Zavala, Julio Martínez, García, Carlos Francisco Martínez Moreno, Fredy Cauich Carrillo, and the author of this book. This edited collection is perhaps one of the most important compilations currently available on Freemasonry in México. It provides key information on the subject as well as detailed information about various aspects of Freemasonry in México. That volume invites the reader to think of Mexican modernity from a different perspective, considering its alterity, contradictions, political culture, and peculiarities.[34]

RITUAL IN THE SERVICE OF THE STATE

Every nation has need of the public theater, fabricated ritual, and foundational fictions by which they promote a national and emotional discourse vital in the construction of a national imaginary.[35] Mexico is no

---

34 Ricardo Martínez Esquivel, Editor; *Historia mínima de la masonería en México,* Texere Editores, 2021.

35 See B. Anderson, *Imagined Communities, op. cit.*; Victor Turner, *Ritual Process, op. cit.*;

exception. In fact, Mexico's rulers have been quite effective in the creation of symbols, rituals, texts and discourses, all of which have a great impact upon this construction.[36] Of course there have been a certain number of Masonic acts performed publicly that have come to be associated with the images of Mexico's presidents. The square and the compass of Freemasonry are emblems that appear frequently on the floral arrangements placed on the tombs of Juárez, Díaz, Madero, Cárdenas, as well as those of other heroes entombed in the national pantheons and monuments, or in the very *Rotonda de los Hombres Ilustres* (Pantheon of Illustrious Men) of Mexico. One commonly sees magazines or other periodic publications that depict prominent Mexican political figures, both past and present, in their relationship to Freemasonry. Another example of the Masons' political participation is the public declaration of support the organization purchases either in national or regional newspapers on behalf of favored candidates aspiring to certain political posts.

As this investigation unfolds, one sees that indeed the Masonic elite form part of the "theater" of Mexican history. The Masonic lodges were precursors of liberal thought in Mexico and contributed to the development of a political perspective different from that proposed for a conservative Catholic State. Additionally, it was in these lodges that a great part of po-

---

E. Hobsbawm, *Nations and Nationalism Since 1780: Programme, Myth, Reality, op. cit.*; Doris Sommer, *Foundational Fictions: The National Romances of Latin America*, California, University of California Press, 1993; Beatriz González Stephan, *La historiografía literaria del liberalismo hispanoamericano del siglo XIX* [The Literary History of Nineteenth-Century Hispanic-American Liberalism], Havana, Casa de las Américas, 1987.

36 The same thing can be said about other countries, Hungary for example: "Since no nation-state can exist without the presence of a multitude of recognized and officially sanctioned public ceremonies, such theatricality was imitated in numerous similar rituals. The constitution (*alkotmány ünnepe*) was implemented on August 20, 1948, in an effort to detract from attention given to St. Stephen's Day, the pre-Socialist religious festival celebrated on that date; as a consequence, the peaceful Catholic festival was overshadowed by a massive military parade. Thus did August 20 symbolize the identification of the State with the Soviet Union and the Warsaw Pact—the ultimate nation-state—while May 1 maintained internal order by means of the dramatization of the myth of the communist state based on the solidarity of the working class." László Kürti, "People vs. the State: Political Rituals in Contemporary Hungary," *Anthropology Today*, vol. y, num. 2, April 1990, 6. "A public is formed when the connections between culture and social interaction are attenuated, so that people can separate and not be in constant interaction." John B. Thompson, "Symbolic Violence: Language and Power in the Writings of Pierre Bourdieu," in: *Studies in the Theory of Ideology*, New York, Polity Press, 1985 [1984], 86.

litical discourse and practice was created during the nineteenth century. It should be noted that many times, from among the ranks of the Masons, there have emerged certain political elites who have sought to be part of the government. It will also be shown in this book that there has been a great number of Masons who have held high government posts, national as well as regional, and who have influenced the country's politics.

OF PASSWORDS, SIGNS, AND OTHER DEMONS

Although the Freemasons are a secret organization, there are those who prefer the term "discreet." The level of secrecy varies from country to country and from one historical period to another. In Spanish America, where I have carried out the majority of this research, the organization is secretive in the extreme. The image the public holds of this society here is unlike that in other countries, where Masons appear in public and open their libraries' doors to non-members. In Latin America, Freemasonry is extremely political, often highly anticlerical and polemic. Thus, gathering material, analyzing, and interpreting it can be akin to exposing top-secret documents or discussing abortion with the Pope. In some countries, the Masonic institutions are more open than in others. Nevertheless, there is one area in which all of them keep their secret. In the Short Talk Bulletin titled "The Secret," published in December of 1941 by the Association of Masonic Services of the United States (these pamphlets are sent to the lodges for distribution to members), one passage demonstrates that, according to the Masons, there are certain secrets that cannot be translated, and so cannot be spoken:

> The majority of those not Freemasons suppose that the Order has some Great Secret, some hidden knowledge the possession of which marks off the possessors from his fellows and, perhaps gives him access to resources not possessed by the uninitiated. A majority of Freemasons undoubtedly consider that the secrets of the order taught in a Lodge are the component parts of The Secret and find a contended satisfaction in their knowledge [...] What then is The Secret? It is something which cannot be told. He who has it cannot broadcast it to his neighbor. It is far too ethereal for words. None of the half million words of the English language are sufficient, ei-

ther, alone or in any collaboration—not even if they are all used—to express music so another may hear it, the perfume of the rose so another may smell it, the glory of a sunset so another may see it. Music, perfume, color must be experienced to be known; they are not tellable. The Secret of Freemasonry is not tellable in words.[37]

This stance has allowed the Masons to preserve the need to keep the secret from those who are not Masons. Marie Mulvey Roberts points out that "secrecy is concerned above all with what human beings want to protect: the intimate, the dangerous, the profane, the fragile, the sacred, and the forbidden."[38] When one speaks of the secret, Roberts notes, "one is struck by its elusive, amorphous and often invisible nature—it is to be found everywhere and nowhere."[39]

Academic publications on the history of Mexico, as I discuss in this section, are lacking in their references to Freemasonry. Perhaps a reason for this is to be found in the fact that the scholars who are not members of the organization and who are interested in the topic are unaware of the considerable quantity of literature that exists about its history and its rituals. This conceptualization of the secret and of the belief that Masonic activities are totally secret has fomented the dearth of information and of an understanding of the accouterments or symbols of this organization. Two very good examples of this are Kipling's *Kim* (1901) and *El hombre de la rosa* (the English edition of which is titled *The Man and the Rose*) (1928) by Manuel Rojas. Paul Rich states, "Kipling himself didn't completely appreciate its meaning. But the carelessness in the literature surrounding his reference to the so-called 'Royal Craft' seems surprising, given Kipling's interest in the lodges, and their ritual has been well documented."[40] Susan M. Linker states that through the consideration and study of the collective symbols we can gain a better understanding of the texts. She argues

---

37 "The Secret," *Short Talk Bulletin*, Washington, DC, The Masonic Service Association of the United States, December 1941, (3, 7).

38 Marie Mulvey Roberts, "Masonic, Metaphor and Misogyny: A Discourse of Marginality?" in Peter Burke and Roy Porter, eds., *Languages and Jargons: Contributions to a Social History of Language*, Cambridge, Polity Press, 1995, 97.

39 Ibid.

40 Paul Rich, "Kim and the Magic House: Freemasonry and Kipling," in: Marie M. Roberts and Hugh Ormsby-Lennon, eds., *Secret Texts: The Literature of Secret Societies*, New York, AMS Press, 1995, 323.

that in order to appreciate *El hombre de la rosa* fully, one must "study Rojas's symbolism and allegory," since that work, says Linker, "reveals itself to be an arrogantly constructed synthesis of the Masonic ideals and symbols of the Rosicrucians."[41] In short, in order to decipher these matters it is important to study the problems related to the specialized vocabulary of an esoteric theme.

One key to understanding the peculiarity of the Masonic vocabulary is to keep in mind that, although the group from time to time both exerts political pressure and is implicated in so-called "New Age" activities, over its entire history it has been extremely ritualistic. Wherever Freemasonry was established, it was characterized by the importance given to the degrees conferred upon its initiates. In these degrees the candidate has his principal role, passing through numerous tests prior to being granted membership. Thomas C. Warden, in his article titled "Whatever Happened to the Written Word?" states that "Masonic ritual relies upon mouth to ear, as does Masonic education to some extent. But the preponderance of our responsibility—our Masonic tradition, heritage, and history—is essentially and necessarily dependent upon the written word. For the most vivid memory pales by comparison to the faintest ink on a printed page."[42]

Due to the great emphasis Masons place on the practice of the degrees of Freemasonry and their legitimacy as founded in the past, they harbor an obsession for the preservation of those rituals in an utterly unchanged form. The vocabulary has, in effect, been sealed in a time capsule. Many of the words are cited in a magical fashion, and some believe they confer power. This is particularly true of the passwords by which members identify each other. Although the degrees of Freemasonry are presented in everyday language, the passwords are often universal. In this way, every Mason is able to remember when he was given—under highly dramatic circumstances, and after taking a solemn oath—the secret utterance by which he can identify his comrades.

Another aspect is that at times a word or phrase becomes "contaminated" because the world of the "profane" has appropriated these words or

---

41 Susan Linker, "A Collision of Rationalism and Spiritualism in *El hombre de la Rosa* of Manuel Rojas: Decoding the Secret Signals", *Hispanic Review*, num. 68, 2000, 27.

42 Thomas C. Warden, "Whatever Happened to the Written Word?" in: *Short Talk Bulletin*, Washington, D.C., The Masonic Service Association of the United States, August 1978, num. 8, 8.

expressions. One example is the phrase in English "giving someone the third degree," which English-speakers use to refer to the severe questioning to which the police may subject a suspect; in Masonic jargon, this refers to the Masonic third degree, in which the myth of Hiram is presented, perhaps the most important degree of Freemasonry.[43] The "third degree" carries no such colloquial meaning in Spanish; the expression is utilized only in its Masonic sense. These different aspects of legitimacy, of the secret, of antiquity, and of the esoteric meaning described before, help in understanding the notions of invisibility (the name of the translators rarely appear on any Masonic texts) and fidelity that Masonic translation enforced.[44]

DECIPHERING THE BOOK'S CONTENT

This book is divided into four chapters, an epilogue, and two appendices, which correspond to the phases of Freemasonry in Mexico that are proposed herein. Chapter 1, "The Formative Years and the Persecutions (1790–1820)," is split into three parts. First, a brief historical analysis of modern Freemasonry and its development in Europe is undertaken, followed, secondly, by a historical study of this institution in Mexico. In

---

43 "The master's degree is centered upon the idea of death and resurrection. It develops the legend of Hiram, a biblical character. The first book of Kings [5:15-32, 9:10-14 and 22-23], undertakes an extensive discussion of Hiram, King of Tiro, whom Solomon sought out to provide Lebanon with cedars for the construction of the Temple of Jerusalem. But the Hiram of Masonic ritual is far from being the King of Tiro. He was a skilled worker of metals, particularly gold, silver, and copper. The author of the first book of Kings describes him [7, 13-48]. The son of a *tirio*, a bronze-worker, and a widow of the tribe of Nephtalé. "He possessed great ability, skill and wisdom to carry out all types of works in bronze." Solomon brought him to Tiro to work on the Temple's ornamentations, all of which he did. In the first book of Kings, one can appreciate the detail of the works he did to beautify the Temple of Jerusalem. Among other works, the scripture mentions two copper columns, each 18 forearms high, topped with capitals in the shape of flowers. Hiram placed the columns in front of the vestibule of the sanctuary, he named the one on the right Yakin and the one on the left Boaz [I Reyes, 7:21-22]. According to the legend, Hiram the architect had numerous workers at his disposal, whom he divided into three classes, each receiving a salary commensurate with his level of skill. The three classes were apprentice, companion and master; each had its special mysteries and was recognized among its members by the use of words, signs and gestures particular to that class.

44 Guillermo de los Reyes, "The Cross and the Compass: The Influence of the Catholic Religion and Masonry in the Formation of the Mexican Political Thought," in: Nicolás Kanellos, ed., *Recovering Hispanic Religious Thought and Practice of the United States*, Cambridge, Cambridge Scholars Publishing, 2007, 145-146.

the third section of the chapter, Freemasonry's role in the independence movement, which began in 1810, is studied. During this period, scholars and those of the middle class found the Masonic lodges a safe harbor for the insurgency. I propose that the eagerness on the part of Masons to propagate these ideas and to create what they saw as a Masonic legacy based on the liberal European tradition gave rise to disturbances, struggles, and arguments in Mexican politics as well as Masonic life.

Chapter 2, "Political Prominence, Secularization and Anticlericalism (1820-1876)" is divided into four parts. The first part studies the repression and control of the Catholic Church over its colonial subjects and its constant persecution of Freemasonry. In addition, the restriction of freedom of the press headed by the emperor Agustín of Iturbide and the support given it by the Church are discussed in this section. Reaction to this censure greatly contributed to the development of anticlerical philosophies of political thought up to the dawn of the twentieth century.

The second part of Chapter 2 focuses on topics related to the smuggling of prohibited books into Mexico, their distribution, and impact, which takes place as a consequence of the censure imposed by the regime of the day. One example that is analyzed here is *The Freemasons' Monitor or Illustrations of Masonry* in Two Parts by Thomas Smith Webb, one of the most important books in Freemasonry, since it set forth the framework for the practice of some of the Masonic rituals carried out in nineteenth-century Mexico. This book supplies information related to the political and cultural situation in that country, the relevance of translating literary works (both Masonic and non-) in the creation of a Masonic literary canon, as well as its impact on the nationalist discourse, the editorial industry in Mexico, along with editorial traffic and the distribution and smuggling of Masonic books. In addition, the political situation of Mexico in the 1820s is analyzed in this section.[45]

The remaining pages of this chapter study some of the works of José Joaquín Fernández de Lizardi and Fray Servando Teresa de Mier as they relate to Freemasonry, as well as the impact that their writings had on the formation of Mexico's secular discourse and the debate surround citizens' individual liberties. Later there is a discussion of the two most import-

---

45   An abridged version of Chapter 2 has been published in English in G. de los Reyes, "Translating, Smuggling, and Recovering Books in Nineteenth Century Mexico", op. cit.

ant Masonic groups of the epoch, which became Mexico's first political parties. In the 1820s, the power struggle between the York Rite and the Scottish Rite gave rise to a conflict that I call "fraternal war without brotherhood." This war created a separation, not because of questions of ritual or symbolic principles but because of political conflicts. I also discuss the impact that Masonic diplomats and politicians of other countries (such as Joel Poinsett, the first U.S. ambassador to Mexico) had on Mexican national politics. Chapter 2 closes with a discussion of the creation, promotion, and evolution of the myth surrounding Benito Juárez. In this section, I analyze how this historical figure has continued as a founding myth representing laicism and secularization and his impact on the years that followed. The chapter links to the arguments presented in the ensuing chapters, in which a discussion is undertaken of the Distinguished Mexican Mason, Juárez, who is also known as *el Benemérito de las Américas*, in recognition of his work as a statesman and his promotion of secular and liberal ideas. To the Mexican Masons, he is without a doubt the most important Freemason in Mexican history.

In Chapter 3, "The Rule of Porfirio Díaz (the *Porfiriato*), Masonic Unification, and the Mexican Revolution (1876-1917)," I first explore Freemasonry during the time of Porfirio Díaz and the dictator's participation in that institution. We see how Díaz promoted the unification of the lodges of the Scottish Rite into an institution that was called "La Gran Dieta Simbólica." The main reason Díaz encouraged unification, as I state in this chapter, was in order to carry out his plan for national pacification. Díaz knew that he had to gain control of Freemasonry if he was to keep the group's members from creating difficulties for him in his quest to achieve the social order and progress that would characterize his government. For this reason, the dictator Díaz made sure that neither the Masons nor any other institution that might have influence in society was outside his control.[46] Later I present a brief study of the development of Masonic lodges during the time of the Mexican Revolution.

In Chapter 4, "The Post-Revolutionary Period, Decline and Transformation (1917-2010),"[47] I discuss the development of Freemasonry from

---

46   Some of the ideas posited in this chapter are briefly taken up in G. de los Reyes, "Freemasonry and Folklore in Mexican Presidentialism", *Journal of American Culture. Studies of a Civilization, op. cit.*

47   In the model that I propose of the stages of Masonry in Mexico, the fourth phase includes through 2010.

1917 until the time of the government of Carlos Salinas de Gortari. I place particular emphasis on Freemasonry during the Cristero War and during the regime of Lázaro Cárdenas. During that time, the Masons had great power since they could rely on the support of sitting presidents. In this epoch, the anticlerical precepts practiced in Mexican Freemasonry are reinforced.

The next section describes Freemasonry's loss of prominence and the transformation it underwent in the second half of the twentieth century. Here I attempt an explanation of the organization's decline and Freemasonry's situation within present-day Mexico.

In the epilogue, in addition to summarizing and analyzing the material presented in the foregoing chapters, I propose that when one speaks of Mexico's Freemasonry (and this applies to other parts of the world, including the United States), one should speak in the plural—Freemasonries—since the organization has developed along multiple angles and is very heterogeneous and dynamic; I propose that it cannot be viewed, therefore, as a monolithic phenomenon. Some material is included to which, I am certain, few people have had access, and with which, I believe, they should become familiar in order to understand the evolution of Freemasonry in Mexico.

Finally, it is necessary to stress that my intentions in carrying out the study of this organization and investigating it more in depth were strictly academic. As a result, I attempted to remain objective at all times to set aside any type of prejudice or stereotype pertaining to the topic, and to avoid any extreme empathy for it. My goal was always to pose a historical explanation of events so that, later, the reader might be transported to this present day through an objective lens based on historical documents and interviews. Of course, one must mention that all scholarly works are permeated by the subjectivities of those human beings interpreting the facts. This book is no exception. Nevertheless, a strong exercise of objectivity and unbiased interpretation was always present during the period I worked on this book.

It is no secret that Freemasonry created for itself a radical tradition, rooted in the quest for knowledge, tolerance, freedom, and equality; these are the self-same principals and characteristics that Carlos Monsiváis, in his book *Herencias ocultas de la Reforma liberal del siglo XIX*, assigned to liberal thought in Mexico, which should be revisited, rethought, and explored again in depth. Freemasonry, because of the liberal thinking it espoused in Europe, quickly became a key element in Mexico's political evolution,[48] all thanks to the group's ability to bring to their lodges great numbers of the most important men among the political and social elite in Mexico. The Masonic lodges created a space that promoted a secret civil society that significantly influenced the creation of liberal and secular thought in that country.

48   Guillermo de los Reyes, "Freemasonry and Folklore," *op. cit.*, 61.

CHAPTER 1

FORMATIVE BEGINNINGS AND PERSECUTIONS (1790-1820)

Historians have been very quick to deduce that secret plots are irrelevant, inappropriate or impossible to document. [...] But conspiracies abounded. They weren't just the product of paranoia and suspicion. We would be wise to take them seriously.[49]

ON THE ORIGINS OF THE MASONIC ORDER

Although it is not the objective of this book to assign an exact date Freemasonry first saw the light of day in Mexico, it is vitally important to review its origins. In that way, the reader may gain a clearer understanding of the Masonic institution, which remained secret from the time of its formation until not long ago, since it has recently come to be known by those who are not members of its ranks. In this chapter is presented, therefore, a historiographic analysis of the origins of modern Masonry that will allow for a better understanding of its development, as well as the debates that have arisen with respect to its beginnings. According to the most reliable current research on the topic, Freemasonry began in Scotland and later in England, and from there it expanded to continental Europe, including the Iberian Peninsula.[50]

In order to better understand the institution, it is extremely important to take into account the various opinions that form its founding narrative, since these represent a window of access "to know the conditions of life" of this society and to capture the countless forms of expression of "common sense."[51] In short, this chapter presents the various interpretations of these origins, as well as the historiographic discussions as to when Free-

---

49   David Fithian Stevens, "Autonomists, Nativists, Republicans and Monarchists: Conspiracy and Political History in Nineteenth-Century Mexico," *Mexican Studies/ Estudios Mexicanos*, Vol. 10, No. 1, Winter 1994, 266.

50   David Stevenson, *The Origins of Freemasonry: Scotland's Century 1590–1710*. Cambridge, Cambridge University, 1988. See also, Four Hundred Years of Freemasonry in Scotland, The Scottish Historical Review, 90(2), 280-295.

51   See Antonio Gramsci, *Antología, selección y traducción de notas*, Manuel Sacristán, ed. Mexico, Siglo XXI, 1988, 231-232; Gómez, Francisco, *Intelectuales y pueblo, op. cit.*, 101.

masonry emerged as an organized institution. My objective is not to specify an exact period or date on which Freemasonry first appeared. What I
attempt is a discussion of its antecedents, so as to better understand its
evolution in Mexico. Therefore, I focus on this organization's importance
during various epochs of Mexico's history. Many of the most relevant
events of contemporary history have been, while perhaps not brought
about by Masonry, at least influenced by ideas either created or promoted
by the institution's members.As was mentioned earlier, there is a great
discussion regarding Freemasonry's antecedents, both among those who
study it and within its ranks. On one hand, we have perspectives of its
origins that are based on the founding myths and lore of Masonry, which
defend the hypothesis that it dates from the times of King Solomon. In
fact, this camp holds that the Masons were the builders of King Solomon's temple. On the other hand, hypotheses have been proposed that
are based on historical documents as well as their interpretations which,
as with the history of any institution, vary according to how exhaustive
the studies are. Some of these propose Freemasonry began in the Middle
Ages and flourished in the Renaissance; others maintain that it arose at
the time of the Enlightenment, as we will see. Many Masonic authors and
the institution's very members defend the hypothesis of a mythological
past—that is, that they are descended from King Solomon. Meanwhile,
contemporary scholars are inclined toward the hypothesis based on historical documents. Even so, this latter group has not agreed upon the exact date when the first Masonic lodges arose.

Discussions of the Masonic institution's antecedents show that the myths,
legends, and hypotheses attributed to Masonry demonstrate that there is
no single, unified narrative as to its origins. We must rely on a plurality of
narratives that have to be considered together to better understand the
discourse of the organization's beginnings, by combining the foundational fictions with historical evidence. It is, therefore, important to use historiography to arrive at a more complete vision of its origins and their many
interpretations.

In like fashion, with studying the works that have sought to place a precise date on the origins of the Masonic institution, it can be seen that
great inconsistencies exist as to its genesis. There are two principal reasons for this: The organization's secretive nature that it has sustained for
many years, and the persecutions that have been leveled against it, which
have caused many of the founding documents to be either destroyed or

hidden. This situation has made the search for historical documents and evidence of the group's origins difficult.[52]

MYTHOLOGY OF ORIGINS: OPERATIVE MASONRY

The history of Freemasonry can be divided into two periods: operative Freemasonry and speculative Freemasonry. The former is the forerunner of the organization as we know it today, founded in a very remote past and which was the inspiration for all the symbols and rituals of speculative Freemasonry. The latter is modern Freemasonry, and from this we have evidence of its founding.

It is extremely important to see the difference between operative and speculative Freemasonry, since much of the current popular literature, such as Dan Brown's *The Lost Symbol* (2009), *The Da Vinci Code* (2003), and *Angels and Demons* (2000), emphasize operative Freemasonry and promote a fantastical past that, more than anything, forms part of the organization's founding mythology. One of the most popular Masonic interpretations of the group's origins is the one proposed by James Anderson (creator of the Masonic Constitution that currently is used by most of the Masonic lodges around the world), which holds that Masonry arose at the time of Adam and Eve and which, while not daring to attribute it to God Himself, installs it in the earthly paradise. There likewise exist many other legends that attribute the rise of Freemasonry to the construction of the pyramids of Egypt, to the Temple of Solomon in Jerusalem, or rather to the ancient mysteries of India, Egypt, Greece and Rome.[53] It is believed that Masonry is so ancient that it already existed and was practiced in Egypt's pyramids, in the temples of India, in the secret crypts of the Maya, in the Academy of Pythagoras, and in many other secret societies

---

52 It should be made clear that many times the persecutions, especially the ones suffered at the hands of the Inquisition, have helped modern-day scholars, since the archives of the Inquisition itself offer excellent information on the Masonic lodges and their members who were judged by the Inquisition. See Rogelio Aragón, "Contra la Iglesia y el Estado: Masonería e Inquisición en Nueva España," 1760–1820, *REHMLAC+ Revista de Estudios Históricos de la Masonería*, Vol. 3, Nº 1, Mayo 2011-Noviembre 2011, 198-202.

53 During my visits to the lodges of the Valley of Mexico, New York, San Francisco, Palo Alto, and Washington, they all had in some form or another (model, painting, etc.) the representation of the Temple of King Solomon, as well as various Egyptian motifs. Ambelain, *op. cit.* 32; Albert G. Mackey. *The History of Freemasonry: Its Legendary Origins*. New York, Gramercy Books, 1996, 10-17.

of ancient history.[54] Without a doubt, these are some of the explanations that make up the institution's myths and legends. It bears pointing out that not all members of the Masonic order share these interpretations. Many instead conceive of them as founding fables or fictions, promoted by James Anderson himself to lend legitimacy to the idea of the organization as ancient.[55]

These stories help us to understand why modern Masonry has certain rituals or utilizes titles that link it with all the myths and/or legends of its origins.[56] In fact, it can be noted that the practices of certain rituals, language and attitudes, among other things, have their origins precisely in all the interesting Masonic lore that has been transmitted from generation to generation. A considerable number of the rituals that are practiced in Masonic lodges were invented by members of speculative Masonry and are based on that mythological past, lending Masonry an ancient touch.[57] The use of ancestral myths or rituals as an organization's foundation is not the exclusive realm of Freemasonry. In some countries, mythical symbols are used as part of national rituals, as many scholars have discussed, such as Eric Hobsbawm and Benedict Anderson, among others. In Mexico, for example, symbols from the Mayan and Aztec cultures are among the founding symbolism of the nation.[58] As a result, epics and narratives have emerged that have contributed to the construction of a profound nationalism, which has been the object of a body of research and which has had a diversity of influence upon, among other things, Masonry itself (as we will see later); especially as regards the part that refers to the discourses and promotion of secularization, laicism, and anticlericalism.

---

54 Folder presented by the Coordinator of Special Studies, under the direction of the Great Lodge of the Valley of Mexico, titled *La Masonería es...* published by Editorial Herbasa, Mexico, D.F., July 1990; See C.W. Leadbeater. *Historia secreta de la masonería*. Barcelona, Editorial Humanitas, 1998, 23-60, 129-142.

55 Jean Palou, *La Franc-masonería*, Buenos Aires, Dedalo, 1979, 18.

56 There are some orders within Freemasonry that take this name: Order of the Eastern Star, Tall Cedars of Lebanon. Also, on the other hand, the title that Scottish-Rite Masons upon receiving the 16th degree is: Prince of Jerusalem. There are also found the Knights Templar in the York Rite.

57 See Eric Hobsbawm, *The Invention of Tradition*, Oxford: University of Oxford Press, 1983, 1-14.

58 See Guillermo de los Reyes, Heredia, "La rehabilitación del mito en las masonerías mexicana y estadounidense," *Cultura masónica: Revista temática de francmasonería*, Vol. XIV, Issue 49, April 2022: 190-200.

MODERN MASONRY: A HISTORICAL VIEW

The historian of Freemasonry Albert Mackey divides its history into two periods: that before historical records (already presented herein, also known as the operative period) and the historical or speculative period (from which those proofs necessary to corroborate the occurrence of events can be gathered). There is still some debate among Masonic historians regarding the moment at which operative Masonry transformed into speculative Masonry.[59] This is supported with the review of a great number of the works that speak of the organization's origins.

Many European and North American scholars have carried out studies about these origins, and for this reason I do not attempt here an exhaustive study of the topic.[60] My interest is in making a brief historical analysis of sources published in Mexico on this topic that have been little explored, and which present different points of view. Félix Navarrete, in his book, *La masonería en la historia y en las leyes de Méjico* (*Freemasonry in the History and Laws of Mexico*), undertakes an interesting discussion of the history of the Masonic order, specifically in two sources, one Masonic[61] and the other Catholic.[62] According to Navarrete, both of these writings hold that Masonry was born in London on June 24, 1717, when four of London's lodges came together and founded the Grand Lodge. Eugen Lennhoff, himself a Mason, states in this regard that it is not known exactly how these four lodges became the foundation of the organization, but it can be stated with certainty that these were the remnants of an older organization, although there is a lack of objective proof of this idea. Many Masons claim that Masonry is descended of the stonemasons' guilds that

---

59   Mackey, *op. cit.*, 10-11.

60   Margaret Jacob, *The Origins of Freemasonry: Facts and Fiction.* Philadelphia: University of Pennsylvania Press, 2006.

61   See Eugen Lennhoff, *Los masones ante la historia. Traducción directa de la segunda edición alemana por Federico Climent Terrer*, Barcelona, Biblioteca Orientalista, 1931, Section 787.

62   See the book *La masonería según los masones*. Article from the *American Encyclopedia*, translated to Spanish by the Bishop of Sonora; El Paso, Texas, 1933. The translator states "that the sources on which the author bases the article are basically of three types: 1) Masonic manuals published by the Masons; 2) Official newspapers and magazines from various lodges scattered throughout the world; 3) Reports from Masonic directors. If in these documents the Masons have not told the truth, do not fault the Holy Catholic Church and its directors for slandering them or doing them harm." Félix Navarrete, *op. cit.*, 9.

played a very important role in medieval Europe; the interesting part of this hypothesis is that it was unknown in Freemasonry's early days. It would not be until later times that it would be first revealed, by the Alsatian historian from Strasbourg, the Abbot Grandidier, who was not a Mason. Later still, a number of archives containing documents confirming this hypothesis came to light; even so, it has not been possible to gather a body of proof that can definitively answer when and where the syndicate of stoneworkers and gardeners became the Masonic order as it is known in the present day.

On the other hand, according to Navarrete, a Catholic publication on Freemasonry supposedly holds the true history of this organization that has caused such great problems for the Catholic Church. This journal is thought to present "the documentary history of Masonry and the authentic oral tradition, which comprise the basic sources from history, cleared of all manner of fallacies and in agreement with what some responsible Masonic historians demonstrate."[63] Despite a certain negativity toward Freemasonry on the part of its author, the arguments presented concur with other, Masonic sources.

What the sources do agree on is that since the beginning of the Middle Ages there existed all over Europe certain guilds into which workers would group according to their specialty, whether merchants, artisans, or professionals. In England during this time, the most powerful of these guilds was that of the builders or masons (the word meaning stoneworker in both English and French). The word *francmasón* (Spanish for Freemason) is derived from the French *francmaçon*; *franc* means "free" or "frank" (in the sense of "exemption"), and *maçon* means builder. So *francmasón* (Freemason) means "self-governing builder."[64] There are those who claim that the English word *freemason* was the first such word used within the ritualistic Masonic context. They also state that when Freemasonry arrived in France it was translated to French as *francmaçon* and was later adopted to Spanish as *francmasón*. This book takes the position that the word's origins are French and that the English used this French word to refer to the Masonic organization.[65]

---

63   "Historia de la masonería universal," in *Información sobre masonería y otras sociedades secretas*, Vol. I, September 1981, 23-25.

64   From Pando Villarroya, *Diccionario de voces de la masonería*, Mexico: 1996, 15.

65   See L. Fray and R. Arús. *Diccionario Enciclopédico de la Masonería en México*. Mexico: Ed. Valle de México, 1977, 10-15.

Freemasons were specialized builders with knowledge of architecture, who cut stone to make up the "freestone" wall in a specific and particular manner. The work of masons (bricklayers), in contrast, was simpler and involved only the breaking of stones. Guilds were formed in Germany and in England. A guild, during those times, focused on protecting the interests of its members, and was an instructional school where knowledge of the construction arts was inculcated, both in theory and in practice. They also served the purpose of safeguarding such secrets as they acquired over time, concerning both the art of construction as well as the process of teaching it. To avoid the infiltration of the guild by outsiders, each group acquired a secret code, such as a particular handshake or phrase, or other signs of recognition that only members understood.

All of the members of these guilds[66] met regularly in places termed lodges (the literal meaning of which is habitation or quarters and which Spanish-speaking Masons adopted as the corresponding *logia*). The lodge, or *logia* is a gathering of an unspecified number of Masons organized in accordance with the rules and practices accepted and followed by the Masonic organization. The lodge is the fundamental workshop of Masonry; it refers both to the place where the meeting is held and to the meeting itself.

These lodges had a hierarchical structure divided into three groups: the apprentices, who were those just beginning in the art of construction, a group in which some stayed several years, until their knowledge and experience allowed them access to the next group; the fellows, made up of members with more practice and greater experience in the construction arts; then, as they reached a certain level, they entered the rank of master, similar to modern-day engineers and architects.[67] As a consequence, Blue Masonry is made up of the three first degrees: apprentice, fellow, and master Mason.[68] It can be said with certainty that the majority of the

---

66   The members of the lodges were called masons or freemasons. Acosta states that "the masons are those who, by meeting the required conditions and fulfilling the necessary formalities for it, are admitted as members of the brotherhood by the initiation ceremony and are written as such in the corresponding registers of the Order." Humberto Acosta. *Normas instructivas para aprendices*. Mexico, Editorial Memphis, 1963, 12.

67   Ibid., 23-24. See Humberto Acosta, 14-20; Pedro Álvarez Lázaro. *La masonería, escuela de formación del ciudadano: La educación interna de los españoles en el último tercio del siglo XIX*. Madrid, Universidad Pontificia Comillas, 1996, 41-53.

68   As we will see in this book, Freemasonry has a wide variety of grades and Rites, even though there does exist a fundamental unity within the order, which is called Blue

world's Masons hold one of these three degrees, since, according to information available about the world's lodges, the majority of Freemasonry's initiates either make up or have achieved one of these degrees.[69] In this same way, there were many kinds of guilds in New Spain whose members held the degrees of apprentice, fellow, and master mason. Unfortunately, the exact relationship between such guilds and Masonry has yet to be proven. It is possible that Freemasonry imitated these guilds and therefore also acquired their main (and more recognized) symbols: the square, the compass, the hammer, the apron, and the term "workshop," which is used to refer to the society. These have been the symbols of the organization throughout time.[70]

There are authors who argue that "because of the need to travel and to understand other countries and customs, the Freemasons came into contact with different ways of thinking and different political organizations, which afforded them an exceptionally broad point of view regarding the religious, philosophical, economical, social, and political problems of their epoch. They had to acknowledge equal rights, men of other nationalities, creeds and races; this laid the foundation for the humanist principles of the nascent order."[71] This statement of one of the educational publications for new members of the craft shows that the romantic perception promoted by the Masonic order was unified, without divisions, and that Germans as well as Englishmen belonged to the same group and heard the same history. In practice, the order took on particular and specific characteristics in accordance with the place it had developed, as well as its historical, political and social context. As we have stated, the rituals practiced by every Mason in the world are the first three degrees that make up so called Blue Freemasonry.

With the passing of time, people not necessarily interested in architectur-

---

Masonry or Symbolic Masonry, that includes the three first grades: apprentice, fellow, and master.

69 See *Proceeding of the York Rite Lodge in Mexico*, 1950.

70 Navarrete, *op. cit.*, 11. See Jean Mourgues. *El Pensamiento Masónico. Una sabiduría para occidente.* Translation, Liliana Priasta. Madrid, Kompás Ediciones, 1997, 125-162. Arthur Edward Waite. *A New Encyclopedia of Freemasonry (Ars Magna Latomorum) and of Cognate Instituted Mysteries: Their Rite Literature and History.* Int. Emmit McLoughlin. New York: Random Houst, 1996; F.T.B. Clavel and John Trutch. *Manual del francmasón.* Madrid, Ediciones Alcántara, 1999, 17-54.

71 *La masonería es, op. cit.*, 27.

al construction continued to be admitted to the lodges. On the death of Oliver Cromwell, the newly crowned King of England showered favors upon the members of the guild in thanks for their support. Later, in 1688, as the result of the Glorious Revolution (1688–1689), William of Orange rose to power and thus began the Hanover Dynasty; because of this, the Freemasons enjoyed great political participation, which transformed them into political parties. As can be seen, from before the time of the founding of the first Grand Lodge, Masons were already coming together in lodges. These meetings had as their principal theme and objective the discussion of and the group's participation in politics.

In England there arose great changes, among the most important of which was the consolidation of Parliament's supremacy over the monarch and the creation of a new doctrine called liberalism. Because of the current interest of the age in knowing all the latest scientific and technological advances of the world, it is said that the English empire wished to establish a secret mechanism by which it could obtain information about everything that went on beyond its territories. It was for that reason that the decision was made to use these lodges of "masons" as a point of departure in the creation of this secret society. During those times, the Masonic lodges were made up principally of politicians and shopkeepers; nonetheless, they were not very well organized.[72] The purpose for the formation of these lodges was principally political and answered to the interests of an elite that little by little was taking shape and, from that moment, was acquiring power.

Anthony Sayer and John Theophilus Desaguliers were among those who, in their roles as Masonic leaders, began to organize and unite the lodges. Sayer was Grand Master in 1717 (several sources agree that he was the first Grand Master); Desaguliers assumed the post of Grand Master in 1719. It was on June 24, 1717, that four lodges came together and created a federal democratic body termed a Grand Lodge, which was headed by a Grand Master. From that moment on, Masonry is said to have entered

---

72   It should be mentioned that on the question of England's interest in creating secret societies throughout the world: as we mention here there is no evidence of this, nor does the source where this statement is made offer proof. Therefore, there is no proof at all presented that Masonic lodges were seen as a foundation for these secret societies. For the purposes of this research, it is not necessary to present definitive proof of Freemasonry's origins, but to present the different opinions and arguments that have arisen about it, to compare them and to present the works in which it relates with any influence to national politics. See *Información sobre la masonería y otras sociedades*, 25.

its modern age, since it was then that there was created an organism to which all lodges owed obedience, and this organism had the ability to create other lodges. It is from this that the concept of a lodge's regularity arises. Bit by bit, such a concept began to acquire great importance, and the Grand Lodge of England became the regulating organ of other Grand Lodges. For that reason, as new lodges arise, they try gradually to achieve the status of regular. There later arose several changes and disagreements; nonetheless, Masonic configuration did not drastically change.[73]

In the various sources dealing with the beginnings of modern Masonry, independent of their specific tendencies, we can see that they agree that it began on June 24, 1717, with the arrival of the Grand Lodge of England[74] (although they differ as to who was the first Grand Master). However, this does not mean that Masonic activities were begun at the moment the Grand Lodge was established. Even so, 1717 should be considered the date that marks the beginning of modern Masonry; even this brings a better understanding of the topic.

So it is that 1717 is the official date of the institutionalization of speculative Masonry; the establishment of the Grand Lodge of England marks the formal beginning of this institution. It is important, nonetheless, to consider David Stevenson's research, which proposes that Masonry began in Scotland at the end of the sixteenth century and was established in England 29 years before the Revolution of 1688. This thesis has been accepted by Masonic scholars such as Jacob, Rich and Ripley, among others, since it offers convincing evidence of Masonic lodges established informally in Scotland. It is important to mention that scholars Susan M. Sommer and Andrew Prescott in a recent article argue that there is not enough evidence to support that the foundation of the Grand Lodge of

---

73   On the other hand, Robert Ambelain, in his book *El secreto masónico*, points out: "Generally, the beginning of modern Masonry is placed at June 24, 1717, the date of the foundation of the Grand Lodge of London, for which four London lodges met in the inn at The Apple Tree, in Covent Garden. By majority vote, Anthony Sayer was elected Grand Master. It is unknown whether he was a gentleman. Now, beginning in 1721, Freemasonry will choose its Grand Masters from among the aristocracy, beginning with the Duke of Montagu. The (very high) obligation of believing in God, the Great Architect of the Universe, extended to all and, beginning in 1723, English Freemasonry admitted Jews to its ranks. Among these, Falk Sheck and Resh Galuth (whom they called the Prince of Exile, or Exilarca) stand out." Ambelain, *op. cit.*, 34.

74   See A. Mellor, *El secreto masónico.* Barcelona: A.H.R., 968, 47-65; Álvarez Lázar, 42-43.

England was in 1717, rather their research shows that perhaps it was established in 1721. However, even after their great discovery, Sommer and Prescott conclude:

> At the end of the day, does any of this matter? After all, we are only discussing about four years. What difference does it make if we say 1717 or 1721? In itself, not a great deal, but the important point is that in investigating these matters we are improving our understanding of the social, political and cultural context of freemasonry in the early eighteenth century. If we believe that freemasonry has played a significant role in society and that one period in which freemasonry made a particularly important contribution to human development was that of the Enlightenment, then the exploration of the way freemasonry emerged in a modern form in the taverns and coffee houses of London is an important and urgent matter.[75]

After this brief historical outline about the origins of modern Masonry and knowing that the purpose of this book is not to discover the organization's exact date of creation but rather to situate it in historical context, it can be stated that Masonry arose in Scotland at the end of the sixteenth century, as Stevenson states. The first Grand Lodge, following the modern definition of the term, began its work in England sometime between 1717 to 1721. Later, James Anderson was chosen to craft the Constitution and the by-laws that took effect in 1723, and to which some reforms were made in 1738. This bit of information is important because Anderson's Constitution is the forerunner of all Masonic Constitutions in the world. As a consequence, it is to be expected that these laws govern all the lodges of the world.

Immediately after modern Masonry was established, those among its ranks early on were noblemen and bishops of the Anglican Church, landowners, merchants, military leaders (especially of the navy), as well as royalty. Ambelain states that "England inclined outward. Obviously, Masonry would be one of the weapons necessary to be able to infiltrate

---

75   Susan Sommer & Andrew Prescott, "1717 and All That," 22-23, 1717-And-All-That-Prescott-Sommers.pdf (quatuorcoronati.com) access, May 22, 2024.

the new economic and liberal policies, which had certain very attractive principles."[76]

Freemasonry was gradually expanding into different parts of the world, beginning in London, where the first Grand Lodge physically was located, until it was a force not only in England but in the whole continent. The Masonic order enjoyed great success due to its distinguished members, including members of nobility and of the British Royal Family initiated as Masons. Between the years 1739 and 1772, certain internal conflicts arose that gave rise to the organization's splitting into two Rites: the Ancient and Accepted Scottish Rite and the York Rite or Rite of the Royal Arc. Freemasonry expanded quickly to other countries. It appeared in France between 1721 and 1732, achieving extraordinary growth. At this time "new rites were formed, and philosophical degrees were created, which was a poorly received innovation in other countries, since it infringed upon the Old Charges, which had been solely responsible for the establishing of the first three degrees."[77] These lodges founded in France were tied to the Enlightenment and to the development of the Encyclopedia. The Nine Sisters Lodge, for example, was created in 1776 by several men of the Enlightenment, among them the philosopher Diderot, the mathematician D'Alembert, and Voltaire himself.[78] In 1773, the restructured Grand Lodge of France took the name Grand Orient of France. Nevertheless, a number of Lodges contested these reforms and formed a National Grand Lodge known as the Grand Lodge of Clermont. These Lodges joined the Grand Orient in 1799, the Grand Orient of France was created, which took a different road from the Freemasonry of Great Britain. Later, the Grand Orient established lodges in South and Central America with the same revolutionary leanings.

In 1751 a new Grand Lodge was established in England, with different principles. Its members called themselves Yorks, or Old Masons, since they maintained they were descended from the Grand Lodge established in York in 1726. In 1813, they succeeded in getting the Grand Lodge of

---

76 Ibid., 26. See Facsimile from Jaime Anderson. *La Constitución de 1723. Compilación de las Marcas (Landmarks) de la masonería*. Silas H. Shepherd. INt. and Notes Pere Sánches Ferré. Translation Federico Climent Terrer, Barcelona, Editorial Alta Fulla.

77 Masonry began with the first three grades: apprentice, fellow, and master Mason, and later instituted the other grades, depending on the Rite.

78 David Gueiros Vieira, *"Liberalismo, masonería y protestantismo en Brasil, siglo XIX,"* in Bastian, *op. cit.,* 44.

England to adopt its forms of ritual. Many claim that here is where the York Rite first appeared.

The Grand Lodge of London gradually extended its influence in Great Britain. In 1717 its jurisdiction encompassed four lodges; in 1726, 63 lodges; and in 1733, 126. In the year 1725, the Grand Lodge of Ireland began its works, and 11 years later the Grand Lodge of Scotland was created. In the 1730s, masonry expanded to the British West Indies, the Antilles, and to the North American British Colonies.[79]

Nevertheless, not all Masonic groups had followed this movement. As time passed, more independent lodges were established, which took shape without the prior authorization of the Grand Lodge of England. The first lodge of this type was founded in Paris in 1725, while the Grand Lodge of France was established in 1732. There were also several military lodges, which started this movement in France with the arrival of King James II of England. In 1733 the royal order of Freemasonry was created, which took the name Grand Orient of France, representing close to 400 lodges. On November 7, 1894, the Supreme Council of the Scottish Rite granted autonomy to its blue lodges, which had developed the first three degrees and authorized their union with the Grand Lodge symbolic of Scotland.[80]

Friction occasionally occurred during this expansion between the different obediences, and sometimes between the Masons that made up their membership. Nevertheless, according to agreed-upon Masonic regulations, if one obedience accepts and welcomes another or, to the contrary, if it denies and/or rejects it, "does not change at all the brotherhood that unites the members of both."[81] In the same way, Freemasonry began to

---

79   Ambelain, *op. cit.,* 34-45.

80   Ibid.

81   In practice, this is far from true. In my visits to different lodges throughout Mexico and the United States, I observed that, as Ambelain states, some Lodges are recognized while others are not; but the fraternity among the members is not the same; most of the time simply no fraternity exists at all. For example, in San José, Yucatán, I visited two lodges. At one, I could not do any interviews because it was always closed, with a sign that read: Ancient and Accepted Scottish Rite. I did have the opportunity to visit the other lodge, and while there, I asked the Grand Secretary what the relation was that they had with the Ancient and Accepted Scottish Rite Lodge that was about a kilometer distant, and he replied that it was an independent lodge that by mistake was called Ancient and Accepted Scottish Rite Lodge, and that his lodge was the one that truly belonged to this Rite. I cannot really say that the two lodges were in con-

expand to the British colonies in America, and the colonizers quickly established Masonic lodges in their respective colonies. Little by little, Masonry expanded across the world.

Freemasonry, as it began to extend through the different regions, began to acquire certain particular characteristics according to the place where it was established. Every group continues to practice the same rite and to belong to the Intercontinental Convention. Even so, in the majority[82] of cases, there is variation in the language, lodge design, etc. (though always remaining faithful to what was called the Mother Lodge, according to that location.

At the time of its origins, the ranks of the Masonic order were open to any who wished to join; but it was gradually becoming a more selective organization, more exclusive, only for a select group. This can be seen in the case of Latin America as well as the United States, England, France, and Italy. This characteristic made the Masonic institution both peculiar and greatly influential in politics.

Thus, Freemasonry became a sort of "political preparatory school," in which members of the European elite formed political cadres, utilizing the lodge as a platform to advance their interests. Some of the Latin American insurgents/educated who traveled throughout Europe and the United States came in contact with the Masonic ranks and in those capitals were initiated into the organization, importing it to the Spanish colonies and founding Masonic lodges that later played an essential role in independence movements, in the definition of the young republics and, in the case of Mexico, in the secularization of the state.[83] Therefore, in the following section, a historical analysis of Freemasonry's origins in Mexico is undertaken, along with its development in the young Mexican republic.

---

flict, but I could see the lack of recognition of one lodge of the other, and in addition I could observe that there was no kind of brotherhood between the members of the two lodges.

82 Not "in every case," because on certain occasions the lodges of country X that expand into country Y continue to function as if they were in country X. For example, in San Francisco, there are several Asian or Mexican lodges that carry out their work in the native languages of their members. In Mexico, some York Rite lodges even continue to perform their works in English. In another example, in the building housing the Grand Lodge of New York, there are some lodges that work in German, others in French, Russian, Spanish, etc.

83 See José Antonio Ferrer Benimeli, ¿Bolívar Masón? Revista de Historia 16, num. 96.

This analysis is fueled by the Inquisitorial proceedings that offer a wide range of information about Masonry's existence, as well as the persecution that Masons suffered at the end of the eighteenth century.

A BRIEF HISTORIOGRAPHICAL DISCUSSION OF THE ORIGINS OF FREEMASONRY IN MEXICO

The history of Mexican Masonry in the eighteenth century still has not been written. Clearly, this organization's origins are tied to the development of Masonry in Spain. Some consider a lodge in Gibraltar in 1727 to be the beginning of organized Masonry in the south of Spain. In 1728, there was a lodge in Madrid whose Grand Master was a representative of the Stuart Pretender.[84] In 1749, a lodge in Cádiz claims to have had the impressive number of 800 members, and by 1750, there existed more than 100 lodges in Spain. This information has been promoted, particularly among the masonic historians, although there is no evidence that there were that number of members of the lodges of Cádiz during that time. There also is a bit of confusion due to the creation of co-Masonic organizations which, although the ritual and symbolism of Freemasonry influenced them, did not formally belong to it. To find out more about the genesis of Freemasonry in Mexico, it is necessary to dig into the Mexican Inquisition records and the anti-masonic narratives promoted by the Catholic church, as will be discussed in the following section.

THE VATICAN VS. MASONRY, AND ITS IMPACT ON MEXICO

Freemasonry's expansion occurred despite Pope Clemente XII's issue, in his Bull of 1738, *In eminenti*, in which he excommunicated all Freemasons

---

84 "No one speaks well of the Duke of Wharton. They call him dishonest, irresponsible, capricious, and some even label him disloyal to England. He joined the Roman Catholic church in 1728, and it is commonly supposed that he was the founder of the *Gormogons*, a group that never succeeded in doing anything but attempt to ridicule Freemasonry. Finally, he joined the Franciscan Order and died in misery in 1731 at the age of 33 years. He is punished in the *moral essays* of the Pope, Epode I ['Wharton, the disdain and marvel of our times, whose passion to govern was a lust of Worship.']." Henry Coil, *Coil's Masonic Encyclopedia*, William Mosely Brown *et al.* eds., Macoy Publishing & Masonic Supply Company, Richmond (Virginia) 1961, 470. "In 1726 he left England, never to return, and the following year found himself fighting against the British in the Siege of Gibraltar. For this he was banned from England and stripped of his title and properties in 1729. In the same year he formed a lodge in Madrid that listed until 1768..." William R. Denslow, *op. cit.*, 1958, 314.

and reserved to the Pope himself the power to absolve them. In 1751, Benedict XIV's papal bull (*Providas*) repeated Clemente XII's mandate.[85] From its very beginnings, Freemasonry in Spain has been considered by the Catholic Church to be a heretic organization, especially because of its secretive nature, and for this, it has been a target of attacks by the Church. There have been reactions to this by Masons and their sympathizers. This sentiment spread to the overseas territories, particularly to the Masonic organizations created in America by the Spanish and French lodges. This continues to the present day, with a distancing that oftentimes is more a question of tradition than of any official stance by either group.

In 1751, Spain's King Ferdinand VI outlawed Masonry, partly due to the report made by the Catholic priest José Torrubia. That report told of the Masonic rituals and of some of the things that went on in the lodges. Father Torrubia, on papal authority, was granted permission to take the Masonic oaths and to gain credibility for having joined Masonic lodges in Spain.[86] Torrubia's report continues to be very important in its impact, being one of the most-used criticisms against Masonry. It could be said that many of these events, to a greater or lesser extent, were duplicated in New Spain, since Masonry was outlawed there, too, and there was great paranoia on the part of the Church against the institution (not a unilateral sentiment).

There is evidence that Masonry was scattered throughout many parts of the Spanish Empire. Two Masons were prosecuted in 1756 in Manila. Elsewhere, in 1762, when the British captured Manila, attempts were made to hold military lodge meetings in the *Catedral de Intramuros*. In fact, this military lodge was organized by members of the Gibraltar Lodge.[87] In 1816, the Spanish Regency Council of the Indies issued a Royal Open Letter against the Freemasons:

> One of the most serious perversions that afflict the Church and the State is the growth of the order of free-masons, so often outlawed by the pontiffs, sovereigns, and

---

85   Ibid., 48, 68.

86   William R. Denslow, *op. cit.*, Vol. IV, 248.

87   Christopher Haffner, *The Craft in the East*, District Grand Lodge of Hong Kong and the Far East, Hong Kong, 1975. "The Archbishop of Manila wanted to completely destroy the Cathedral for its desecration, but he never got authorization from Spain to do that, and the Cathedral stood until the Second World War." *Idem.*

by all the Catholics of Europe [...] it is to the advantage of the spiritual wellbeing of the faithful and for the peace of nations the prevention, with the most scrupulous vigilance, of meetings of these type of people; and having already discovered in the Indies several of these evil secret religious societies [...] order and decree that all judges in the regular royal jurisdictions of these possessions [...] to proceed against the aforementioned freemasons.[88]

In the Spanish territories, Freemasonry was considered a political threat. One Catholic author blames the organization for the loss of the Philippines:

It is a paradox of history that Spain itself, especially after the revolution and the dissolution of all the orders in 1835, has begun to weaken its own position in the country by supporting Freemasonry. The association of the Philippines with lodge brothers in the United States and in the neighboring countries in Asia [...] brought about the independence movement, and, lately, to the surprise and disappointment of all parties involved, brought on the American occupation of the country.[89]

Another observer finds in Masonry the root of the Church's difficulties in Spanish America during the nineteenth century: "The class now in power, that had been so strongly affected by Freemasonry, found themselves to be still unready for rational laicism—most constitutions still incorporated Catholicism as the State religion—but they were in favor of the most important principles of the Enlightenment."[90] Opposition to the Masonic organization was quite severe, particularly on the part of the Church, who saw the Masons as a rival, a threat to its interests.

THE INQUISITION PERSECUTES THE MASONS

The Mexican Inquisition persecuted several individuals who defended that the organization of Freemasonry was a positive thing. Among them

---

88 Ibid., 12.

89 Ibid.

90 Roger Aubert, et al., *The Church Between Revolution and Restoration*, Trans. Peter Becker, Burns & Oates, London, 1981, 169.

were Juan Laussel, Manuel Zumalde, Pedro Burdales and Fray Servando Teresa de Mier. In 1785, a Mexican, Manuel Zumalde, along with a Frenchman and an Italian, were tried for suspicion of being Masons and for defending the organization.[91] The proceedings are found in the National Archives of Mexico and were also published in 1932 by the Mexican Office for Domestic Affairs under the title *Los precursores ideológicos de la Guerra de Independencia: La masonería en México, siglo XVII [The Ideological Precursors to the War of Independence: Masonry in Mexico, Seventeenth Century]*. This collection is a significant contribution to the study of Masonry because it catalogs several of the inquisitorial cases related to this topic, which serve as examples of Masonic persecution by the Church and, therefore, clearly illustrate the Catholic Church's attitude via an anti-Masonic discourse that had been already developed in Europe. At the same time, Inquisitorial proceedings provide information about Masonry's antecedents in New Spain. Rangel describes such a dynamic in a very peculiar way:

> Inevitably, to the Spanish dominions in America, Freemasonry arrived, where it tried to block and annihilate the Tribunal of the Holy Inquisition, only achieving this in part. In the Archive that belonged to the Tribunal of Mexico are found the consecutive causes of a Filipino, an Italian, and two Frenchmen being Freemasons, which are today published and will serve for the formation of Freemasonry's history in Mexico.[92]

The author also mentions that the inquisitorial cause in Manila against the Filipino Manuel Zumalde is due to the fact that the jurisdiction of the Inquisition of New Spain extended all the way to Central America and the Philippines. These proceedings demonstrate that in the eighteenth century in Mexico, and in other parts of the Spanish Empire, there existed indications of Masonry.[93] The persecution of the organization had taken

---

91   Denslow, *op. cit.*, IV, 364.

92   *Archivo General de la Nación Ramo Inquisición* (National Archives of Mexico, Inquisition Department), cause of faith of Don Manuel Zumalde, Sergent Major of the Manilia Provincial Militia, for propositions and suspicion of Freemasonry, 1780. See also Nicolás Rangel, *Los Precursores ideológicos de la Guerra de Independencia: La masonería en México, siglo XVIII, Vol II*. Mexico: National Archives of Mexico Publications, Vol. XXI, National Graphics Workshop, Mexico, 1932, VI.

93   For reasons of adequate space, we cannot go into detail in every one of the processes,

form in an effort to prevent its expansion and the accumulation of the power it had by that time amassed in Europe.

At the time of the arrival of Don Juan Vicente Pacheco de Güemes, second Count of Revillagigedo, the migration of French subjects to New Spain was well known. These migrants came from Paris and settled on San Francisco Street, where they opened hairdressing salons and shops dealing in *haute couture*. As examples of this, we find Pedro Leroy, Nicolás Bardet, Vicente Lulié, Juan Malveret, and Pedro Burdales, the last of which arrived in Mexico sometime between 1782 and 1784 and undertook several journeys through Querétaro, Molango, and Mextitlán.[94] In Molango he struck up a friendship with a priest and an ecclesiastical judge from that parish who, in the presence of Burdales, issued a panegyric on Masonry, and at the same time published various other pamphlets that "might be prohibited by the Holy Office." The priest José Ignacio Muñiz, who feared that someday Burdales would stand before the Tribunal of Faith, preferred to denounce him.

The priest from Tlachichonol questioned the priest from Molango because of the denunciation the latter had leveled against Burdales and the relationship he maintained with him. The examinee stated:

> That Burdales not only worshiped Masonry as a legitimate sect, but also said that those who attacked it were mere stupid novices and that the most notable men were Masons, such as the Archbishop and the Viceroy; that the society proposed establishing a lodge in Mexico, and that all its members had agreed to nominate the Viceroy as *Hermano Mayor y Venerable*; it was he who offered money and a room at the Palace, protecting the Masons.[95]

Burdales said in his statement that the Enlightened Dr. Alfonso de Haro y Peralta, who governed the Church and was the Viceroy, was not only affili-

---

even though the information provides material enough for a future investigation of the topic. Ferrer Benimeli touched briefly on the study of these processes in his majestic work: *Masonería e Inquisición de Latinoamérica durante el siglo XVIII*, Caracas, Universidad Católica Andrés Bello, 1973.

94   José A. Ferrer Benimeli, *Masonería e Inquisición, op. cit.,* 1973, 46.

95   National Archives of Mexico, Inquisition Department, Process against Pedro de Burdales, hairdresser and pedestrian, 1793. Rangel, XXIX.

ated with Masonry but, indeed, was its protector. Nicolás Rangel analyzes the Frenchman's assertion and says that "Sr. Dr. Alfonso de Haro y Peralta ... was born in Cuenca in 1729. Of extraordinary value from an early age, he solidly possessed philosophical and theological knowledge, as well as in different languages."[96] And Haro should have played an important role "before a corrupt and frivolous Court, where *chischibeismo* reached even some members of the Roman clergy, such as the Italian cleric Antonio Bonavita, Priest of Ayacapixtla."[97] These testimonials demonstrate the Church's aforementioned paranoia on the subject of Masonry. One needed only to express their support for the organization for the Inquisition to persecute them. Sometimes to speak in favor of Masonry was just as damning as it was actually to be a Mason (as was the case with Lizardi and Fray Servando, as we will see in the next chapter).

As for the Masonic rite, it should be mentioned that during the reign of Charles III, in Naples his minister, the Marqués de Tanucci, was given the task of fomenting and directing Freemasonry. The king, rather than adjudging the Freemasons guilty as he might have been expected to do, instead ordered that Don Genaro Pallatini—the president of the *Rota* who had ordered Freemasons to be apprehended—be put on trial. The principal Italian cities, including Rome, were home to a goodly number of lodges, of which the most enlightened men of the country were members. It would not be surprising that Sr. Haro was a Mason nor that being in Mexico he had decided to encourage the organization's development by offering a location he owned for their use.[98]

What catches one's attention is that Burdales, being in the same situation as Laussel, who also was persecuted by the Inquisition on suspicion of practicing Masonry, was allowed to go to Europe, without being required to stand before the Tribunal, while Laussel did not enjoy the same good fortune. Might it have been that they didn't want the names of the Archbishop and of the Viceroy to come to light, as well as those of several other well-known people? It is a pity that Burdales did not confess all that he knew about Freemasonry, because if he had, perhaps we would now have more information about this organization's development in Mexico.

---

96 Ibid.

97 Navarrete, *op. cit.,* 28.

98 This location was the Palace occupied by Ventura López, with a back door that opened onto Santa Teresa Street. See Rangel, *La masonería en México Siglo XVIII*, and Zalce and Rodríguez, 4.

Juan Laussel was Viceroy Revillagigedo's senior chef.[99] When he arrived in Mexico, he was one of the frequent attendees in the clock shop of the Frenchman Juan Esteban Larroche, the place where the most enlightened of the French residents of Mexico met, as well as the most forward-thinking Spaniards and Mexicans. In such places, encyclopedic books were read, along with other printed material from France and Holland, and these were discussed with great enthusiasm. Laussel was condemned for having said "it is cowardice to confess that he has never done so: he has affirmed that he indeed is a Freemason, and that is a good thing."[100] Rangel points out that Don Vicente F. Vidal immediately burned the books, without leaving a list of them. He told the Secretary of the Inquisition about them, that they were, "English; German; and only one French, Rousseau's Letters Written From the Mountain, unbound and timeworn; and a few small notebooks, twenty or thirty; that he burned on the patio of his home, as he saw they were of little or no value.[101]

It is quite likely that the liturgies, manuals, and statutes that Vidal burned were related to Masonry. In addition, Laussel stated that in the home of the watchmaker, he had recognized Dr. Durrey, the hairdressers Lulié and Du Roy "by the decreed signals of the fraternity" and it was there that the summer solstice of 1791 was celebrated. On August 9, 1795, the Inquisitors Juan de Mier y Villar, Antonio Bergosa y Jordán, y José Ruiz de Conejas sentenced Laussel to be taken to Spain, and from there to one of the prisons of Africa for three years.[102]

The documents and materials that exist today about the origins of Masonry in Mexico provide no exact information as to the year it began operating in that country, even though Inquisitorial proceedings bear testimony to Masonry's presence in New Spain at the end of the eighteenth century. Although they do not provide a precise date, it is known there was already debate over Masonic activities during that time. Also, as has been pointed out, the proceedings reveal the negative attitude the Church had toward Masonry. It can be argued that the majority of the Inquisitorial proceedings go hand-in-hand with other accusations having to do with

---

99   Ferrer, op. cit., 52.

100 National Archives of Mexico, Inquisition Department, Trial of Juan Laussel, Senior Chef of the Count of Revillagigedo, 1794. See also Rangel, 210.

101 National Archives of Mexico, Trial of Juan Laussel; Rangel xxx-xxxi.

102 Ibid.

the "abominable" French influence, or the "heretical" thought of certain authors. Because of that, it is not true that Masonry was the Church's sole target; more than anything, it was part of a group of "heresies" that, in the imaginary of the Church, were an assault against religious principles. A Masonic publication mentions that during the time of the Spanish Empire, "The Holy Office categorically prohibited masonry in the territory of New Spain. Transgressors—and, on many occasions, pseudo-transgressors who were reputed to be Masons, with vaguely harmful objectives —were punished by severe and inhuman means—among others, being burned alive.[103]

This prohibition was due specifically to the growing attitude of paranoia beginning in Catholic Europe because of the growth of Masonry from England to Spain. During the eighteenth century, as mentioned before, several papal bulls were issued against the Masons, and the Inquisition tried at all costs to prevent Masonry's expansion overseas. Nonetheless, this prohibition did not prevent the formation of Masonic lodges in the American territories, as we shall soon see.

THE FIRST LODGE IN MEXICO: A HISTORIOGRAPHIC PERSPECTIVE

Three classic works from within the Masonic ranks outline the history of Freemasonry in Mexico. They are: *Historia de la masonería en México desde 1806 hasta 1884* (*History of Masonry in Mexico from 1806 to 1884*) published in 1884, by José María Mateos (one of the founders of the Mexican National Rite); *Una contribución a la historia masónica de México* (*A Contribution to the Masonic History of Mexico*) published in 1899 by Richard Chism[104]; and *Apuntes para la historia de la masonería en México* (*Notes on the History of Masonry in Mexico*), published in 1950 by Luis J. Zalce y

---

103 "Commentary on Masonry," s.a., *Acción del saber* 1 (March 93/94): 8.

104 Chism states that he wrote his book because he found various "histories" of Masonry in Mexico, published in the United States, which were quite far from the reality, and that they falsified and distorted the true events of the history of Masonry in Mexico. Chism states: "Having a profound indignation against these opinions, I began to study the Masonic history in Mexico at some length; by searching everywhere the information that has survived the years of revolutionary tumult and armed invasion in which Mexican Masonry was born and developed, to coordinate this dispassionately and without distortion, forming the narration of the facts as best I could, in light of the documents I've been able to acquire." Richard Chism, *op. cit.*, 15-16.

Rodríguez. The vast majority of books about Masonry in Mexico cite one or more of these sources to some degree. Since so few works contain information on the origins of the first lodges in Mexico, these sources have become obligatory, particularly for their historical richness.

Mateos and Chism mention the existence of a lodge on *calle de las Ratas* in Mexico City. In addition, the masonic historians assume this lodge arose after a group of Mexicans who "were found tied hand and foot, sunken in the most complete lethargy that tyranny could cause"[105] were able to form a lodge. Mateos points out that the history of this lodge has not been preserved, so we do not have the specific details of the event. Chism mentions that the lodge belonged to the York Rite since the Grand Lodge of England established four lodges in Spain: one in Madrid, another in Cádiz, and two in Gibraltar. Chism is inclined to believe that the lodge that Mateos considers to be the first in Mexico was a political center since the latter shows us that it was in that lodge that the idea of Mexican independence was begun.[106]

On the other hand, masonic historian Zalce y Rodríguez presents a different date for Masonry's start in Mexico from that of Mateos and Richard Chism. He says this on the subject:

> Thus established as dogma, the only lodge of which Mateos tells us, it is understood that it met in Number 5 on the former *Calle de las Ratas* (*Ratas* street), which is now Number 73 Bolívar Street in Mexico City, and that it was established by Don Enrique Muñiz [...] The house in question was the home of Don Manuel Luyando, city alderman; due to that position, it is believed that other aldermen, such as the Marqués de Uluapa and the Trustee *Licensiado* Francisco Primo de Verdad y Ramos, were also members of this lodge. [While] Mateos [...] admits that no document exists that can "officially" establish its origins or its provenance, nor its duration, nor anything

---

105 Mateos, *op. cit.,* 15.

106 Ibid., p. 607. See Richard E. Chism, *Una contribución a la historia masónica de México,* 217-219. Additionally in this same section, Chism says that the history of this lodge (the one on *calle da las Ratas*) was lost in the Mexican War of Independence, and that it is not known where the lodge got its charter, if it ever had one, or if it was only a group of Masons that rebuilt the original right of Freemasonry.

about "if it might have any political purpose," he relates
the names of those who were said to have comprised
it: don Gregorio Martínez; Feliciano Vargas; Miguel
Domínguez; Miguel Hidalgo y Costilla, Parish Priest of
the *Congregación de los Dolores*; and Ignacio Allende.[107]

In any case, it is possible that Enrique Muñiz had been initiated in one of
the four lodges that depended on the Grand Lodge of England and that
later he had brought together those born on the Iberian Peninsula and
the so-called *criollos* (sons of Spaniards born in New Spain) for Masonic
as well as political interests. Masonry's antecedents date from the end of
the eighteenth century. Perhaps the lodge on *Calle de las Ratas* is the first
lodge known with certainty to have existed. Nevertheless, as has already
been seen in the case of the Inquisitorial archives, there is evidence that
Masonic activities appeared before the creation of that lodge.[108]

A Masonic lodge did indeed convene in Larroche's house. One reason
they met in private homes during those times is that it allowed members
of the viceroyalty to appear not to be involved, particularly with meetings
of this type. Such individuals were motivated to take many precautions so
as to avoid being discovered and persecuted by the Inquisition. An exact
accounting of the organization's members and its circumstances would
have been impossible to obtain except under the rigorous discipline of
a carefully organized and directed lodge. The use of symbols and other
means of recognition, in those times, was only practiced in the lodges, before beginning their works, "so that it was certain that the person was not
a profane who was inquiring. Because the asking by the use of such signs
is a particularly Masonic way that eludes even the best profane observer."
Therefore, "a celebration of the solstice, such as the one in the summer of
1791, cannot be arranged except by an organized lodge."[109] For anyone

---

107 Chism, *op. cit.,* 8.

108 "We must correct the primacy that Mateos and Chism award the Lodge on *la calle de
Ratas.* From 1782 to 1784 and in the ensuing years, the activities of certain French im-
migrants, suspected by the Inquisition, were evident; the meetings in the watch shop
of Larroche ... where those present recognized each other by the signs established
by the fraternity and that the celebration of the summer solstice in 1791 was held.
All this is known from authentic documents, which are testimonies within reach of
any researcher, located in the National Archives of Mexico so that we can with complete confidence know that it was in the watch shop of Larroche that the first Masonic
Lodge met that we know of to this point." Ibid., 7-8.

109 Chism, *op cit.,* 8.

who has read the declarations of the Holy Inquisition,[110] in which one sees how the accused resisted answering certain difficult questions, it is not unreasonable to think that Larroche, Burdales, and their colleagues comprised a Masonic lodge.[111]

On the other hand, the chronicler of Mexican Masonry, Grand Master Jaime Ayala Ponce, in his book *Introducción a la francmasonería* (Introduction to Freemasonry), mentions that Masonry appears in Mexico beginning in 1771, and that the *criollos* and nationals met in the house of Don Juan Esteban Larroche, where the ideas of the encyclopedists were discussed. Ayala makes no reference to any document or other evidence that might corroborate Masonry's beginnings in Mexico in 1771; Ayala simply proposes it as the date, without presenting any proof. As for the meetings at Larroche's house, Ayala agrees with the opinion of Luis Zalce.[112]

In this way, Masonry began to spread throughout America in the eighteenth century (it began in 1733 in the United States). Thus, one wonders why it arrived so late in New Spain. Evidently, the Inquisition played a large part in this. The point I argue is that although a Masonic movement as broadly organized as in other parts of the world did not take place in New Spain, there was a Masonic presence there at the end of the eighteenth century. So, Masonry expanded through Spain from the first half of the eighteenth century, and its members had a great interest in spreading it throughout the New World, as did those residents of New Spain who had been initiated in Philadelphia, London, Madrid, Cádiz, or Paris. It is for that reason that it can be proposed that the first Masonic activities in Mexico became apparent after the end of the eighteenth century and not beginning after 1806 as Mateos and other authors have stated.[113]

As Michael Meyer and William reveal, "the Masonic meetings were, of course, carried out in secret and, since the lodges were inviolable, all of the machinations could be hatched behind closed doors, with little fear of being exposed."[114] This statement shows the strategy employed in Europe,

---

110 See one of the most comprehensive works on this topic, José A. Ferrer Benimeli, *Los Archivos, op. cit.*, 100-115; 637-654.

111 Chism, 9.

112 Jaime Ayala Ponce, *Introducción a la francmasonereia I*, Mexico, Recca, 1983, 97.

113 Félix Navarrete mentions in his book, cited previously, that Freemasonry in Mexico began at that time.

114 Michael C. Meyer and William L. Sherman, *The Course of Mexican History*, Oxford: Oxford University Press, 1991, 317.

which certainly spread to New Spain by creating a tradition of tight secrecy and mystery around the organization.

According to William R. Denslow's work, Fausto Ehuller and the Aragón brothers have the distinction of having established (in the nineteenth century) the first modern Masonic lodge in Mexico City. It is also mentioned that the founders of the lodge sought out various insurgents, among them Miguel Hidalgo, who joined them in meetings.[115] Denslow, one of the most quoted scholars of Masonry in the United States and the rest of the world, provides neither documents about initiation nor about the formation of the lodge. However, there are coincidences between that which this author describes and that which Chism (especially) and Mateos say.

It is important to pause for a moment to explore the affiliation with the Masons of Miguel Hidalgo and other insurgents. The only evidence available on this topic is that which Masonic chroniclers provide us. There are historians in Mexico who do not share that opinion and others who assure us that the father of that country did indeed take his place among the ranks of the Masons, alongside other enlightened men. We know that Miguel Hidalgo met secretly with other rebels and that they had the so-called plots for independence. Evidence also exists that Hidalgo was very close to some members of the Masons and that he, too, was persecuted by the Inquisition. It is plain that the Inquisition's judgments handed down on this man were not motivated by his Masonic involvement. Nevertheless, it is yet another coincidence of his possible Masonic affiliation with the *Cura de Dolores*. It is not the purpose of this book to point out those who were and those who were not Masons. However, a pause to provide the foregoing explanation is merited since Hidalgo's Masonic affiliation is a very controversial topic and should be studied more in depth.

As will be explained later, a great part of Freemasonry in Mexico derives from what is called Scottish Rite. This has been one of the most important and popular of the Masonic rites systems. In many countries, including the United States and Canada, the Scottish Rite is highly respected and possesses no political character. Nonetheless, its public image has not always been a positive one, as can be seen in a published denunciation presented more than a century ago, which posits the following:

---

115 William R. Denslow, *op. cit.*, 13.

The Scottish Rite has its origins in the hearts and minds of Presbyterians; of tyrannical renegades, of Jews, who retained nothing of Judaism but whose hate for Christ, along with the Jesuits, conspired against Europe's freedoms for the overthrow of the government of France. Its first home in this country was the city of the Nullification, Secession, and Rebellion; in Charleston, South Carolina, in 1801, 13 Jews and three Protestants, Mitchell, Dalcho, and Provost, who had received them from France, pretending to find them in the constitution given by Frederick the Great. If Satan had chosen the time, the inventors, and the place of this Rite, undoubtedly, he would have chosen the same.[116]

The same critic (J. Blanchard, then rector of Wheaton College of Illinois), believed that the Scottish Rite had a political structure based on that of the Southern empire headed by the rebel politician Aaron Burr who, between 1805 and 1806, was implicated in mysterious negotiations in the territory of Mississippi. Burr was accused of creating an empire of slaves to the west and south of the Mississippi River, which would have included Mexico and Central America. He was also accused of treason, and part of the evidence used against him was written in Masonic language.

The fact that Burr was a member of a Masonic lodge and that some of his associates were Masons, together with the use of letters with Masonic language, was enough to convince conspiracy theorists that there was support by Burr and the Masons for the creation of a new country between the United States and Mexico:

> All things taken together, that the mind should be weak, ignorant, or worse; which does not see, in the Charleston Supreme Council of 1801 and the Ancient and Accepted Scottish Rite, a devil's government with a devil's gospel; and this arose in the underground lodges, in the harsh words of Lamartine, the "Catacombs" of a new ritualist religion which, in the *Champ de Mars*, was one of a naked woman, a Goddess of Reason.[117]

---

116 J. Blanchard, *Scottish Rite Masonry Illustrated,* Vol. I. Charles T. Powner, Chicago, reptd. 1979, 29.

117 Ibid.

Such opinions do not guarantee the existence of adequate amounts of material on the relationship between Masonry and politics in Mexico. However, they do demonstrate the arguments that were generated against it, and the accusations that were made against it, discrediting it as a politicized institution.

In the next section, we will discuss the means by which Masonry remained active during the Spanish reign in Mexico; we will also see how, during the time Guadalupe Victoria was president, this secret organization occupied a central place in Mexican politics. Victoria's presidency stands out for the appearance on the political scene of political and Masonic groups, the Yorks and the Scottish.

MASONRY IN THE TIME OF MEXICAN INDEPENDENCE

As we delve more deeply into the study of the Mexican insurgency that began in 1810 and of the various ideologies and political antecedents that influenced the conscience of those directing and commanding the operations of the independence movement, we understand Masonry's great intellectual importance to this entire process.[118] At the time the ideas expounded that would contribute to the development of the consciousness required for revolutionary change, as took place in the times following the unrest and mobilization of the independence movement, a Freemasonry very close to these ideas can be discerned. The evidence reveals the permanent presence of men belonging to Masonic organizations of the various rites and dependencies, as was the case with Guadalupe Victoria who, with the help of the York Masons, succeeded in becoming Mexico's first president. These men were determined to awaken the peoples of Mexico and take them into battle, a difficult and tireless task that took more than a half-century to bear fruit.[119] During this period, Masonic groups begin to meet regularly, and important persons are found among their ranks. Because of the lack of information, it cannot be stated with absolute certainty which texts, documents, or campaigns were influenced by Masonry. What can be confidently stated is that there was Masonic participation in politics, in the insurgency, and in the decision-making of the Independence movement. It is fitting to note that one should be very cautious about making claims as to who might have been among the Masonic

---

118 Alfonso Fernández, *op. cit.*, 5.

119 Ibid.

ranks, since there is no evidence; but by seeing Masonry's great presence in the events of the time, one can deduce some of the participants.

Hans-Jürgen Prien observes that although the Masonic groups were not pursuing political objectives, they did exercise certain authority in the "formation of awareness." Bit by bit, the ideas that developed in the lodges were setting the stage for independence. In this regard, Hans-Jürgen Prien argues that "although there was a natural opposition of interests between Freemasonry and the patriarchy of the Roman Catholic Church [...] a considerable part of the native Latin American clergy manifested its adherence to Freemasonry because this was the representative indicator of the struggle for independence."[120] At the end of the eighteenth century and the beginning of the nineteenth in Spanish America, it was customary that educated persons of the upper class, as well as intellectuals, researchers, priests, and military men, would meet to discuss, study, and propagate the documents that opened up the new ideas of freedom and independence. It has been clearly shown that Masonic meetings counted many such persons among their members. To prevent their being discovered, considering the politics of the Inquisition, members of the Masons would always organize themselves in secret lodges:

> Such societies were disguised as "Fraternal Associations," "Brotherhoods of Charity," "Patriotic, Scientific, Philanthropic Societies," etc. This allowed them to operate legally, influence the social environment, meet to study, and commit to these new ideas without arousing suspicions, attract and initiate members, and create new Masonic groups.[121]

In this first stage of Mexico's history, Masons risked their fortunes, their freedom, and tranquility for the goal of multiplying their action for the whole country,[122] a clear example of Masonic participation in the move for independence, as several of the insurgents were an active part in the independence movement. These men did not abandon their understandable drive (and in some cases Masonic interest) to be independent of Spain. And the persecution of the Masons and the paranoia that it

---

120 Hans-Jürgen Prien. "Protestantism, Liberalism and Freemasonry in Latin America during the Nineteenth Century: Research Problems," in Bastian, 22.

121 Ibid., 6.

122 Ibid., 7.

caused did not stop a number of clerics from being initiated into the organization.

Some Masonic sympathizers point out that it had a great influence on the intellectual elite during independence. One demonstration of this is presented by Fernández Cabrelli in his book *La francmasonería en la Independencia de Hispanoamérica* (*Freemasonry in Hispanoamerican Independence*), where he cites Antonia Zúñiga, who argues:

> The link between the *criollos* and the cultural, political, social and Masonic centers of Europe of the day cannot be denied; as well as the role that these centers or societies played in Hispanoamerica facilitating the new ideas of liberty, democracy, republicanism, and emancipation or, if you prefer, independence. The *criollos* who were able to come to Europe—among them Miranda, Bolívar, San Martín, Belgrano, Alvear, Mier, Nariño … and so many others—steeped in the political cultural currents in vogue during those times in Europe, returned to *las Indias* with new ideas and decisions to accelerate the process of emancipation.[123]

Although this is the opinion of a member of the Masons, that it alludes to Masonry giving rise to the movement for independence in America is similar to what one of its enemies proposes, i.e. Primitivo Ibáñez, who states:

> The various causes that influenced the American insurrection, some produced by Masonry with this objective, such as the parliamentarianism of the Courts of Cádiz; liberalism, which in terms of doctrine is none other than Masonry […] claims for Masonry the honor of having initiated the treason of separating Spain from its empire in the Americas.[124]

These opinions reveal the tendency toward two extremes: to either defend or to criticize Masonry's role in Mexican independence. Its influence can be seen reflected in the construction of an opinion in favor of

---

123 "Aproximación a las llamadas logias Lautaro," *Hoy es historia*, No. 23, September-October 1987, Motivideo. Quoted in Ferrer Benimeli, 16.

124 Ferrer Benimeli, 17.

independence and in its active participation in the struggles undertaken toward it. At the same time, this proves the interest that Masonry has inspired in a small group of researchers, essayists, historians (both Masons and non-), especially Latin Americans, and the equality of their opinions when referring to the role of Masonic influence in American liberation movements of the nineteenth century. Masonic, anti-masonic, and profane authors alike recognize that the presence of Masonry and its followers contributed to the preparation and development of revolution in the Americas.[125] The influence of Masonry can be appreciated mainly in the works directed against it since, owing to its censure and persecution, there are no extant Masonic apologist texts from before the time of independence. These, as we will examine in the next chapter, appear later, after the 1820s.[126]

---

125 Primitivo Ibáñez, *La Masonería y la pérdida de las colonias*, Burgos, 1938, 14.

126 It should be noted that Freemasonry was not the only group that contributed to the move for independence. Many forces added to this movement.

CHAPTER 2

POLITICAL PROTAGONISM, SECULARIZATION AND ANTICLERICALISM (1820–1876)

Rome, political, enlightened and tolerant, will bring to our
religion many advantages that it has been noted to lack, for
various popes not deigning to give to God that which belongs
to God, and to Caesar and to the people that which belongs to
them ... His Majesty banishes from us wrath and vengeance
in the name of religion, so that one day the Christian and the
Hebrew, the Moor and the Gentile, the Protestant and the
Roman, are touched by the kiss of peace ... [127]

THE CATHOLIC CHURCH AND CENSURE

From colonial times, the Catholic Church has been an institution that has enjoyed broad power and influence within the Mexican political system. The process of evangelizing practiced by the conquistadors either Christianized or conquered the imaginary of the colonial subject, since despite the resultant syncretism, the Church had a great effect upon the regulation of political discourse and control of the colonized. During this time there was no separation of Church and State. Through his representatives in New Spain, the king controlled part and the Church controlled the other, the most important of which was control of the bodies and minds of the colonialized subjects. The friars and priests were given this task; both the Church and the Crown had this job of Christianization and control, evidenced by the installation of the Holy Inquisition. [128]

In the beginning, both the Church and the Crown dedicated themselves to carrying out their respective charges, but gradually the Crown realized that the Church was acquiring greater power. It also noted that colonial subjects were influenced primarily by the guidance of the clergy, with the

---

127 José Joaquín Fernández de Lizardi. "Segunda Defensa de los Francmasones." In *El laberinto de la Utopía: José Joaquín Fernández de Lizardi, una antología general.* México, Fondo de Cultura Económica-Fundación para las Letras Mexicanas, UNAM, 2006, 250.

128 See Nancy Farriss. *Crown and Clergy in Colonial Mexico, 1759–1821: The Crisis of Ecclesiastical Privilege.* Athlone, 1968; Alberro, Solange. *Inquisición y sociedad en México, 1571–1700,* México, FCE, 1988.

monarchy seen as a distant authority that separated them from society. The ideas of the Enlightenment that began to develop in Europe, and which traveled rapidly to the New World, also contributed to the Crown regaining control of its subjects. Also, the Bourbon reforms gave the Crown greater control in several areas formerly controlled by the Church.

Faced with this, the Church began to shore up its power over the various publications and books that were printed in or came into New Spain. Little by little, this contributed to its becoming an organ of censorship and control over what was read in the colony at about the time of independence. The relevant point here is that many aspects of the Mexican political imaginary were brought about by the strict censorship that the Catholic Church—by means of the Inquisition—imposed upon the editorial industry and, especially, the free dissemination of ideas. In this regard, the Mexican writer José Emilio Pacheco notes:

> For reasons of Christianity against paganism and of sexual morality, they deprived us of Greece as they stripped us from the Bible to impede "Protestant contagion." There is not enough space available to illustrate how much the Inquisition perpetrated this cultural cleansing in New Spain by bringing us through the back door into a model of social organization that was breaking up in Europe but that would be rooted in the new continent for more than three centuries. The first fruits of this *cordón sanitario* [sanitizing cordon] that Spain placed around its territories was avoiding the "Lutheran heresy" and its consubstantial right to examine questions of faith by means of believers having direct access to the Bible.[129]

Pacheco clearly describes the impact that the Inquisition had on the New World and how it contributed to repression and achieved a great degree of control over society. Such control emerged with tremendous force at the beginning of the Conquest and continued throughout ups and downs of the colonial period, though never disappearing from the political and social panorama.

Despite the relative lessening of the Church's control, it continued to ex-

---

129 Cited in Carlos Martínez García, "Docetismo Mexicano," in *La Jornada* [México], April 19, 2000, 14.

ercise power into the nineteenth century. An example of this is the Plan of Iguala, or the Plan of Three Guarantees,[130] in which Catholicism was recognized as the only religion that could be practiced in Mexico.[131] As a consequence, in the First Constitution of Independent Mexico (1824), Catholicism was confirmed as the young republic's only religion.

As mentioned previously, the Catholic Church controlled literary production as well as the editorial industry during the colonial period, even into the first years of Mexico's independence. For several centuries this institution censored certain books because they were considered offensive before God and the Catholic religion. When the Church lacked direct power, it did everything possible to lobby for its views to be heard so that censorship would be carried out. We can see an example of this in the royal Printing Regulations, which specify that:

> The multitude of books that directly attack the Holy Catholic Apostolic Roman religion, by different authors and with different titles, flood this Court and other places in the Empire, have powerfully caught the attention of the State Council. Various sessions have dealt with the legal means that Your Majesty should consult in order to stop the torrent of evils that the introduction and circulation of such books will doubtless cause the entire Nation.[132]

---

130 The Mexican Plan of Three Guarantees, proclaimed in 1821, was a foundational agreement that aimed to secure Mexico's independence from Spain. Created by Agustín de Iturbide and Vicente Guerrero (one of the leaders of the Yorkinos), it was based on three main principles or "guarantees": a) Religion – Roman Catholicism would be the official religion; b) Independence – Mexico would be independent from Spanish rule; c) Unity – Equal treatment and unity among social classes and ethnic groups. These guarantees formed the basis for the Army of the Three Guarantees, which helped secure Mexico's peaceful transition to independence.

131 "The Plan of Iguala treated separation as a fait accompli, although at the beginning this plan was nothing more than a proposal that Iturbide hoped would unify the nation. It has an air of authority that would lead one to at least reliably suppose that it was a fundamental law, accepted without error by the nation in general–especially after being endorsed in the Treaty of Córdoba. Iturbide faithfully adhered to what he interpreted as its three basic points: the creation of a moderate constitutional monarchy, the protection of the Church, and the protection of those Spanish who remained in independent Mexico." Timothy Anna, *El Imperio de Iturbide*, México, Alianza Editorial, 1991, 17.

132 Imprenta Real, *Reglamento,* 26 de septiembre de 1822, British Library.

In like fashion, in the Rules published by Iturbide on September 26, 1822, there was included a list of books recommended for censure for attacks on the Catholic Church and the faith of the Mexican people. Among them were included:

Guerra de los Dioses (War of the Gods)

Compendio del origen de todos los cultos por Dupuis (Compendium of the Origin of All Cults by Dupuis)

Meditaciones sobre las ruinas, ó lo que comúnmente se llama: Ruinas de Palmira (Meditations on the Ruins, or What is Commonly Called: The Ruins of Palmyra)

El Citador (The Summoner)

La sana razón, ó el buen sentido, ó sea las ideas naturales opuestas á las sobrenaturales, así en su edición de Ginebra de [1]819, como en la de Madrid de [1]821, y cualquiera otra. (Sound Reason, or Common Sense, or Natural Ideas Opposed to the Supernatural, in both the 1819 Geneva Edition and the 1821 Madrid Edition, and Any Other).

El Compadre Mateo, ó Baturrillo del espíritu humano. (Mateo the Godfather, or Medley of the Human Spirit).

Cartas familiares del ciudadano José Joaquín de Clara Rosa á Madama Leocadia. (Familiar Letters from Citizen José Joaquín de Clara Rosa to Madam Leocadia)

Carta de Taillerand Perigot al Papa. (Letter from Taillerand Perigot to the Pope)

El sistema de la naturaleza, y su compendio (The System of Nature, and Its Compendium).

El Monitor Masónico (Freemason's Monitor)

In like fashion, Iturbide, influenced in great part by the Church, proposed the creation of a regulation that prohibited freedom of the press. In light of this, a commission of political representatives of Congress was created to analyze Iturbide's proposal. The commission—principally made up of liberal and moderate representatives, many of them Masons—decided that a proposal against freedom of the press was an affront against a fundamental human liberty. Perhaps this insistence on the part of the Church to restrict freedom of the press was one of the main causes of an anti-clerical attitude that developed among many Masons. Though during the time of the Inquisitorial persecutions there were still no organized Masonic lodges in Mexico, Freemasonry was already well developed there by this time. The attitude of the Church generated great tension and clearly shows the distancing that arose between these institutions beginning in this period. It is fair to say that this tension between the Church and Free-masonry would last until the twentieth century [133]

The Church exercised some of its control by means of censorship and per-secution of books it considered unsuitable for colonial subjects. Mainly Masonic books were on this list of banned books, and it was prohibited either to publish them or to bring them into the country. This control, censure and repression imposed by the Church during colonial times, to-gether with the restrictions imposed by Iturbide, engendered a sense of rejection by society, and this brought about the clandestine circulation of books and magazines that the Church did not allow.

This discontent also gave rise to clandestine movements that informed social organization, and which at the same time favored the creation of an anti-censorship political culture; this in turn motivated society to seek ways and means of fighting this prohibition of the circulation of books, and particularly of ideas. In like fashion, it should not be overlooked that although Mexico had become an independent nation, the Catholic Church continued to influence decision-making and wielded the political power to constrain freedom of the press.

Despite the tireless attempts of Iturbide and his group to limit such pub-lications, they did not have great success. The editorial industry did de-velop and did achieve notable growth. [134] Also, many among the popula-

---

133 And I would dare to say from some statements of members of Freemasonry that it is still latent in the twenty-first century. See, Juan de la Serna y Echarte et al., *Dictamen de la Comisión de Libertad de Imprenta, leído en el Soberano Congreso en la Sesión del 9 de mayo y mandado imprimir por S.M.*, México, Imprenta de Benavente y Socios, May 9, 1822, Document contained in the British Library.

134 Nicolás Kanellos. "Hispanic American Intellectuals Publishing in the Nine-teenth-Century United Status: From Political Tacts in Support of Independence to Commercial Publishing Ventures." *Hispania* 88.4, December 2005: 687-692; De Los Reyes, "Translating, Smuggling, and Recovering Books in Nineteenth Century Mex-ico: Thomas Smith Webb's El Monitor de los Masones Libres: ó, Illustraciones sobre

tion demanded more and more books, which was reflected in this market growth. The number of private libraries, bookstores, literary agents, and binderies grew, as Juana Zahar Vergara's work states:

> The setting through which flowed and mixed books, seminars, newspapers, booksellers, printers and book merchants, and where there were found to be a goodly number of bookstores, book warehouses, subscription agencies, brokers and binderies, continued to be the Plaza Mayor and its surrounding area: Tiburcio (now 2a. calle de Uruguay), Ortega (now 1a. calle de Uruguay), La Monterilla (now 5 de Febrero), el Puente de Correo Mayor (now 3a. de Correo Mayor), la calle del Ángel (now 5a. de Isabel la Católica), Tacuba (the name of this street has not changed).[135]

The repression of freedom of the press, led by Iturbide and the Catholic Church, continued to be an obstacle for the industry's development. The reaction to censure contributed in great measure to the development of anticlerical thought, which persisted in the Mexican political imaginary for a long time. Even so, the publishing industry's capacity was not enough to satisfy internal demand. This was mainly due to the demand of groups interested in the new liberal ideas of Europe and the United States. One of these groups, perhaps the most prominent of the era, was the Masons. In the next section we will analyze the *Freemason's Monitor or Illustrations of Masonry*, one of the most important books to the practice of Masonic ritual and which was, like so many others, smuggled into Mexico. The majority of these books were translated in the United States or in Europe and were then distributed clandestinely in Mexico.

TRANSLATION AND SMUGGLING OF MASONIC BOOKS TO MEXICO

The *Freemason's Monitor* by Thomas Smith Webb (1771–1819), published in 1797, was one of the books of greatest relevance during the eigh-

---

la Masonería." In The Critical Importance of Region: Recovering the U.S. Hispanic Literary Heritage Project Vol. VI. Antonia Castañeda and Gabriel Meléndez, eds. Houston: Arte Público Press, 2006, 143-158.

135 Juana Zahar Vergara, *Historia de las librerías de la Ciudad de México*, México, Plaza y Valdés, 1995, 58.

teenth and nineteenth centuries in the United States (and, in some cases, Europe as well) in the canon of Masonic ritual. This publication mainly described the rituals of the first three degrees, and scholars maintain that it was used both by the Scottish Rite and the York.[136] The *Monitor* was the first Masonic book published in the United States that described the practices of the Masonic degrees. These degrees were conferred in various parts of the nation, particularly in New England, New York, and Pennsylvania, and they testify to the establishment of a new Masonic rite.[137] The Freemason's Monitor established a new system that later expanded into a rite of ten degrees and was distributed in the United States and other parts of the world. Twenty-five years later, the same book was published in Spanish by a well-known publisher of the day (H. C. Carey & I. Lea), in Philadelphia, where there was concentrated a significant number of Masons, as well as exiled Latin Americans interested in the liberal ideas of the times and who, in turn, admired the work of the founding fathers of the United States. The book's first Spanish edition was translated as *El Monitor de los Masones Libres: ó Ilustraciones sobre la Masonería* in 1822 in Philadelphia. This book is one of the first Masonic publications in the Americas and one of the first to circulate (though clandestinely) in the young Mexican Republic.

THE *FREEMASON'S MONITOR* IN MEXICO

In addition to taking place within the walls of universities' libraries and archives, the labor of the researcher unfolds within bookstores (of books both new and old). It was in May of 1998, in an antique book store in Mexico City that I discovered the first edition of Thomas Smith Webb's *El Monitor de los Masones Libres: ó Ilustraciones sobre la Masonería* that perhaps was once in the hands of some important Mexican politician, himself a Mason, in 1822.[138] In light of my discovery of this buried Masonic

---

136 Edwin Sherman argues that Webb relied on the 15th and 16th degrees of the Scottish Rite to develop the English rite *Red Cross*. He also proposes that he based the degree of the *Rose Croix* to create the degree of *American Knight Templar*. Edwin Sherman, *Brief History of the Ancient and Accepted Scottish Rite of Freemasonry*. Oakland, California, Carruth & Carruth, 1890.

137 Hebert T. Leyland, *Thomas Smith Webb: Freemason, Musician, Entrepreneur*. Daytona, The Otterbein Press, 1965, 74.

138 After visiting a great number of used and antique bookstores in the center of Mexico City, I came across a copy of *El Monitor* that caught my attention, and from this arises the research that I present in this section. I would like to thank Paul Rich and Antonio

treasure, many ideas and questions came to my mind: By what means did this book arrive in Mexico, since the entry of such books was not permitted in those times? Why had a book on Masonry been translated into Spanish and published in Philadelphia? Not finding their name in the book anywhere, I became curious as to who the translator was. After making a preliminary investigation at the Masonic libraries in Philadelphia and New York, I discovered that there are two known Spanish-language editions of the book, both published in the United States in 1822: the one mentioned above and a second one, entitled *Monitor ó Guía de los Franc-Mazones, Utilísimo para la Instrucción de sus Miembros é Información de los que desean imponerse en sus principios* (Thomas Smith Webb's *Freemason's Monitor, or Illustrations of Masonry* is the title of the book in English, the Spanish versions change the original title), published in New York City. Although both editions will be referred to in this section, the greater part of the discussion will center on the Philadelphia publication. In the next few pages, I will focus on answering the foregoing questions.

Additionally, I will analyze the Spanish translations of Webb's *Freemason's Monitor*. Regarding the book's translations, I have discovered that in each of them the translator is invisible. This anonymity arises from the tendency, typical of the day, to view the translator as an unimportant part of the process, but principally because of the Masonic tradition of secrecy and originality. Further, I will explore Mexico's political situation in the 1820s, particularly with regard to the smuggling and distribution of Masonic books to Mexico, since documents uncovered in the Philadelphia archives dealing with this topic bring to light a wide variety of political and social questions that it is vitally important to discuss.

THE EVOLUTION AND TRANSLATION OF THE *FREEMASON'S MONITOR* IN THE NINETEENTH CENTURY

Thomas Webb was one of the founding fathers of Masonry's York Rite. According to Leyland, the York (or American) Rite is a Masonic Rite created in the United States because of the need for a "strong national and state organization to preserve, invigorate and propagate the then de-

Lara for sharing some information related to this topic and for co-publishing a work on the topic with me. I also thank Regina Bendix for her invaluable comments and suggestions related to theories of translation as a cultural practice. Likewise, I extend my thanks to Antonia I. Castañeda and A. Gabriel Meléndez for their comments and suggestions on my analysis of the *Monitor*.

tached, uncontrolled and sometimes nebulose ceremonies that now are known as the capitular degrees and the Templar orders."[139] Aware of this, Webb persuaded others to unite and form this new Rite. Although other Masons may have understood the need to create a new Rite, they never translated this need into action.

Thomas Webb realized the importance of having the rituals in print form to facilitate the practice of Masonic ceremonies. He therefore published *The Freemason's Monitor or Illustrations of Masonry in Two Parts, by A Royal Arch Mason K.T., K. of M.* in Albany, New York, by Spencer and Webb in 1797. With this book, Webb contributed much to the practice of Masonic ritual in the United States and other parts of the world. From the time it first appeared, the *Freemason's Monitor* became a catechism of York Rite ceremony.[140]

In the various editions of this publication there appeared different prefaces regarding which edition was the first. The version of the preface that was believed to be from the "original" is actually from the editions between 1805 and 1818. The edition most reproduced of all of those that emerged during the nineteenth century was that of 1818, which was the last edition that Webb read and revised.

As we have begun to reveal here, Masonry in Mexico in the first half of the nineteenth century played a dominant role in the various doctrines of the Mexican independence movement. The fact that the first political parties (the *yorkinos* and the *escoceses* [the Yorkist and the Scottish]) were two distinct Masonic groups is no coincidence. This would explain much about Masons' great interest in knowing more on this subject. The organization's popularity in other parts of the world, along with the constant persecution of its members, fueled the interest of liberals in Mexico (as well as that of a great number of moderates and conservatives) to enter into the ranks of this institution. It is for this reason that the demand for Masonic publications was generated.[141]

---

139 Leyland, *op. cit.*, 69.

140 Translation practices of the Masonic canon have not stopped; in fact they have increased, especially due to constant immigration. In Mexico, the Grand Lodge of York often confers degrees in English, although the rest of the state and national lodges work in Spanish. In many countries some expatriates conduct their rituals in their native language. In the case of the United States, one can easily find Mexican Masons who practice their Masonic rituals in Spanish.

141 See Rich and De los Reyes 1995 & 2002. Also see De los Reyes 1997.

Before continuing into the subject of illegal importation of Masonic books into Mexico, I wish to note how organizations and groups create a certain internal unity. There are many ways governments, organizations and groups go about this. One of the most efficient means of pursuing this objective is by the creation of a literary canon. This was precisely the method that the Freemasons employed, upon recognizing that there was a demand, since such a canon contributed to a certain extent to the institution's unity and success. This process began with members of the order who were forced out of the country and who felt the need to or the interest in practicing the rituals of Freemasonry. As was previously mentioned, the order grew tremendously during the eighteenth and nineteenth centuries. Initially, the Masonic canon was transmitted orally, and later in written form.

In his book *Imagined Communities: Reflections on the Origin and Spread of Nationalism*,[142] Benedict Anderson states that the romantic nationalists create imagined communities that go on to promote the same language, the same symbols that gave cohesion to the building of nations. Freemasonry's precursors also used the same methods, or "cultural artifacts," as Anderson calls them, which "became modular, able to be transplanted, with varying degrees of self-awareness, to a great variety of social settings, to merge and be merged with a correspondingly wide variety of political and ideological constellations."[143]

Masonry utilized these cultural artifacts to create a sense of brotherhood and unity within its ranks. This begs the question: Who were the ones to develop the use of this kind of cultural strategies/artifacts, the Masons or the romantic nationalists? It is not my objective to answer this chicken-or-egg question, particularly since many of the Mexican republic's founding fathers were Masons. What we can say is that Masonry instigated a universal movement that shared the same symbols, language and rituals. Masonry's promotion as a universal movement influenced the development of the cultures of printing and of translation.[144] The Masons have used this method to promote their rituals and to create and expand their influence in various parts of the world. The *Freemason's Monitor* is a classic

---

142 Anderson, Benedict. *Comunidades imaginadas*. Madrid: Trama editorial, 1997.

143 Benedict Anderson, *Imagined Communities, op. cit.* 4.

144 Lawrence Venuti, *The Translator's Invisibility: A history of Translation*. Nueva York: Routledge, 1995 100. See, Guillermo de los Reyes, "Translating, *op. cit.*, 143-158.

example of translation, as well as a part of the strategy to begin building a Masonic canon and to promote its rituals.

The study of the translations into Spanish of Webb's book leads us to the conclusion that they can be taken as faithful translations, using Walter Benjamin's approach, and the translators invisible as defined by Lawrence Venuti. According to Benjamin, accuracy—a traditional theme in the field of translation—promotes "the freedom of faithful reproduction and, in its service fidelity to the world."[145] For his part, Venuti defines invisibility as the translation in which the translators receive minimal—or no—recognition for their work.[146] Both elements fit perfectly with the Masonic tradition and practice of originality, secrecy and tradition. Beginning with the approaches of Venuti and Benjamin, we will analyze the translations of the book studied in this chapter and the context of the time in which it was published.

As noted previously, there are two versions of Webb's book published in Spanish in 1822. One is titled *Monitor ó Guía de los Franc-Mazones, Utilísimo Para la Instrucción de sus Miembros é Información de los que desean imponerse en sus principios* (*Freemason's Monitor or Guide, Very Useful for the Instruction of its Members, and for the Information of Those Who Wish to Enter Initiation*—note that the title in Spanish is different from the original in English mentioned above) New York, Joseph Desnoues, and the other one *El Monitor de los Masones Libres: ó, Ilustraciones sobre la Masonería, por Thomas Smith Webb, Gran Maestro Pasado de la Gran Logia de Rhode Island* (*The Freemasons' Monitor: or, Illustrations on Masonry, by Thomas Smith Webb, Past Grand Master of the Rhode Island Grand Lodge*, Translated from English to Spanish) Philadelphia, H. C. Carey & I. Lea. The book's title differed significantly in its two translations. The Philadelphia edition is almost a literal translation from the English version. The New York edition is similar, but its impression is not so literal. In it, the translator attempted to demonstrate the book's purpose in its title: a use-

---

145 Walter Benjamin, "The task of the Translator" Rainer Shulte y John Biguene. *Theories of Translation: An Anthology of Essays from Dryden to Derrida*. Chicago: University of Chicago Press, 1992, 78. This problem is a consequence of the way the text was translated following the notion of 'fidelity', which in one "traducción de palabras individuales casi nunca puede reproducir completamente el significado que ellas tienen en el original" ("translation of individual words can almost never completely reproduce the meaning of those in the original.") Benjamin, 79.

146 Lawrence Venuti, *The Translator's Invisibility*, 8.

ful and informative manual for every person who wanted to be part of the order. One word in the title that merits attention is Freemason. In the Philadelphia edition, this word was translated literally as *"masones libres"* (free = *libre*, masons = *masones*). In the New York edition the translator suggests a new word—*Franc-mazon*—similar to the word in French. This was probably the first occasion this word was used in Spanish.

The two editions appear to be translations of the 1818 printed edition by Cushing and Appleton in Salem, Massachusetts. In fact, the majority of the English editions were taken from the same version. As I pointed out earlier, this was because it was the last edition that Webb corrected and, it would seem, the one considered among Masonic circles as the best developed, due to the care taken during editing and to its design. The editions in Spanish feature an illustration opposite the title page, an image that reveals to us a creative interest on the part of the editor of the Spanish-language version. This picture appears in many Masonic books from the eighteenth and early nineteenth centuries. I believe that the editor included it for the purpose of demonstrating a famous illustration representing the majority of symbols and elements used to confer the basic Masonic degrees.

El Monitor ó Guía de los Franc-Mazones features a preface that is different from that of the Philadelphia edition. This preface is not a translation of the English-language version. The book contains no signature or translator's name anywhere. This edition has a note on the first page that says "escrito en inglés por un Franc-mazon y traducido al Castellano" ("written in English by a Freemason and translated to Castilian"). Here we are dealing with an invisible translator, a situation that was quite common during those times, as mentioned earlier. Venuti argues that "invisibility" is one of the prevailing characteristics of translators both in the United States and in the United Kingdom after the seventeenth century.

It is certain that such invisibility of the translator is amplified in the context of the Masons. Masonic translations in the nineteenth century rarely reveal the name of their translators. Of prime interest was maintaining the author's name as if he or she were the only contributor to the work. By doing so, the idea was that any translated text should be "judged acceptable by most publishers, reviewers, and readers when it reads fluently, when the absence of any linguistic or stylistic peculiarities makes it seem transparent, giving the appearance that it reflects the foreign writer's personality or intention or the essential meaning of foreign text—the appearance in other words, that the translation is not in fact a translation, but the original."[147] This idea remains prevalent in Masonic circles to the present day.

The preface of the New York version portrays Masonry as a universal order, in which "all men were born brothers," the differences in the languages they speak, the clothes they wear, the countries in which they live, and their position in society being accidental. They believe that "the whole world is just a replica, in which each nation is like a family, and each individual is like a son: having everything ready for the *sapientisimo* Grand Architect of the Universe."[148] This statement is echoed in the characteristics with which Benedict Anderson imbues the creators of imagined communities. In this preface we can see the enormous appeal of Masonry, which attracted men to the order and caused them to create new lodges in which to practice the American Rite in Latin America and to create an imagined community of universal Masonry.

There is evidence of considerable freedom in the manner in which these books were translated, particularly the New York Edition. In fact, it seems that accuracy was forgotten when the purpose of the work was to promote and attract new members. One purpose of the book in its Spanish form was to transmit Webb's rituals to the new Latin American nations and to Spanish-speaking Masons within the United States.

We must now turn to one of the questions posed at the beginning of this section regarding the *Monitor* published in Philadelphia: Why would an editor in the United States produce a book on Masonry in Spanish? Initially a curiosity arose in me regarding Matthew Carey's Masonic affiliation, since he was a devout Catholic who published religious books. However, during that period it was not unusual to see liberal Catholics closely associated with Masonry. In fact, there were those who were both Catholic and Mason. Steven Bullock mentions that Masonry helped Carey in his book-selling business, since his Masonic activities gave him contact with potential clients. Carey states in one of his letters that Bullock included in his book: "Hope to vend some tomorrow at the Masonic meeting 16 miles from here." Two months later, Carey noted, "Tomorrow I set off to Newton to be ready to utter the Masonic Oration—God grant I will sell Bibles, etc..." Bullock states that Carey's identification as "a Ma-

---

147 Ibid., 1.

148 Webb, New York, iii.

sonic brother on his publications similarly served commercial purposes, underlining his moral authority and encouraging fraternal patronage."[149] I do not fully agree with this statement, since it can't be known whether Carey joined the Masons for commercial interests only. Although being a member of this institution helped him in his business, we can go so far as to say that Matthew Carey joined the ranks of the Freemasons to nourish his business enterprise.

In 1822 Matthew Carey retired and left control of his editorial house to his son-in-law, Isaac Lea. Carey and Lea seem to have had the respect of the Grand Lodge of Pennsylvania.[150] Additionally, the initiative for the publishing of the *Monitor* in Spanish was due to their sympathy for the rebellions that were taking place in Spain's colonies in the Americas; they published several books in Spanish as well as a Spanish dictionary.

Another reason the book was published in Castilian could have been due to demand for it that came from the Hispanic community in Philadelphia, in the region, and in the United States in general. The books in Spanish that Carey published were not strictly for export. The Hispanic migrant community in Philadelphia in the period 1810 to 1830 was significant, and a large number of Carey & Lea's publications would have found a readership there. Also, several copies of these publications went straight into Philadelphia-area libraries, where they can still be found.[151] So these three considerations could have been among the reasons Carey published the book.

There is also the possibility, given the great number of them living in Philadelphia during that time, that Latin American intellectuals petitioned Carey to publish the Monitor in Spanish so that they could send it to Lat-

---

149 Bullock, *op. cit.* 198.

150 Carey published nearly 1,100 books from 1785 to 1821, an average of 30 per year. He did not see this progress until 1794 and 1795, the years of Guthrie and Goldsmith. 1796 to 1801 were lean years, after which there was another period of expansion that continued uninterrupted until 1821, except for dips during the War of 1821 and the Panic of 1819. James Green, *Matthew Carey Publisher and Patriot*. Philadelphia, The Library Company of Philadelphia, 1985, 22.

151 This information is based on interviews with Nicolás Kanellos, Professor of Hispanic Literature at the University of Houston and director of Arte Público Press, on November 18, 2004, and David Szewczyk, owner of the Philadelphia Rare Book and Manuscript Company, on November 7. December 1999. See Nicolás Kanellos, "The Hispanic Exile Press in the United Status," 59-84.

in America to help continue the development of Masonic lodges there. Matthew Carey received a series of letters demonstrating this community's interest in Freemasonry. In fact, there are 18 letters at the Historical Society of Pennsylvania that were sent to Carey by F. W. Robinson, his agent in Mexico. The letters were written from August 18, 1822, to the latter part of 1823. One of the letters shows that Robinson, after arriving in Mexico, met Manuel Reyes, a representative of the Emperor Agustín de Iturbide.[152] In the letter, he notes that he assessed Manuel Reyes "about the square and the compass but received no response. I then asked him a number of questions that he answered to my complete satisfaction" (Letter of August 18, 1822).[153] The content of these letters is extremely valuable, not only for their several references to Masonry, but because they expose Masonic books as contraband in Mexico. In another letter to Carey and Lea from Robinson, he states:

> [Include] the prohibited books by placing them at the bottom ... next to the cookbooks ... each box 15 copies of the café _____ 15 of the Monitor and 15 of the Library. Be careful to place the binding and put them in separate boxes and also note how many are bound, to avoid the problem of inspection in Alvarado. Bound books in the same form as Law, Contracts, Cardboard-bound Books are cookbooks ... rustic books are those with paper with
> _____.[154]

It appears that the *Freemason's Monitor* published by Carey & Lea entered Mexico on at least one occasion hidden in a shipment of cookbooks. This was because at the time, as we mentioned at the beginning of this chapter, Agustín de Iturbide had adopted the inquisitorial politics of censure. The letters noted above illustrate the political atmosphere in Mexico during that epoch: political and social repression as well as the persecution of some of the most important intellectuals, such as Fray Servando Teresa de Mier, as can be seen in this letter from Robinson to Carey:

---

152 Emperor Agustín de Iturbide (1783–1824) was a Mexican military leader and politician best known for leading Mexico to independence from Spain and briefly becoming its first emperor.

153 Letters at the Historical Society of Pennsylvania that were sent to Carey by F. W. Robinson.

154 Undated letter, Correspondence from Matthew Carey. Emphasis is mine.

On the first of this M_____ the celebrated Padre Mier, one of the last congressmen whom the Emperor impris- oned, escaped from the convent of St. Domingo, by the agency of a priest[. A]t 4 o'clock in the morning, he took me _____ to the house of a lady who has _____ to pro- tect him, but since the Emp[eror], as exasperated as he is that he should have effected his escape, has made in every direction a search that the ladies _____ fearful that some or another accidents might happen gave the information to the p_____ authority ... and the Inqui- sition.[155]

Another important figure of the time that the agents of Carey and Lea met was the first ambassador of the United States to Mexico, Joel R. Poinsett, who was a very active Mason in both countries. In fact, he was key to the development of the York Rite in Mexico, although not a founder as some have proposed. Robinson mentions that "Mr. Poinsett ... bought sever- al [books] and told me they looked at him with extravagance." There is, therefore, a possibility that Poinsett had asked for copies of the Monitor, as well as other books to promote the York Rite of Masonry in Mexico. This can be interpreted that he was probably instrumental in the distribu- tion, and even the solicitation, of the Monitor. Paul Rich and this author have argued that although Poinsett was not the founder of Freemasonry or, more specifically, the York Rite in Mexico, he helped Mexican Freema- sons create lodges and develop the York Rite.[156]

In summary, Carey and Lea's agent in Mexico kept them informed about the political and economic situation in that country, since both political and economic stability were important to their business. So they estab- lished relationships with the most important political actors of the time, the majority of whom were Masons or supported Masonry. Robinson, for example, knew many of them. He observed up close what was hap- pening in Mexico and sent a report to Philadelphia. Here is an example of these observations:

The revolution which Santa Anna has set in motion with

---

155 Undated letter from correspondence with Matthew Carey.

156 Paul Rich and Guillermo de los Reyes, "Towards a Revisionist view of Poinsett: Prob- lems in the Historiography of Mexican Freemasonry, Part II." *The Philalethes: Journal of the Philethes Society*, 1995, 1-5.

Victoria … you no doubt will have heard, this reaching
you around May ___ now Orleans, it is important that the
desire always _____ say what will be the result of so many
revolutions … Ch___ continue to have on hand those
who may be opposed to the current form of preceding
to inform a solid Gov … this revolution that moves such
evil in the circles where it is found.[157]

From this correspondence between the agent in Mexico and Carey in
Philadelphia, we can affirm that there was communication between what
was happening in the two republics, and that the *Monitor's* entrance into
Mexico shows the great interest in spreading the Masonic canon in that
country. Therefore, the Masonic question is not separate from the political, and we find ourselves in a situation where the actors of the one cannot
be studied separately from those of the other.

The study of the *Monitor* is an example of the way many prohibited publications entered Mexico. It is in turn a demonstration of how, paradoxically,
the censorship of the day contributed to a need to know; the consequent
introduction of forbidden material; and the ultimate development of a political culture and a subversive literary canon that would go on to influence
the national and political discourse of the period. So this contributed to
a better understanding of the ways in which the materials that helped develop ideas circulating in Mexico were distributed. The *Monitor* also gives
us another element that can illuminate the political situation of the time
and the ways these ideas developed, were transmitted and were distributed
during that time. In other words, since the *Monitor* is a translation, investigating who the translator might be, as we shall see next, will allow us not
only to understand the art of translation as a tool for transmitting ideas, but
it also will reveal to us elements of the politics of the day.

IN SEARCH OF THE TRANSLATOR

Knowing the identity of the translator—or translators—of the *Monitor*
can help us to have a more complete picture of the Masonic publications
and their translations into Spanish during that period. Also, searching not
only for the authors' names but also those of the translators can be of
great help in the recovery of other publications. But these are instances of

---

157 December 2, 1822, letter from correspondence with Matthew Carey.

the invisible translator, since there is no recording of the name(s) of the translator(s) that appears in any of the various Masonic bibliographies of the period.

As one example, there is no such reference in Kent Walgen's article "Una bibliografía o impresiones del Rito Escocés en pre-1851 Luisiana" ("A Bibliography, or Impressions of the Scottish Rite in pre-1851 Louisiana"). Walgen describes all the Masonic books that held content meaningful to the Scottish Rite that had been published within the actual borders of the United States. He presents each bibliographical entry, including the author, the title, where the work was published, the editorial house, the date of publication, quotes from the referenced works, the location of copies of the work, the topic, and general notes. He does not provide any reference to the Spanish translators of any of the editions.

In the Philadelphia edition, one note mentions that "the author of this note is not a Mason, but a man who speaks for evidence of the sense of reason." At first, I thought that the note would contain certain information about the translator, but this was not the case; its purpose was only for propaganda or recruitment. It basically describes the size of the lodges in the United States during that time. It also mentions that the members of the lodges are the most prominent citizens, "the first men of the nation, whose morality, talent and character places them in the highest posts in society."[158] Therefore, the translator criticizes those who say that the Masons are responsible for the problems and destabilization in Europe—"These are blasphemies and ignorance"—and points out that "the streets on which the Masons live are never stained with the blood of the citizens; private property is respected, and men find, in these countries, a place where they participate and carry out all social virtues. In these places, there is nothing but action, industry, and honor."[159] It is evident that the translator is utilizing that note to discuss the situation in Mexico and the rest of Latin America during that period, particularly the problem between the conservatives (who followed the traditional Spanish model) and the liberals (who followed the United States and French Revolution model). It is not difficult to see that his note is a call to join the Masons in the American model.

Carefully studying the books published in Philadelphia by Carey and Lea,

---

158 Webb, *op. cit.* 290.

159 Ibid., 291.

publications contained in the Historical Society of Pennsylvania, and those of the Recovery Project of the Hispanic Literary Heritage of the United States at the University of Houston, I found a number of works translated from English to Spanish, and from French to Spanish, by Edward Barry. Among these books is, *El solitario o el misterioso del monte (Le Solitaire)* by Charles Victor Prévot Arlincourt,1822; *El espíritu del despotismo en honor a Simón Bolivar, Presidente de Colombia,* 1822 (The Spirit of Despotism in Honor of Simón Bolívar, President of Colombia); *Jachin y Boas, o una llave auténtica para la puerta de la Francmasonería* (Jachin and Boaz, or An Authentic Key to the Door of Freemasonry), 1822; *La vida de Jorge Washington, Comandante en Geje de los Ejércitos de los Estados Unidos de América en la Guerra que estableció su independencia y su primer presidente,* 1826 (The Life of George Washington, Commander-in-Chief of the Armies of the United States of America in the War that Established Its Independence and Its First President). These books contain the same elements of the *Freemason's Monitor.* They were published and translated in Philadelphia from English to Spanish or from French to Spanish during the 1820s, three by the same editorial house, (the last was published by the publishing house R. Desilver), and all carefully edited.

After going through the many telephone directories of those days and the names of translators, I found eight men with the name Edward Barry, the majority of whom it was easy to eliminate from the list because of their profession or other characteristics. However, two of them remained as the possible translator. Motivated by the interest in searching for the translator(s) of the Monitor, I decided to examine the evidence more closely, and I found that one of the Edward Barrys was 12 years old when the Monitor was published in Spanish, leaving Edward Barry, the Colombian consul in Philadelphia, as the most probable candidate as the translator. So, after a broad investigation, I am able to conclude that the consul Edward Barry was the translator of the Philadelphia edition of the *Monitor.* In spite of the fact that the editorial house of Carey and Lea had several English-Spanish translators, Barry was who translated the majority of the Masonic material during the 1820s. He translated other works from English to Spanish in the following years. Paul Rich and Antonio Lara note that Edward Barry had a strong connection with Matthew Carey, and that during that time numerous copies of the *Monitor* were sent to Colombia and to Mexico.[160]

---

160 Rich and Lara, "Continuing Adventures in Masonic Bibliography," Heredom: *The Transactions of the Scottish Rite Research Society* Vol. 8 (1999-2000): 219-223.

During the 1820s, Philadelphia was, without a doubt, an intellectual hub, where people from all over the continent traveled to learn about freedom and democracy. As a political, social and intellectual center of a new nation, Philadelphia was an inspiration to Latin American intellectuals who wanted to fight for their countries' independence. Additionally, as Rich and Lara point out, Philadelphia "was a center for the publication of polemic books in Spanish, given that the emigrant community took advantage of the freedom of the press to advance the cause of independence from Spain."[161] One fine example of the publishing industry in Philadelphia is none other than the *Freemason's Monitor*.

This one publication has cast a light on the study of Masonry in Mexico and Latin America, as well as on the study of Mexican intellectual life during the first years of the 1820s. The recovery of this book shows the secrecy, the ritual, and the politics of Masonry in Mexico. Also, one can learn about the sociopolitical situation in that country and the control that the government had over materials published and distributed during the first years of that decade. The two translations of the *Monitor* that I have described in this article were published in the same year and in the same country, but in different cities (Philadelphia and New York), under different titles. This fact points to a vibrant interest for Masonic publications in Spanish, both in the United States and in Latin America, as well as the demand and possible competition between editors to publish and to translate such materials.

Again, the names of the translators do not appear anywhere in these books. The accepted standard during that period was to keep the translator invisible to the reader, while at the same time the Masonic order sought to preserve the accuracy of the texts. Masonic scholars obsessed over the originality and the ancient tradition that Walter Benjamin tells us about; they had great interest in promoting the rituals and preserving them in written form. Perhaps it was the translator's own decision to keep his name secret. In the case of the *Monitor* published in Philadelphia, I have concluded that the Colombian consul Edward Barry was the translator. The discovery of the translator's name has led me to other Masonic publications and materials of the period. This has encouraged me, and I hope other researchers as well, to discover who translated the New York edition and so continue the recovery of Masonic publications in the nine-

---

161 Ibid., 267.

teenth century. Both versions in Spanish, as we saw with the Philadelphia edition, give rise to numerous questions. These questions can help us to delve further into the topic and find answers that may help contribute to a better understanding not only of Freemasonry's history in Mexico, but to the history of Mexico in general. Of course, there is no way to know who translated the books without seeking out the archives and the bibliographical records. It is therefore very important to promote the recovery of those texts in order to learn about the social, cultural, and political context of the period, so as to understand Mexico's present and anticipate its future. The study of Freemasonry in Mexico and the rest of Latin America during the first half of the nineteenth century is enormously important because of the role of this organization in the country's independence and in the formation of the young Mexican Republic. This publication is only an example of what can be learned about Mexican history through the study of Masonic texts.

TWO LIBERALS DEFEND FREEMASONRY: LIZARDI AND FRAY SERVANDO

As we saw in the previous section, censorship contributed to the development and free circulation of liberal ideas. Added to this, many scholars chose to publish books and magazines to disseminate such ideas, some of them criticizing the government's attitude that impeded their free circulation. These also criticized the attacks on Masonry, some of them refusing to remain silent and responding to these acts of aggression, as was the case with Joaquín Fernández de Lizardi (1776–1827) and Fray Servando Teresa de Mier (1767–1827). Both of these men had a great impact on the writings and thought of Mexican liberals. Likewise, they reacted severely against the ecclesiastical attacks on Freemasonry and themselves, becoming defenders and sympathizers of the order and in turn contributing to the evolution of the anticlerical political discourse.

Fernández de Lizardi was excommunicated in 1822 for his work "Defensa de los Francmasones" ("In Defense of the Freemasons"), in which he criticized the Catholic Church for its treatment of and attacks on Freemasonry, arguing that a dialogue was necessary to review the facts without fanaticism. That same year several papal attacks against the Masons were again published in Mexico. Faced with this situation, Lizardi responded with his "Segunda Defensa de los Francmasones" ("Second Defense of the Freemasons").[162] In this reply to the Church, Lizardi emphasizes:

> You assume that I defended the Freemasons: this is an
> error, because I did nothing more than make some ob-
> servations about the Bulls of the Holiest Clemente XII
> and Benedict XIV, wherein they are condemned by the
> Church's severest sanctions, without having met them
> and only because of suspicions, but without being able
> to prove any crime. And is that not the final test of secu-
> lar or ecclesiastical despotism, to impose punishment for
> the mere suspicion of a crime? What would we say if a
> king ordered all those who went about wrapped in a cape
> to be hanged, basing such order on the idea that if they
> weren't carrying something they'd stolen underneath the
> cape, they wouldn't be muffled in it? Well, this is precise-
> ly the nature of these pontiffs' condemnations, founded
> only on the idea that Masons work evil because they hide
> from the everyday lives of men.[163]

Lizardi's direct and careful words demonstrate the strategy that he is em-
ploying, not of defending the principles and mission of Masonry, but
rather criticizing the Church for baselessly accusing citizens merely for
belonging to a group but having committed no crime. It can be interpreted from Lizardi that he is being cautious since he had been excommunicated, and it is clear that he does not want to aggravate the situation;
but neither is he diluting his point nor betraying his ideals, and therefore
chooses to base his argument on the injustice being committed against
the Masons. This is clearly seen repeated in another part of his writing:
"Now you see, my friend, that this paper has nothing to do with a defense
of the Freemasons; and while conceding that the Bull in question was
founded by rights, I am not in favor of it. I am only setting about impugn-
ing its basis as wrong."[164]

---

162 See Torcuato S. Di Tella, *National Popular Politics in Early Independent México, 1820–
1847*, University of New México Press, Albuquerque, 1966, 57, 88, 90.

163 José Joaquín Fernández de Lizardi. "Segunda Defensa de los Francmasones". En *El
laberinto de la Utopía: José Joaquín Fernández de Lizardi, una antología general*. Fondo
de Cultura Económica, Fundación para las Letras Mexicanas, UNAM, México, 2006,
238.

164 Ibid.

The sanction of excommunication was quite severe and was not to be taken lightly, which shows the persecution and censure that Masonry endured in those times and which contributed, paradoxically (as mentioned previously), to its very development. In a letter that was published as a preface to the "Segunda defensa de los francmasones," the person who sent it, with the initials Y. M., writes to Lizardi:

> Therefore I implore you, and exhort you, to forswear your errors and to reconcile with the Church. This, far from being unseemly for you, will elevate your merit in the thinking of sensible folk by confirming your religiousness and Catholicism; since all men make mistakes, we can also abjure our mistakes when we become aware of them. David lost nothing by confessing his guilt, nor St. Peter, nor Mary Magdalene, nor St. Augustine, nor so many sinners and penitents that we venerate at the altars; and neither would you lose anything by imitating them … The true friendship that I have for you teaches me to try to warmly persuade you thus, wishing that your spirit become tranquil once it is absolved of censure.[165]

In addition to receiving efforts to persuade him from Church sympathizers or persons who were aware of the gravity of the situation in such an extremely Catholic country, Lizardi had the support of other intellectuals who were furious with the attitude of the Church. More than defending Freemasonry,[166] they were against what was, according to them, the inalienable right of freedom of the press. Also, Lizardi stressed that other publications had spoken in favor of Freemasonry, as was the case with *Examen crítico de las causas de la persecución de los francmasones, y explicación de las bulas de los Sumos Pontífices Clemete XII y Benedicto XIV*,[167] and that the writers of that and other works had not received such a severe sentence.

---

165 Ibid., 237.

166 It is worth mentioning that some people did not publicly defend Freemasonry, as they preferred to keep their Masonic affiliation secret. We have no evidence indicating that was the case for those who supported Lizardi, but we cannot rule this out.

167 *Examen crítico de las causas de la persecución de los francmasones, y explicación de las bulas de los Sumos Pontífices Clemente XII y Benedicto XIV.* Madrid, Imprenta de Vega y Compañía, 1820 (one of the copies is in the library of the *British Museum*).

Pablo de Villavicencio, in his *Defensa del Pensador Mexicano*,[168] *o sea reflexión sobre su causa y estado* (*Defense of the Mexican Thinker or Reflection on His Cause and Condition*)[169] and Rafael Dávila in his *Justo castigo y destierro del Pensador Mexicano* (*Just Punishment and Exile of the Mexican Thinker*)[170] spoke out against Lizardi's excommunication. Just as Lizardi himself explains in his *Second Defense*, these intellectuals did not defend Freemasonry; more than anything they appealed for Lizardi's right to defend his opinion and to fight against such injustices.[171] They argued that the defense of the Mexican Thinker should be heard and that reflecting upon the Masons and reflecting upon their rights to oppose some mandate of the Catholic Church were not the same thing.[172] They also criticized the punishment imposed upon Lizardi as excessive, since Mexico was an enlightened country, in which citizens' self-expression should not be impeded under religious pretext. Part of the defense that these authors mount for the Mexican Thinker is based on the arguments that he himself presents in the *Second Defense*. Lizardi had support from the intellectual community, Masons as well as non-Masons; and the following year, the Audiencia de México,[173] after hearing Lizardi offer a formal apology and ask forgiveness, rescinded the excommunication.

The papal bulls criticized by Lizardi in his writings, as well as the writings

---

168 José Joaquín Fernández de Lizardi was called "El Pensador Mexicano" (The Mexican Thinker) because he was a prominent intellectual and journalist in early 19th-century Mexico. He earned this title through his influential work as a writer and social critic, using his pen to address and critique the political, social, and cultural issues of his time. Lizardi adopted the pseudonym "El Pensador Mexicano" to reflect his role as a thinker committed to promoting Enlightenment ideals, such as reason, liberty, and justice. His writings often challenged colonial authorities and supported Mexican independence, as well as advocated for reforms in education, governance, and social equality. His most famous work, "El Periquillo Sarniento," is considered the first Mexican novel and one of the earliest examples of social satire in Latin American literature.

169 Pablo de Villavicencio. *Defensa del Pensador Mexicano, o sea reflexión sobre su causa y estado*. México, Imprenta de Betancourt, 1822.

170 Rafael Dávila. *Justo castigo y destierro del Pensador Mexicano*. México, Oficina de D. José María Ramos Palomera, 1822.

171 Dávila, 2.

172 Villavicencio, 2-3.

173 The Real Audiencia de México was one of the most important governing bodies of colonial New Spain (modern-day Mexico and parts of Central America) during the Spanish colonial period. It was established in 1527 by the Spanish Crown and served as both a court of law and an administrative council.

themselves and the essays in support of Lizardi against his excommunication, are examples of the period of transition in the midst of which the young Mexican Republic found itself a year after its independence. But it was not just a political transition that was taking place. A transformation in the citizens' imaginary was also occurring, since the unthinkable was beginning to happen: the open criticism of the almost untouchable ideas of the Church. Additionally, we can see the ground that Masonry was gaining as an intellectual organization, with a great presence within the country, particularly among the enlightened elite. María Eugenia Vázquez points out that many of these texts bear testimony to the breaking down that was happening in "the political culture, and in general in the understanding of the world and of society, as the religious and political spheres separated."[174] Also, within the Masonic lodges this struggle helped achieve a greater organization within the ranks, and also contributed to the formation of an informal alliance between the Masons and the intellectual community.

We may then argue that from that moment, and inspired by the papal bulls, the seeds of secularization and laicism began to be sowed, not just within the ranks of the Freemasons, but also among the citizens, especially those who opposed Church control and the limitation of the rights that the inhabitants of the young nation considered vital. Both the laws and the government, as Vázquez Semadeni points out, "had ceased to have a transcendental goal of souls' salvation, and began to appear as those in charge of safeguarding certain rights and freedoms of the citizenry now that these were no longer necessarily predetermined by religious precepts nor by divine law, but which were the result of a national debate among equals."[175] Society, especially intellectuals such as Lizardi, fearful for citizens' rights and freedoms, reacted against the Church's paranoia and its aggression against Masonry, which indirectly affected citizens' rights generally. This is clearly reflected in the pamphlet that the Mexican Thinker published in 1826 under the title "Verdadera defensa de los masones" ("True Defense of the Masons"), in which he argues:

It has had to do with the persecution of our brothers, reaching such a level

---

174 María Eugenia Vázquez Semadeni. "La interacción entre el debate público sobre la masonería y la cultura política 1761–1830." Doctoral dissertation, Colegio de Michoacán, Centro de estudios históricos, 2008, 143–44.

175 And Lizardi completes: "whoever they may have been, the bull forbids us from favoring those similar to us, the Masons." Ibid., 153.

of fanaticism as to exhume the body of a military officer only for the holy and indispensable errand of extracting from his coffin the gloves that his friends had tossed in as a final show of affection ... Error and malice have always pursued these noble reunions [of the Masons] and have sought to discredit their constituents by any means at their disposal; whether by taking advantage of the simplicity of a number of popes, coercing them into shining the light of the Vatican on the Masons, imagining them to be enemies of the Catholic religion, or by arousing the hatred of kings as enemies of the state.[176]

The process of secularization brought about by situations such as this gave rise to the citizens' beginning to realize that it was the duty of the State and not of the Church to regulate matters concerning freedoms. Lizardi, as did other intellectuals, used his pen to criticize the attitudes of the Church and of Senator Cevallos, who had supported the prohibition of Masonic meetings. The Mexican Thinker appealed to the laws of the Constitution of 1821 to strengthen his argument, advocating as a last resort for the freedom of association and freedom of the press. The debate that originated as a defense of Masonry—or as Lizardi said it, a publication "to assist and encourage our fellow man,"[177]—contributed to the development and promotion of the debate against censorship, by means of books, pamphlets, magazines and newspapers.[178] The precedent set in the public space contributed to forming a vision of a modern political system that had a great impact on the imaginary and on the new political culture that promoted the separation of Church and State; it also, as we have seen, sowed the seeds of laicism and secularization. This is noted in the Lizardi quote that serves as the epigraph of this chapter:

> Rome, political, enlightened and tolerant, will bring to our religion many advantages that it has been noted to lack, for various popes not deigning to give to God that which belongs to God, and to Caesar and to the people that which belongs to them ... His Majesty banishes from us wrath and vengeance in the name of religion, so that one day the Christian and the Hebrew, the Moor and

---

176 Lizardi, "Verdadera defensa de los masones. Folleto, México, 20 de mayo de 1826. En El laberinto de la utopía, *op. cit.*, 270.

177 "Segunda defensa," 239.

178 Vázquez Semadeni, "La interacción... *op. cit.*, 153.

the Gentile, the Protestant and the Roman, are touched
by the kiss of peace ... [179]

Like Lizardi, Fray Servando Teresa de Mier was a defender of the Masonic organization and of other similar organizations. Fray Servando was also the target of accusations by the Church, specifically the Inquisition, which tried him in 1816. During the proceedings, Mier stated that he did not belong to the Masons but to an organization called Lodge of Reasonable Gentlemen, whose objective was to fight against Napoleon's troops. The Society of Rational Knights, as it has also been called, was a paramasonic or co-masonic organization founded by the Argentine Mason Carlos María de Alvear and counted among its members Latin Americans concerned with the prospect of independence, such as José de San Martín. Fray Servando, in his many confessions, provided numerous details in the matter, attempting to deflect attention away and to confuse the inquisitors with countless details and opinions. Exactly what the Inquisition's judgment was is unknown; apparently a decision was reached, and Mier was expelled from Cádiz.[180]

Teresa de Mier criticized the Inquisition for persecuting and condemning the Masons. He also stated that the inquisitors' cause was in vain, since they would never be able to wipe out such a vast group of persons as those constituting the Masonic ranks. He spoke of this in his *Memorias* (*Memories*):

> The inquisitors are mistaken, directing all their effort against the Freemasons. And it is indeed a large undertaking if they think they will destroy them, because in England and in the United States, there are one hundred thousand [Masons], there are eighty or ninety thousand in Germany, not many less; in France, seventy thousand; in Italy, sixty thousand; in Spain and Portugal, thirty thousand.[181]

---

179 "Segunda Defensa," 250.

180 Christopher Domínguez Michael, *Vida de Fray Servando. México*: México: México, Era, CONACULTA, INAH, 2004, 381-385.

181 Santiago Roel, ed., *Memorias de Fray Servando. Escritas por él mismo en las cárceles de la Inquisición de la ciudad de México, el año de 1819*, Impresora Monterrey, S.A, Monterrey, 1946, 130. It is important to note that these are not accurate numbers. The purpose of the author was to show that Freemasonry was a very influential organization during that time.

Fray Servando Teresa de Mier shared the vision of the Masons about religion, since they saw it through the lens of freedom, tolerance and respect, but they opposed the Catholic Church's overwhelming control, as well as its excessive wealth and its many possessions. It should be noted that although it may not always be carried out in practice, the official view of the Freemasons with regard to religion is one of respect, tolerance and freedom; in contrast to what their enemies promote and to the idea they have created, the Masons are not atheists. They believe in the Grand Architect of the Universe, and during that period in particular, no evidence can be found that any of them were either very religious or promoted atheism.[182]

In his *Memorias*, Teresa de Mier pays homage to Freemasonry, since this was a society that he admired but to which, according to him, he did not belong. Such enthusiasm was due to Masonry's work during the French Revolution. On the other hand, its persecution at the hands of the Inquisition inspired Mier to describe Masonry in the manner that can be seen in this Cervantine apology:

> Among the Freemasons, all meetings dealing with political matters are detested as going against the institution. It is a universally beneficial society, one of inviolable brotherhood or friendship. If I had been a Mason, I would not have undergone so many times of hunger and hardship. A Mason, in whatever country chance casts him, finds himself with as many friends and benefactors as there are Masons ... It would be vanity to attempt to wipe out this organization: public interest will support it. Men, tired of loathing and persecuting each other because they are from a different nation, religion or ideology, or because of the whips of despots and fanatics, have invented this means of fellowship and encouragement against the caprice of fortune.[183]

---

182 Fray Servando Teresa de Mier, *Memorias de Fray Servando Teresa de Mier,* Alfonso Reyes, editor, Instituto Nacional de Estudios Históricos de la Revolución Mexicana, México, 1985, 336.

183 *Memorias,* 142. For more information on the life and work of Fray Servando see Christopher Domínguez Michael, *Vida de Fray Servando.* In my opinion this is the most complete work available on Dr. Mier.

Both Masonic thought and the censorship and persecution of the organi-zation greatly influenced Mier. His thinking is interesting, since he was a liberal Catholic who sympathized with the Freemasons (a trait that is not difficult to spot among the intellectuals of this period).

As we have seen, Fray Servando was among the ranks of the Rational Knights (Caballeros racionales) and not a Mason; even so, the latter group inspired the former, at least in the area of ritual. The members of the Reasonable Gentlemen had to undergo an initiation process and to practice rituals, among other details similar to those of Masonry. During that time, various political, philosophical and ritualistic inclinations de-veloped, along with religious ones. This contributed to the fact that many among the educated class of the time, among them Mier, had been influ-enced by numerous hybrid tendencies. The ideas of Fray Servando are an example of a hybrid thinking that, beginning at about that time, devel-oped in Mexico due to the influence of the Catholic Church and liberal ideas arriving in Mexico from the United States and Europe. In Father Mier's case, he experienced these ideas firsthand, since he had traveled to these places while in exile.[184] Mier and Lizardi, among others, were in-tellectuals advocating secularization. Servando Teresa de Mier is a great example of hybrid political thought that combined religious and secular aspects; such thought would go on to characterize an important group of intellectuals in the nineteenth century.

Whether directly or indirectly, there is no doubt that Masonic thought had an impact on Mier, Lizardi, Dávila, and Villavicencio, along with oth-er intellectuals and politicians such as José María Luis Mora, Valentín Gó-mez Farías, and Benito Juárez. Most of them were Masons or members of paramasonic groups, but even though some did not belong to any such group, liberal and secular thinking was transmitted indirectly by means of a lay discourse that reacted to the excesses, prohibitions, and control of the Catholic Church during that time.[185] Freemasonry, like Catholicism, contributed elements to the political thought that predominated in the first half of the nineteenth century.

The liberals that comprised the ranks of the Masons and the groups sym-pathetic to them promoted the Masonic ideas that allowed and supported the discussion of political and religious ideas with a certain degree of free-

---

184 See Guillermo de los Reyes, "El compás y la escuadra..."*op. cit.*, 9.

185 See Octavio Paz, *El Laberinto de la Soledad*, México, FCE, 1990.

dom. Freemasonry during the first decades of the nineteenth century in Mexico, as well as prior to then in other parts of the world, had been recognized as an institution that promoted liberal and revolutionary ideals. For that reason it is important to mention that the intellectuals and politicians of the time, such as Lizardi—and, later, Juárez—and their cohort, recognized that the Masonic institution had cooperated enormously in the consummation of independence and had been key to the overthrow of Emperor Iturbide. This does not mean that the intellectuals of the time were blind to Freemasonry's missteps nor to the rivalries that existed among the various Masonic groups. But at the same time, they were aware of the ideals this transnational organization espoused in addition to those which the group's leadership practiced.

FRATERNITY WITHOUT BROTHERHOOD: YORKS AND SCOTTISH[186]

During the nineteenth century, Freemasonry in Mexico consisted primarily of the Scottish Rite. The two rival groups of Mexican Freemasonry in the first half of the nineteenth century were called Scottish and York (*Escoceses* and *Yorkinos*). These two terms have been frequently used in textbooks of Mexican history, but it is unclear whether either their authors or their readers fully understand the meaning of the terms. The terms Scottish and York should not be understood in the sense Freemasonry currently gives them, but rather in the sense of their meanings within the context of the nineteenth century. On occasion, both groups followed the Masonic rites of continental Europe (which are commonly referred to as Scottish), which causes great confusion for persons not familiar with Freemasonry.[187]

---

186 In this book I will not discuss the development of the Mexican National Rite since there are classic works that analyze it. See: José María Mateos, *Historia de la masonería en México de 1806 a 1884* and Richard Chism in his book *Una contribución a la Historia Masónica de México*; V. Ventura Anaya, *Orígenes del Benemérito Rito Nacional Mexicano y causas que motivaron su fundación y Constitución de la Confederación de Grandes Logias Simbólicas del B. R. N. M.*, México, 1957. Ventura Anaya points out that the Mexican National Rite emerged from two meetings due to the struggle between the York Masons. The first at the beginning of January 1826 between Miguel Ramos Arizpe, Andrés Quintana Roo and Fray Servando Teresa de Mier with Vicente Guerrero, Minister of War; and the second, a week later between them and Guadalupe Victoria, President of the Republic. *Idem*, 4-6.

187 "It should be noted that in France until almost the middle of the seventeenth century, the word 'Scottish' or 'Scots' as an adjective was rendered 'Ecossois.' This and other ar-

The term "York" (that is referring to the York Rite), in the sense that it was used at the beginning of the nineteenth century, described a "simple" form of Masonry that only included the first three degrees. The term "Scottish" (that is referring to the Scottish Rite), is more difficult to contextualize; but with a simple explanation it is easier to understand and follow its complex system which during that time was considered the more elaborate of the Masonic degrees.

At the end of the eighteenth century and the beginning of the nineteenth, there was great confusion as to which rite corresponded to which degrees. Albert Pike, the great Masonic scholar, in *Morals and Dogma* describes the Scottish Rite as a system of morality veiled in allegory and illustrated by symbols. He emphasizes that the teachings are designed to inspire enlightenment and self-improvement among its members, guiding them through a journey of moral and philosophical development. Pike highlights the importance of progressing through the degrees to gain deeper insights into truth, virtue, and the nature of existence, while also exploring themes of duty, justice, and the higher ideals of humanity.[188]

The nineteenth century can be identified as the period in which Masonry was consolidated in Mexico. It was tenacious; its members' interest in participating in politics was great. By the same token, that century was a period in which there originated a marked division among the Masons, a time in which there surely was fraternity without brotherhood.

In 1821, Agustín de Iturbide was proclaimed emperor, thanks to the help of the clergy. The Masons, especially the most liberal among them, roundly opposed this and, in fact, tried unsuccessfully to prevent it.[189] In 1824,

---

chaic French terms [appear now] as 'Ecossais.' The two words of course have the same meaning." A.C. F. Jackson, *Rose Croix: The History of Ancient Accepted Rite for England and Wales*, rev.ed., Londres, Lewis Masonic, 1987 [1980], xii.

188 Albert Pike, *Morals and Dogma* of the Ancient and accepted Scottish Rite of Freemasonry Prepared for the Supreme Council of the Thirty Third Degree for the Southern Jurisdiction of the Jurisdiction of the United States and Published by Its Authority, Charleston, 1871, reprint L.H.Jenkins, Richmond (Virginia), 1930, 326.

189 In 1821, Mexico achieved independence from Spain after an 11-year struggle that began with the Grito de Dolores in 1810. The final phase of the independence movement was led by Agustín de Iturbide, who formed the Plan of Iguala, which called for an independent constitutional monarchy, equality between Spaniards and Creoles, and Roman Catholicism as the state religion. The Treaty of Córdoba, signed in August 1821, officially recognized Mexico's independence. Soon after, Mexico declared itself

in the young Mexican Republic, an apparent stability began to take hold
in country during the presidency of the Mason Guadalupe Victoria. A
great number of political activists, interested in being part of a Masonic
group with more liberal ideas perhaps far from Spanish conservatism, so-
licited the Grand Lodge of New York by open letters to install the lodges
"Libertad," "Independencia" and "Federación" (Freedom, Independence,
Federation), forming the "Gran Logia Nacional de México" (National
Grand Lodge of Mexico).[190] This lodge came to be made up exclusively
of liberal-minded men. As such, they had numerous confrontations with
the Scottish lodges, the majority of whose members were monarchists
and conservatives.

In 1824, Ferdinand VII of Spain issued a decree that outlawed Masonry
for its being, in his opinion, the main cause of the disturbances in New
Spain and Spain. The king's concerns seem to have been based on the opposition apparently shown by some Masons to the monarchy in Spain. In
addition, the many conflicts and disagreements that the Catholic Church
had with the Freemasons played an important role in Ferdinand's lack
of sympathy toward the Masonic organization; the conflict between the
Yorkist and the Scottish gave the king further reasons to dislike the Masonic lodges.

The revolt against President Guadalupe Victoria in 1827 included a large
number of members of the Scottish Rite, supported mainly by Vice-pres-
ident Nicolás Bravo. The York line was under the leadership of the president.[191] One curious fact that still makes the study of this historical period
difficult is that the protagonists of such movements frequently changed
sides for political convenience, or were members of both groups, which
creates tremendous confusion.

Although many Mexican patriots were involved in Freemasonry, several Masons of the United States had a close relationship with York Rite
Masons in Mexico. Robert Gould, who wrote about the history of Freemasonry in different parts of the world, gathered information about the

---

a republic, transitioning from Spanish colonial rule to self-governance, but the early
years were marked by political instability and power struggles.

190 See Zalce y Rodríguez, *op cit.*

191 It is important to note that by no means did all members of the Scottish Rite that Bravo supported switch to this rite. On the other hand, there were certainly some Yorks
who were loyal to Victoria.

relationship established between the Grand Lodge of Louisiana and the lodges of Veracruz and Campeche in 1816 and 1817, and in Alvarado (Veracruz) with the Lodge of Pennsylvania in 1824. Most of the Masonic conflicts were as a result of the clash between the Scottish and the York Rite Masons.

In order to understand this conflict, it is important to provide a brief context. In the 1820s, shortly after Mexico gained independence, the *escoceses* and the *yorkinos* became heavily involved in the country's political landscape. These groups represented different ideological and political visions for Mexico's future, and their rivalry significantly influenced Mexican politics. On the one hand, the Scottish Rite Masons were a more conservative group and supported a centralized government. They were often aligned with the old colonial elite and sought to maintain strong ties with the Catholic Church and uphold traditional hierarchical structures. The *escoceses* advocated for a more controlled and elitist governance that would limit radical social reforms. On the other hand, the York Rite Masons were more liberal and supported federalism, democratic reforms, and broader citizen participation in government. The *yorkinos* received support from the United States (both from the Masons and the government) and pushed for separation of church and state, land reforms, and decentralization of political power. They represented a more progressive vision for Mexico, appealing to those who sought change and modernity.[192]

The conflict between these two factions fueled political instability throughout the decade. Each group influenced government policies by aligning with different leaders and promoting their members for positions of power. The rivalry became a proxy for larger debates over Mexico's direction as a newly independent nation, setting the stage for ongoing struggles between conservative and liberal forces throughout the 19th century

It is instructive here to briefly consider the career of Nicolás Bravo (1786–1854), who was president of Mexico from 1842 to 1843; in 1846, at the time when he was the leader of the Scottish Rite, he supported Emperor

---

192 Robert Freke Gould, *The History of Freemasonry: Its Antiquities Symbols, Constitution, Customs, Etc.*, Vol. VI, T.C. & E.C. Jack Edinburgh, n.d., 370. The book published by Gould first appeared in 1903. See George F. Adams, "Freemasonry in México," *Philalethes*, Vol. XXIII No.3, June 1970, 54. See also, María Eugenia Vázquez Semadeni, *Op cit*, 2010.

Iturbide; in 1823 he had been among those who brought him down. He rebelled against his fellow Mason, President Bustamante, just as he had given the order to execute General Vicente Guerrero, who was the leader of the York Masons.

Lucas Alamán, a prominent Mexican statesman of the day, a historian with a broad knowledge of the political persuasions of—and who maintained a close relationship with—the leaders of the time, wrote that the United States government appointed Joel Poinsett as its first representative to Mexico. Poinsett had as one of his goals the establishment of a new Freemasonry in México. This new Freemasonry had a formidable conflict with Scottish Rite Freemasonry. Alamán expressed strong opposition to Poinsett's involvement in Mexican affairs, particularly as regarded the establishment of York Rite Freemasonry. Alamán viewed Poinsett's actions as intrusive and detrimental to Mexico's sovereignty, criticizing him for promoting a foreign Masonic order that, in Alamán's view, sought to undermine Mexico's traditional institutions and political stability. Alamán's writings reflect his belief that Poinsett's interference through Freemasonry was a significant factor in the political turmoil of the era.[193]

In *10,000 Famous Freemasons*, William R. Denslow provides a concise overview of Joel Poinsett's involvement in Mexico during the 1820s. Denslow notes that Poinsett, serving as the first U.S. Minister to Mexico, actively engaged in the country's political affairs, particularly through his promotion of the York Rite Freemasonry. This involvement was perceived by many Mexicans as undue interference, leading to significant tensions. Denslow highlights that Poinsett's actions contributed to the establishment of the term "poinsettismo" in Mexico, denoting unwelcome foreign intervention.[194]

These perspectives underscore the complexities of Poinsett's diplomatic mission, where his efforts to influence Mexican politics through Masonic channels were met with resistance and suspicion, reflecting the broader challenges of U.S.-Mexico relations of the time. Alamán describes the establishment of the York Rite in Mexico and names the key figures who contributed to its founding. On the other hand, José Fuentes Mares states

---

193 Lucas Alamán. *Historia de México*, México, Editorial Jus,V, 760; See also, Eric Van Young, *A Life Together: Lucas Alaman and Mexico*, 1792–1853, Yale University Press, 2021.

194 Denslow, IV, 375.

that it was the United States' plenipotentiary minister, Joel Poinsett himself, who started the York Rite in Mexico. According to Fuentes Mares a document exists in the Washington National Archives that Poinsett wrote to Rufus King, in which he states quite clearly that it was none other than Poinsett who founded York Rite, and he says so himself in a letter containing the following passage:[195]

> Dear Sir: An unimportant occurrence moves me to write to you again about the topic to which my last communications referred. But small things, as you know, sometimes lead to very serious consequences in the political field. With the purpose of offsetting the fanatical Party in this City (Mexico City, D.F.) and, if possible, spread more widely the liberal principles among those who must govern the country, to help and to inspire a certain number of respectable persons, men of high rank and consideration, to form a Grand Lodge of Ancient York Masons. So it happened, and a numerous group of the brotherhood happily dined at my home.[196]

King showed the letter he had received from Poinsett to Mr. Canning, and replied to Poinsett in the following manner:

> Except for a Mr. Canning, who considered your question in all its aspects, and although he did not condemn them outright, he did observe that the establishment of Masonic lodges lent itself to misinterpretations from the point of view of political interference [...] With this sole exception, I find nothing worthy of objection in the correspondence.[197]

As this correspondence shows, the origins of the founding of the Masonic rites in Mexico are shrouded in mystery, which seems inevitable given the nature of the organization. There was no Masonic unity, not even in the time after Mexican independence in 1821. Mexico at the time found itself in revolutionary ferment, which atmosphere fueled the growth of

---

195 See Félix Navarrete, *op. cit.,* 34.

196 José Fuentes Mares, *Poinsett, Historia de una gran intriga,* México, Editorial Jus, 1951, 125-126.

197 Ibid., 130.

different expressions of Masonry and a swarm of Masonic ideologies and philosophies.[198] As contrasted to the arguments of Fuentes Mares and those of many other historians, here it is suggested that Poinsett did not create Freemasonry in Mexico. What the first U.S. Minister to Mexico (Poinsett) did was support a group of Mexican Masons in their efforts to win the recognition of Masonic authorities in the United States.

Poinsett, as Lucas Alamán rightly states, apparently utilized the York Rite as a means to reinforce his diplomatic mission.[199] The British minister who was a diplomat in Mexico during the 1820s, Henry G. Ward (1797–1860), was biased in favor of the Scottish Rite, hoping to receive trade concessions; for his part, the Colombian ambassador had been an officer of the Scottish Rite in Cartagena and supported Ward's position. The participation of foreign politicians within Freemasonry was extremely important since they ultimately were key to the Mexican lodges' receiving recognition from other countries. In addition, this allowed them to establish relationships and exchange Masonic materials as well as other books banned in Mexico.

This foreign interference coincided with the growing resentment among Mexican patriots toward the Scottish Rite which, together with its supposed European affinities, was seen more as working toward commerce and position rather than for the good of the community. In this regard, Poinsett's decision to employ Freemasonry as a tool to achieve his interventionist politics was the beginning of a long relationship between Masonry and Mexican politicians, the effects of which had been viewed so variously by scholars—for good or for ill, depending on where you looked.

The branch of Freemasonry that finally won more adherents was Scottish Masonry. Scottish Rite Masonry of that era was characterized by its great number of degrees.[200] As we have seen, it has occasionally been anticler-

---

198 Raymond Estep, *Lorenzo de Zavala (Profeta del Liberalismo Mexicano)* México, 1949, 107. In this matter, the origins of Freemasonry in Europe remain a mystery. See Paul Rich's comments on the work of C. N. Batham "The Origins of Freemasonry (a New Theory)," *Ars Quatuor Corononatorum*, Vol.106, 1993, 45.

199 This relates to Alberto Carreño's discussion regarding the importance of unofficial relations in Mexican-North American affairs. See Alberto María Carreño, *La Diplomacia Extraordinaria en México y los Estados Unidos, 1789–1947*, Vol. I, México, Editorial Jus, 1961, 7.

200 Degrees that in the early 19th century, we may add, were sold by traveling charlatans

ical and stands in contrast to the less politically open Masonry prevalent in Great Britain and its territories, and emphasizes the first three degrees of the blue lodge: apprentice, fellowcraft, and master mason.[201] It was this type of Scottish Freemasonry that became an extraordinary enemy of the Church in Mexico as well as in some European countries:

> Even if one were a critic of a "global conspiracy," one would not consider Andriano Lemmi, who was a Grand Master of the Italian Freemasons with his pathological hatred of the Catholic Church, as representative of all the lodges, and the distinction was made between the Roman organizations and the others, it should be mentioned that we are talking about the intellectual leaders of the period, who set off on an impious war against the Catholic Church, with scant regard for how the humanitarian ideals of the movement would be judged. This and Freemasonry's victories within Catholicism, especially in Latin America, forces one to consider the impact and intensity that the Catholics' struggle against the Freema-

---

and staged for public ridicule by the Freemasons' opponents. See "A Brief History of the Anti-Masonic League of Dublin, Popularly Called The Illegitimate Prince Mason and Designated by Themselves 'The Grand Chapter of Ireland'; with a few Comments on the Mendacious Slander, Styled 'A Few Words on the Degree of the Rose Croix,' Published by this Grand Chapter: Also Some Observations on the Part Played by the 'Quarterly Magazine of the Freemasons' in Propagating and Circulating said Slander," Published from Original Documents by Verax, Dublin, 1844.

201 The Blue Lodge, also known as the Craft Lodge, is the foundation of Freemasonry and confers the first three degrees of the fraternity. These degrees are: 1) Apprentice: This is the first degree, where a candidate is initiated into Freemasonry and introduced to its fundamental principles and symbols. It represents the beginning of a journey of moral and spiritual development, focusing on the virtues of morality, truth, and brotherly love; 2) Fellowcraft: The second degree represents the candidate's advancement in Masonic knowledge and understanding. It emphasizes education, the development of the mind, and the study of science, art, and nature. This degree encourages members to seek wisdom and improve themselves; 3) Master Mason: The third and final degree is the culmination of the Blue Lodge experience. It teaches important lessons about mortality, virtue, and the immortality of the soul. The candidate learns deeper Masonic teachings and is given full membership, with the privilege of participating in all the rights and responsibilities of the fraternity. These degrees form the core of Masonic teachings and lay the groundwork for further exploration in Freemasonry, such as in the York Rite or Scottish Rite, see, Albert Pike, *Masonic Formulas and Rituals: Transcribed by Albert Pike in 1854 and 1855*, edited by Arturo de Hoyos, and Ronald A. Seale (Foreword), Westphalia Press, 2020.

sons had in stimulating the consolidation of the latter group's consciousness against the enemy. Even Leo XIII, in his encyclical Humanum genus, differentiates among the Sectarores—who, according to him, though they are not without fault, do not participate in malicious acts and do not have a clear image of what the ultimate goals of Freemasonry are. But the encyclical begins with a reference from the Invida Diaboli and ends with a petition to the episcopate of the world to take this "diabolical pestilence" (impuram luem) up by the roots, since such a malignant attack as theirs requires an equally malignant defense [...] Leo XIII repeats the prohibition of membership, under threat of excommunication proclaimed by his predecessors.[202]

Because of the persecution of the Freemasons, as well as the censorship and intrigues on the part of the Church, a strong anticlerical feeling can be seen developing in Mexico, which will become the core value of Mexican Freemasonry.

Today, the term Scottish Rite as it is used applies generally to a system of 33 degrees. Some of the degrees of modern Scottish Rite were practiced in some form in Mexico at the beginning of the nineteenth century, according to some persons who traveled through Europe in the nineteenth century and who are said to have held a high degree within the Mexican Scottish Rite. The first of these Masons was Joseph de Glock-D'Obernay, who appeared in Paris before 1819, claiming that he had obtained the 33rd degree in New Mexico and Spain. He spent some time in England, where he pestered the Grand Master of the United Grand Lodge of England, the Duke of Sussex, and then went to Jamaica, where he collected (and apparently kept) membership dues.[203]

Paris is another city that during that time appears to have been a refuge for Masonic figures from the New World, as there is evidence that during the 1830s a representative of the Scottish Rite in several of the Spanish possessions in America was there. His name was Henri Dupont Frank-

---

202 Roger Aubert, et al., *The Church in Industrial Age*, Londres, Burns & Oates, 1981, 216-17.

203 Jackson, *op. cit.*, 143-55.

lin, and he had the "Golden Book,"[204] in which the records were kept of those who received the higher degrees, such as the 33rd degree. In the Paris of this decade there also lived a gentleman who was called Count de Saint-Laurent, a rather flamboyant South American, who had apparently commanded part of the Mexican navy, and who claimed the title Great Sovereign Commander of the Supreme Council of New Spain; he also claimed to possess documents signed by Frederick the Great of Prussia, which he had obtained from a Viceroy of New Spain.[205] De Glock, Franklin and Saint-Laurent were involved in attaining degrees only of interest to a few, and it is unlikely that many of them, who in Mexico were called Scottish Masons, received the full complement of advanced degrees of what is today known as Scottish Rite.

In 1820 the members of the Scottish Rite in Mexico belonged to the upper classes: the nobility, the militia, and the Catholic clergy. In spite of the fact that the Masons of the Scottish Rite were fond of belonging to a conservative group, they opposed not only the monarchy of Spain but also that of Iturbide (1822–1823). This appears not to have had any ideological basis, since further on, during the conflicts between the Scottish and the Yorks, the Scottish Masons were characterized as being "centrists," who favored an autocratic government. The Yorks, who by 1828 had 102 lodges in Mexico, were identified with federalism and an insurgent liberalism.[206]

The degrees conferred both by the Scottish Rite as well as the York Rite were probably only the first three degrees. The Yorks, as I mentioned earlier, had the support of Joel R. Poinsett, former Grand Master, Lieutenant of the Grand Lodge of South Carolina, and the United States Minister to Mexico. In 1826, Poinsett had obtained the Charters for York lodges from the New York Grand Lodge (to be given by those established in Mexico that were following the York Rite). These authorizations were definitely

---

204 The book where Freemasons record the names of members who have attained higher degrees is often referred to as the "Book of Gold" or the "Golden Book." This book is traditionally used in some Masonic lodges, especially in the higher bodies like the Scottish Rite, to maintain a registry of distinguished members and those who have achieved elevated ranks or honors within the organization.

205 Jackson, 77-80. "All one can say is that the declaration that came from Mexico can be rejected and that there is a convincing story that the original was burned in America." Ibid., 81.

206 H.T. French, "El Lugar de la Masonería y la Logia Holanda No.1 en la Fundación de la República de Texas," *Transactions, Texas Lodge of Research*, Vol. XXI, June, 22, 1985 – March 15, 1986, 158-59.

for the blue lodge, or the first three degrees, and not for the "superior" degrees.[207]

A CONFUSION OF TERMS

Mexican historians have used the terms Scottish and York indiscriminately, without taking into account their variable meaning. In nineteenth-century Mexico, the name Scottish seems to apply to the lodges that were working with the first three degrees and were made up primarily of conservative Spaniards. Later on, this term came to be used to refer to the European and anticlerical nature of the lodges, instead of merely referring to the rite.

The term "Scottish Mason," used to describe the secular Masonry practiced in Mexico, confers a connotation that is too general and generic. The spirit of Mexican Freemasonry is one of a Latin Scottish Freemasonry, characterized by outrageous uproars, repeated schisms, and vigorous agitations, generally absent from the Victorian Masonic lodges, and simply nonexistent in the secrecy of modern-day Anglo-Saxon lodges. Latin Masonry frequently insists on doing certain things that Anglo-Saxon Masons consider either irregular or illegal. The same turns out to be true for the political governing body: The history of the Mexican nation is no more peaceful than that of Mexican Freemasonry.[208] Anglo-Saxon Freemasonry has had its quarrels and divisions and, in a way, all of Freemasonry is an atavistic memory of quarrels; and the degrees continue to be the remnants of past disputes.[209] K. W. Henderson, a world authority on the different masonic systems, points out that "Mexico is the most diverse country in the world, Masonically speaking. It possesses close to 30 Grand Lodges [...] The task of producing a single synopsis of Mexican Masonic history would be almost encyclopedic."[210]

Following Poinsett's successes, the York Masons accomplished little until 1846. On January 2 of that year, General Mariano Paredes had himself designated President of the Republic by a committee that he himself had

---

207 Ibid., 159.

208 Henry Wilson Coil, *Coil's Masonic Encyclopedia*, William Moseley Brown *et al.* eds., Richmond, Macoy Publishing & Masonic Supply Company, 1961, 412.

209 "In every European country, local circumstances produce significant differences in the success and social influence of Freemasonry, and these are worthy of consideration." Robert, *Mythology of the Secret Societies*, 43.

210 K.W. Henderson, *Masonic World Guide*, Lewis Masonic, Londres, 1984, 155-56.

appointed. Paredes thought that a better defense against the United States was that the committee be backed by the Masons. In the face of this, a group of liberals, influenced by the Grand Lodge of Jalisco, got the backing of the military (José María Yáñez, Guadalupe Montenegro, and Santiago Xicoténcatl), deposed the governor and reinstated the Constitution of 1824. The Mexican-American War (1846–1848) was a parenthetical on the road of Masonic evolution in Mexico. During that time, the French residents in Mexico founded the lodge *Les Hospitaliers de deux Mondes*, which received the Charter of the Grand Orient de France (Great Orient of France) in 1850.[211]

In 1855 the triumph of the Ayutla Revolution[212] took place and, with the help of the Masons, Juan Álvarez was designated President of Mexico. Once the *Asamblea Constituyente* (Constituent Assembly)[213] convened, it ruled in favor of Ignacio Comonfort, with the understanding that he would cleave to the liberal foundation and to the principles of the *Reforma*[214] for those who fought so hard for the Rito Nacional Mexicano (Mexican National Rite). Later began the downfall of the Mexican National Rite, brought about in part by the Three-Years' War and the fact that its political objectives and principles had been exhausted.

BENITO JUÁREZ: CONSTITUTIVE AND SYMBOLIC MYTH

Benito Juárez is considered to be the most distinguished Mason in the history of Mexico. He is also known as the Benemérito de las Américas (The

---

211 "Comentarios sobre...", *op. cit.* 9.

212 The Ayutla Revolution (Revolución de Ayutla) was a pivotal movement in Mexican history that began in 1854 and aimed to overthrow the dictatorship of Antonio López de Santa Anna. This revolution was named after the Plan of Ayutla, a manifesto proclaimed on March 1, 1854, in the town of Ayutla, Guerrero, by liberal leaders Juan Álvarez and Ignacio Comonfort.

213 The Asamblea Constituyente in Mexico refers to the Constituent Assembly, a body convened to draft and adopt a new constitution for the country. One of the most significant of these assemblies was the Constituent Assembly of 1856–1857, which created the Constitution of 1857. This assembly was called after the triumph of liberal forces in the Ayutla Revolution and was primarily composed of liberal leaders and intellectuals.

214 The Reforma profoundly reshaped Mexican society, limiting the influence of the Catholic Church and establishing the foundations of a secular, democratic state. However, the country remained politically unstable and vulnerable to foreign intervention, leading to the subsequent French invasion and the establishment of the Second Mexican Empire under Maximilian of Habsburg.

Meritorious of the Americas), which honorary title reflects Juárez's significant contributions to democracy, justice, and the defense of national sovereignty, not only in Mexico but also as an inspiration throughout the Americas. There is a great number of articles, books, monuments, busts, and the like, dedicated to him. Beyond any doubt, Juárez is the most celebrated of the Masons. His work for the secularization of Mexico and the development of the lay state have also been carefully analyzed. It is for this reason that the anticlericalism arising in Mexico during the Juárez regime is often mentioned. In this section, therefore, I shall not revisit what it has already been said many times about Juárez and the separation of church and state. What I wish to examine instead is the impact of this leader as a symbol or icon of Mexican Masonry, and his development and promotion as a constitutive myth.

As a reaction to the attacks by the Church and to the prohibition of Freemasonry, one of the most common demonstrations of antipathy toward and disagreement with the Catholic Church was that of becoming a part of the Masons. This was true in the 1820s and continued for many years. During the Juárez presidency, Mexican Freemasonry expanded considerably. We can safely say that Juárez's presence contributed to the development of Mexican Masonry in his time, but it has also had an impact on the Masonic organization in later years, since the figure of Juárez has become a symbol of secularization and laicism that are two very important elements for Mexican Masons.

Before talking about the impact of Juárez as constitutive myth, I will give a brief analysis of his Masonic credentials. There are various hypotheses as to the location and date of Juárez's initiation into the Masons. On the one hand, Ramón Martínez Zaldúa claims that he was initiated in the *Respetable Logia Simbólica "Espejo de las Virtudes" del Oriente de Oaxaca* (Respectable Symbolic Lodge of the Orient "Mirror of the Virtues" of Oaxaca), of the York Rite between 1833 and 1834. On the other hand, Rafael Zyas Enríquez proposes that Juárez belonged to the Mexican National Rite and obtained the Ninth degree within this rite, which is equivalent to the 33rd degree of the Ancient and Accepted Scottish Rite.[215] Albino Lázaro Chávez concurs with Rafael Zayas and suggests a more detailed description of Benito Juárez's affiliation with Masonry. Chávez argues that once the Constituent Assembly had elected Juárez as a Rep-

---

215 Ramón Martínez Zaldúa, *Historia de la masonería en Hispanoamérica. ¿Es o no religión la masonería?*, Costa Amic Editores, Barcelona. España, 1967, 56.

resentative (Member of Congress), before he left for Oaxaca to take the post as Provisional Governor of that state on January 26, 1847, the Benemérito de las Américas took advantage of his time in Mexico City to be initiated as a Mason. The above sources who state that Juárez was initiated into the Masons in Oaxaca provide no evidence to support this. The main source of information about Juárez's masonic initiation is the "Funeral prayer read by the Andrés Clemente Vázquez in the Iturbide Theater, on the night of August 21, 1872, for the Masonic funeral rites of C. Benito Juárez." In fact, the majority of scholars, as does Albino Lázaro Chávez, rely on this source. In this "Prayer," Clemente Vázquez describes the initiation as follows:

> It was January 15, 1847. In the Senate in Mexico City, decorated simply for the occasion with the symbols of Masonry, a man, still youthful, waited calmly in the chamber of reflections, which had been prepared to receive a Mason of the very respectable Mexican National Rite. That man was the senator to the general congress for the State of Oaxaca, and his name was BENITO JUÁREZ. Many of the members of the lodge from workshop num. 2, entitled Independencia, should recall the solemnity of that ceremony. Present were Manuel Crescencio Rejón, the Pericles among our orators; Valentín Gómez Farías, patriarch of democracy, and in those times incidental president of the Republic; Pedro Zubieta, minister of State; Pedro Lémus, commander general of the Federal District and of the State of Mexico; José María del Río, Fernando Ortega, Tiburcio Cañas, and Francisco Banuet, senators; Agustín Buenrostro, former governor of the Federal District; Joaquín Navarro, Official Mayor of the Ministry of State, and senator; Ambrosio Moreno, former town representative and now Minister of the Supreme Court of Justice; Miguel Lerdo de Tejeda, who would later stand beside 'Hércules' Juárez, the Achilles of the Reforma; and many other very distinguished military and scholarly persons.[216]

---

216 Andrés Clemente Vázquez, "Oración fúnebre leída por el Lic. Andrés Clemente Vázquez en el Teatro de Iturbide, la noche del 21 de Agosto de 1872, con motivo de las Exequias masónicas del C. Benito Juárez," México, Tip. de la Escuela de Artes y Oficios, en Guadalupe, Zacatecas, 1892, 4-5.

Andrés Clemente Vázquez also adds that the Masonic name that Juárez received was Guillermo (William) Tell.[217] The information offered in the "Funeral Prayer" shows that Juárez's rite of initiation was not only attended by important persons from the political and intellectual spheres but was also carried out in a very important and symbolic building. This prayer has contributed substantially to the creation of the Juárez myth, and it offers to those who were not present a description of Juárez's initiation that reveals it to have been comparable to a coronation. So the initiation featured all the necessary ritualistic elements to make it such that it surely impacted those who were there, and those who have read of it and have continued to contribute to the creation of the myth. According to scholars of ritual theory such as Victor Turner, Émile Durkheim, Roy A. Rappaport, and others,[218] successful rituals require a defined physical space for the ritual to be practiced, dramatic and performative elements, structure, repetition, an audience as observers and judges, symbolism, the feeling of belonging, of unity, and of transformation. The description offered by Clemente Vázquez of Juárez's initiation includes all of these elements. Thus, the creation of the Juárez myth was supported by an important ritual of initiation.

Additionally, it stands out among other ceremonies for several reasons, among them: being the initiation of Benito Juárez, the space where it was carried out (the Senate Chamber in Mexico City), and the members of the

---

217 Carlos Francisco Martínez Moreno, in his work "Juárez masón: Hipótesis en torno a una polémica histórica inconclusa. Primera parte" carries out an excellent analysis based not only on the "Oración fúnebre" but also on the medals and other Masonic clothing of Juárez and presents a very accurate and well-documented hypothesis about the initiation of Juárez, who according to the evidence we have was initiated in the Mexican National rite, but Martínez Moreno argues that according to Juárez's clothing, it is likely that he was also given decorations from other Masonic rites. Carlos Francisco Martínez Moreno, in the work of Juárez Mason: Hypothesis around an unfinished historical controversy. First part. Paper presented at the 1st National Meeting of Master's and Doctoral Students in History: History and current debates, January 9, 2006.

218 See Émile Durkheim, *The Elementary Forms of Religious Life*, trans. By Karen Fields, NY, The Free Press, 1995 (1912); Roy Rappaport, *Ritual and Religion in the Making of Human Kind*. Cambridge, Cambridge University Press, 1999; Victor Turner, *The Ritual Process: Structure and Anti-Structure*. New York: Aldine de Gruyter, [1969], 1995; Catherine Bell, *Ritual: Perspectives and Dimensions*, Oxford, Oxford UP, 1997; Roger Abrahams, "An American Vocabulary of Celebrations," in *Time Out of Time: Essays on the Festival*, Alessandro Falassi, Ed. Albuquerque, The University of New Mexico Press, 1987.

audience, such as Valentín Gómez Farías, Manuel Crescencio Rejón, Miguel Lerdo de Tejada, José María del Río, among other important political and Masonic figures of the time. It can be stated that this ritual, as much for the moment in which it took place as for the reading and repetition of the funeral prayer, has had an impact not only during those times but also in the present day. I would emphasize that Juárez's initiation has contributed to the mythification of the man and has transformed him into the Mason par excellence. This was due in large part to the fact that Juárez was consolidated in the official discourse as the leader of the secular movement. In the same way, the national postrevolutionary discourse of the twentieth century underscored the secular value of the Mexican nation and hoisted the image of that leader as representative of the separation of church and state. Therefore, the Masons have benefited from this success; they have also promoted the figure of Juárez for his contribution to the secularization of the country and because this allows Masons to be a part of the struggle through the figure of Juárez. The Masonic historian Luis Zalce y Rodríguez expresses the perspective on Juárez held among the ranks of the Masons which, in my opinion, has been key to the creation of the myth:

> To the great Mason Benito Juárez, exceptional builder of a country, not an idealistic theorizer nor an orthodox ritualist, who, because of his constructive activities gave freedom to a people that had lived chained by its ancestral fanaticism, a characteristic of the races that mixed in its formation, because of ignorance [...] and in that almost superhuman process of building, Juárez revealed what can be seen as the result of the practice of fundamental virtues, which are the synthesis of the commandments of our Order: fraternal love, support, and truth.[219]

There is no doubt that Benito Juárez was deeply involved in Freemasonry, which significantly influenced his political ideology and actions. Juárez's Masonic beliefs were evident in his leadership during the War of Reform (1857–1861), where he implemented policies that diminished the Catholic Church's influence and promoted civil liberties. His commitment to Masonic principles of equality and justice was also reflected in his resistance against the French intervention and the establishment of the Second Mexican Empire under Maximilian I. Juárez's legacy within Free-

---

219 Zalce, *op. cit.*

masonry is profound; numerous lodges and Masonic bodies in Mexico honor his name, and he is venerated as a symbol of the fraternity's values. His life exemplifies the integration of Masonic ideals into national governance and the pursuit of societal reforms.

There exists a noteworthy similarity between the mythic patriotism realized in the lodges of Mexico as well as in other parts of Latin America or the United States. The Masonic temples of today use pictures of Juárez extensively, to the same extent that the lodges of the United States use pictures of George Washington, or those of South America pictures of Simón Bolívar. The growth of the legends surrounding Juárez is similar to that of those surrounding Washington. However, there is a great number of patriotic myths that are being cultivated in the present day: "The myth of Juárez is not the only historical myth that exists in Mexico. It is one among many that have been created to serve various political and social purposes." Charles A. Weeks explores how figures like Benito Juárez have been mythologized to embody national ideals, often simplifying complex histories to promote unity or legitimize political agendas.[220]

It should be noted that the majority of myths associated with Masonry state that the nation has been naturally blessed such that its success has been an act of divine intervention marked by fortuitous coincidence. Freemasonry helps to promote a modern version of the magical king with a kingdom graced by the gods.[221] In *The History of Freemasonry*, Robert Freke Gould discusses the origins of the U.S. flag, noting that some accounts have been embellished over time. He observes that the narrative surrounding the flag's creation has been "woven into a somewhat flowery version," indicating that certain elements may have been romanticized or mythologized. Gould emphasizes the importance of distinguishing between documented facts and later additions to the story, highlighting how historical events can be transformed into national myths through repeated retelling.[222]

There is no evidence at all that General Washington or any other person

---

220 Charles A. Weeks, *The Juárez Myth in Mexico*, Tucalosa, The University of Alabama Press, 1987, 135-36.

221 For a convincing example of the use of ritual in politics see Douglas Brooks-Davies, *The Mercurian Monarch: Magical Politics from Spenser to Pope*, Manchester University Press, 1983, 1.

222 Robert Gould, *History of Freemasonry*, Vol. 1, New York, Charles Scribners' Sons 1936, 48.

was thinking of the Masonic lodge when they designed the American flag, but this story shows how Masonry wrapped itself in nationalist clothing. It should come as no surprise to discover that this was seen by many leaders who were Masons as a way to legitimize their leadership. This relationship conforms to what Charles Webb says about Mexican political life and the use of myths:

> Due to the fact that myths simplify certain things, governments use them to explain complex situations and to communicate with the citizens. There are also groups outside the government that use the fabrication of myths to eulogize or criticize the government currently in power [...] The governments of Mexico have exploited the wealth of persons and events from its history to attempt to assure the commitment to the nation and to its leaders [...] which they have achieved.[223]

Many scholars, including Victor Turner, Roger Abrahams, Doris Sommer, Beatriz González Stephan, and Benedict Anderson, have extensively argued that literature, myths, and legends serve as crucial instruments in the creation of foundational epics and national narratives. These narratives often function beyond mere storytelling; they play a fundamental role in shaping collective memory and national identity. By weaving together cultural symbols, historical events, and heroic figures, such narratives craft a sense of shared heritage and purpose among members of a nation. Victor Turner's work highlights the performative nature of cultural rituals and how they reinforce social structures, a concept that extends to how myths and epics function in the national context. Roger Abrahams emphasizes the power of oral traditions and folktales in creating a unifying cultural ethos, while Doris Sommer explores how literature serves as a medium for nation-building, particularly in Latin America, where fiction has often interacted with political agendas. Beatriz González Stephan addresses the way literary and cultural texts have historically contributed to the consolidation of state power and the construction of a national image. Benedict Anderson's concept of "imagined communities" encapsulates how national identity is constructed through shared stories and cultural symbols that give people a sense of belonging to a broader, yet intangible, community. Myths and foundational epics, in this view, are more than

---

223 Charles A. Weeks, *The Juárez Myth in México*, 9.

cultural artifacts; they become powerful tools for legitimizing political authority and reinforcing state ideologies. They provide historical depth and moral justification for the rule of political leaders, casting them as the protectors of national values and as heirs to a mythologized past. By doing so, these narratives perpetuate the idea of a continuous and unbroken national destiny, which is often used to garner loyalty and unity among the populace.[224] In sum, literature and cultural myths are deeply interwoven with political discourse, supporting the creation and perpetuation of national ideologies that legitimize leadership and strengthen the idea of a cohesive nation.

Mexican Masonry has also made use of heroic figures, such as Juárez, whom they have made into the Masonic hero par excellence. Juárez and other notable figures have served a role such that, through them, fantastic and allegorical narratives are believed, which in turn will serve as pillars of the Masonic discourses. Such discourses have helped to legitimize them and have bestowed upon them the respect of those who also need such symbolic capital.[225] Thanks largely to its publicity through Masonry, the image of Juárez has become the representation of laicism and the symbol of secularization. Although the Leyes de Reforma (Laws of Reform) are the text that outline these leanings, Juárez is the symbol of a lay State (a symbol that Masonry has appropriated).[83]

Masonry's myths and legends of its glorious past and its ideologies ema-

---

224 See Victor Turner, *The Ritual Process: Structure and Anti-Structure* (1969); Roger Abrahams, *The Man-of-Words in the West Indies: Performance and the Emergence of Creole Culture* (1983); Doris Sommer, *Foundational Fictions: The National Romances of Latin America* (1991); Beatriz González Stephan, *Fundaciones imaginadas: la narrativa venezolana del siglo XIX y la formación de la nación* (1995); Benedict Anderson, *Imagined Communities: Reflections on the Origin and Spread of Nationalism* (1983).

225 I use the term symbolic capital as inspired by Pierre Bourdieu, referring to the non-material assets that give an individual prestige, honor, and recognition within a particular social context. These assets can include things like reputation, education, titles, or social status. Symbolic capital often converts into other forms of capital, such as economic or social capital, because individuals with high symbolic capital are often treated with greater respect and influence, allowing them to mobilize resources and gain advantages. For example, a respected Masonic title, such as Grand Master, or a prestigious award, or a reputation as a political leader can serve as symbolic capital, giving a person the ability to shape opinions or access exclusive opportunities. Symbolic capital, as Bourdieu operates subtly, reinforcing social hierarchies and legitimizing power structures. See, Pierre Bourdieu. (1986). "The Forms of Capital." In *Handbook of Theory and Research for the Sociology of Education*, edited by John G. Richardson, 241-258. New York: Greenwood Press.

nating from the Enlightenment have helped politicians utilize their Masonic affiliation to achieve legitimacy and to gain supporters. The impact of the Yorks and the Scottish lasted throughout the nineteenth century; that is to say, the relationship between Freemasonry and politics remained close. The seed that was planted then has remained for many years, though not always with the same intensity. The Masonic strategies have contributed to the construction of political discourses that, although they do not themselves necessarily emanate from Masonry, have influenced the political environment as regards the legitimacy of leaders, and have formed part of the imaginary of Mexican society.

EL MONITOR

DE

LOS MASONES LIBRES:

ó

ILUSTRACIONES SOBRE LA MASONERIA,

POR TOMAS SMITH WEBB,

GRAN MAESTRO PASADO DE LA GRAN LOGIA DE RHODE ISLAND.

TRADUCIDO DEL INGLES AL ESPAÑOL.

PHILADELPHIA.
H. C. CAREY & I. LEA.
Año 1822.

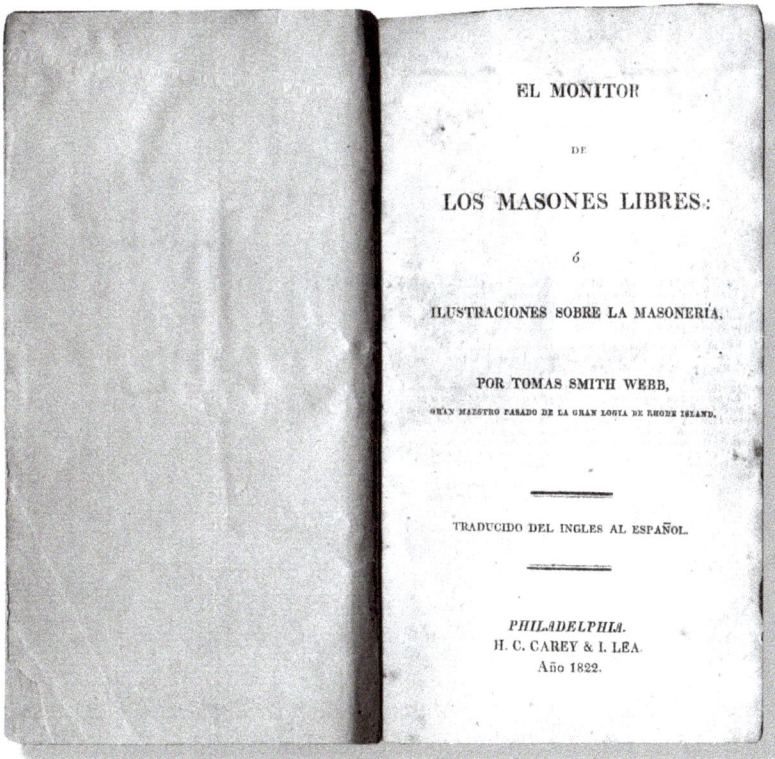

Title page of *El monitor de los masones libres* by Thomas S. Webb (1822). Like this copy, other Masonic books were smuggled into Mexico hidden among Bibles and cookbooks. Many of them were translated and published outside Mexican territory due to censorship imposed by the Inquisition and the government of Emperor Iturbide. This book was published and translated in Philadelphia in 1822.

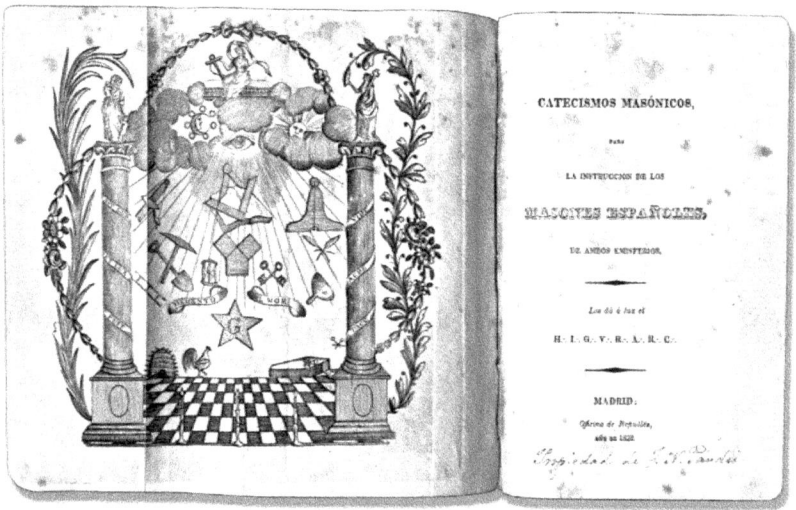

Masonic Catechisms for Spanish Masons of Both Hemispheres (1822). Like *El Monitor de los masones,* this Masonic Catechism arrived in Mexico through smuggling. Many of these books were bound together to facilitate their entry (as was the case with these two publications). This copy was published and translated in Madrid in 1822.

Joel Roberts Poinsett (1779–1851) was a member of the United States House of Representatives and was appointed the first U.S. Minister to Mexico (a U.S. ambassador to Mexico was not appointed until 1896). Poinsett was a York Rite Mason who contributed to the establishment of the York Rite in Mexico (it is worth noting that he was not its founder). The publishing agent who published *El Monitor de los masones* also distributed books to Poinsett.

Benito Pablo Juárez (1806–1872) wearing Masonic regalia. According to the "Funeral Oration" delivered by Lic. Andrés Clemente Vázquez on the occasion of his Masonic funeral, he was initiated as a Mason on January 15, 1847, in the Senate chamber of Mexico City.

Bust of Benito Juárez in the Grand Lodge of the Valley of Mexico. To his right are busts of renowned Masons from Mexico and other parts of the continent. The Benemérito of the Americas is perhaps the most admired and celebrated Mexican Mason by Mexican Freemasonry in general.

Collage of illustrations depicting Masonic symbols, especially of
the York Rite, as well as representations of Masonic rituals.

CHAPTER 3

THE *PORFIRIATO*, MASONIC UNIFICATION, AND THE MEXICAN REVOLUTION (1876–1917)

I have before me the noble and great task that belongs to you: to reestablish the supreme authority of the Constitution, to reaffirm the peace, to protect by its influence all legitimate interests in order to develop the great resources of wealth of this country.[226]

FREEMASONRY IN THE *PAX PORFIRIANA*

After the death of President Benito Juárez, on July 18, 1872, the Congreso de la Unión (Congress) named as interim president of Mexico Manuel Lerdo de Tejada, who was at that time the president of Mexico's *Suprema Corte de Justicia* (Supreme Court of Justice). Later, on November 16, 1872, Congress named Lerdo de Tejada to be the Constitutional President of the Mexican Republic by a majority of votes, for the term that would commence December 1 of that year.[227]

During that epoch there was a variety of trends and ideologies in Mexican society, and because of this, the liberal party divided basically into three branches: the *juaristas* (followers of Juárez), who were the most numerous; the *lerdistas* (followers of Lerdo), a group with a lot of push and energy; and the *porfiristas* (followers of Porfirio Díaz), very active and with a desire for national recognition. Even though Freemasonry by this time had lost some ground because of the heated battles of the 1820s and the War for Reform (*Guerra de Reforma*), its presence continued to be felt in the political realm and with the publication of books and magazines that were distributed among its members and those who were sympathetic to the organization. Therefore, due to the great diversity of political inclinations and having become a type of political party, the Masonic lodges played an extremely important role. The lodges served as spaces in which a great many among the population organized, argued political strategies, and recruited new members. In fact, occasionally, Masonic publications,

---

226 François Xavier Guerra, *México: del Antiguo Régimen a la Revolución*, México, Fondo de Cultura Económica, 1988, 214.

227 "Comentarios sobre la masonería" Acción del saber 1 (marzo 93/94): 115.

as did the meetings in lodges and in the Supreme Council, allowed the distribution of ideas, not only in Mexico but also in other parts of the hemisphere, as Mateos shows:

> In one extraordinary session of the Supreme Council of the 33rd and last degree of the Ancient and Accepted Scottish Rite, duly and legally constructed by the Jurisdiction in the Mexican Republic and convened in Mexico City on April 28, 1868, it was unanimously agreed that the following document be printed and sent to all the great Masonic bodies in the two Hemispheres for their due understanding.[228]

There existed in Mexico a Supreme Council of the same rite that, according to unofficial reports, had been founded in Veracruz in 1860 by a Sovereign 33rd-Degree Grand Inspector named Carlos Laffont de Ladebat; the members of that Supreme Council wanted the two supreme councils to be united, and it was agreed that they would appear for a meeting with all documented justification.[229] As we know, such fraternities had a great political presence in the nineteenth century, as an unpublished manuscript in the Supreme Council of 33 in Washington, D.C., argues. This manuscript speaks of the presence of various Masons and politicians, such as Ignacio Altamirano, who brought politics to the lodge.

(It is worth noting that it was very prestigious for Masons of the time to be a part of these supreme councils. Consequently, it became an honor, since it meant belonging to both the Masonic elite and the political elite at the same time.) The above-noted manuscript is entitled "Impartial Notes on the History of Mexican Masonry by an Old Mason Continuing His March Almost Since the Establishment of the Ancient and Accepted Scottish Rite in the Republic." The manuscript states that there were, nonetheless, many conflicts, rivalries, and quarrels within the different Masonic organs. It states, "this sworn bitter enemy incarnate rite of the Scottish, and pursuing its Jesuit policy of 'divide and conquer,' made its members affiliate in the squalid Bodies of our rite, in order to sow discord and disunion among the brotherhood."[230] So the fraternity without broth-

---

228 Mateos, *op. cit.*, 269.

229 Navarrete, *op. cit.*, 119.

230 A. Velazco, "Apuntes imparciales para la historia de la masonería mexicana por un viejo masón que viene siguiendo su marcha casi desde el establecimiento del Rito Es-

erhood continued, due in large part to the political aspirations among the members. As the Masonic groups came to see themselves as political parties, the rivalry between them grew. The rituals do not necessarily promote such rivalry; primarily it was generated because of the political leanings or external influences upon the lodges.

When Porfirio Díaz came to power by defeating rival groups (1876), he had as a goal the pacification of the country and in this way achieve economic progress in and governability of Mexico. Months after coming to power, Díaz stated, "I have before me the noble and great task that belongs to you: to reestablish the supreme authority of the Constitution, to reaffirm the peace, to protect by its influence all legitimate interests in order to develop the great resources of wealth of this country"[231] (the quote that is the epigraph of this chapter). In these brief lines, Díaz summarizes his strategy, or his so-called *pax porfiriana*—that is, the politics of conciliation that he promoted that allowed him to consolidate his power and that in later times would transform him into a dictator.

During the time that General Díaz was in power, he tried to unify all of the Masonic lodges of the Scottish Rite. The main reason he promoted such unification was so that he could carry out his plan of national pacification, along with the unification of various sectors and institutions. But what caused Porfirio Díaz to amass great power within Freemasonry? What were the strategies he employed? How did this influence the *pax porfiriana*? These are some of the questions that are raised in this chapter. I argue that Díaz, despite having become a dictator, did not completely break with the liberal principles that had been imposed by Benito Juárez, Melchor Ocampo and others, and which Masonry so jealously defended. It cannot be said that this pacification was achieved because Díaz imposed these principles. What he did was to adapt them for his own use and at his own convenience, in order to gain total control and pacification of the country. It was for that reason that his policy of conciliation was so successful and that the Masons did not escape his control.

Díaz understood that an important strategy was to take control of Freemasonry, specifically that part belonging to the Scottish Rite. As was explained in the previous chapter, at the dawn of the Mexican republic, Freemasonry

---

cocés Antiguo y Aceptado en la República." Supreme Council of 33, correspondence between the temple and the Mexican lodges, 1885.

231 Guerra, *op. cit.*, 214.

had a great impact on politics, particularly in the 1920s, with the Yorks and the Scottish acting as the first political parties. Later, this impact continued with the politicized lodges of the Mexican National Rite. During the Juárez epoch, some Masonic lodges, or their members, had considerable influence in the political decision-making process. Díaz viewed such impact cautiously and consequently decided to create a conciliatory politics in order to avoid at all costs anything that might destabilize his government. For this reason, Díaz always made very sure that neither Masonry nor any other institution (such as the Catholic Church) gained political ground without his authorization or supervision. Díaz's strategy, therefore, was to keep them very close to himself, whether directly or indirectly.

The *porfirista* strategy toward the Masonic institution is clearly seen in the correspondence this government sent to international lodges, particularly those in Washington, D.C. and in Paris, France. In these communications one sees a formal or cordial relationship with Díaz's foreign Masonic brothers, an effort to win a certain recognition of the lodges of Mexico. This was important for Díaz, not only so that he might contribute indirectly to the Mexican lodges, but also to show that in Mexico there was peace (apparently), order and progress.[232] Though Díaz during his presidency was not very active within Freemasonry, he did use his affiliation strategically at the beginning of his government.[233]

Within the personal political objectives[234] that Díaz developed, from 1876 to 1911 he sought to gain total control of all the institutions. His conciliatory politics, "carrot or stick," was vital in the identification of all those groups and individuals that might reveal themselves to be against

---

232 It is worth mentioning that since Freemasonry is an international or transnational organization, members of Freemasonry from other places see very closely the situation of their Freemason brothers in other parts of the world.

233 Correspondence with the Grand Orient of France 1876 to 1900. Emilio G. Cantón, Secretary General. Archive of the Grand Orient of France in Paris.

234 The cult that Díaz promoted to himself and his leadership should also be considered, as proposed by Roderic Ai Camp. Camp also talks about the personalist tradition used by Mexican leaders from Porfirio Díaz to Lázaro Cárdenas. The latter was the one who institutionalized the presidency in Mexico. That is to say, it does not matter who the president is; what matters is the title. Therefore, when someone is the head of the executive, they automatically become the most powerful politician in the country. In the case of Porfirio Díaz, with the personalism that he developed, it did not matter if he was the president or not (as was the case in the period 1880-1884 when Manuel González Aldama was president), he always had the power. See Roderic Ai Camp, *Intelectuales y política en México*. Oxford, Oxford University Press, 1996, 32-40.

the government or to oppose him politically. Díaz understood this from the very beginning of his government, when he had to find the economic resources to defeat his political rivals Lerdo and Iglesias and in this way reaffirm his power and preserve his possession of the capital.[235]

There were many factors that permitted Porfirio Díaz to control the Masonic lodges belonging to the Scottish Rite. The fact that the dictator had not been directly involved in Masonic activities (it was the members of the organization who wanted him to join and who asked him to participate in their events) would give him a great advantage, since this afforded him freedom from any close commitments and from any remorse for not carrying out his Masonic obligations. If one looks closely at the important Masonic posts that were awarded to Díaz, such as Grand Master and Deputy Grand Master (it should be noted that in later documents, he appears as honorary Grand Master), one would assume that he was quite involved. However, Díaz's Masonic correspondence with the Lodges of France and of Washington indicate that it was mainly his Masonic brothers who tried to get the president to participate and to get involved for the benefit of Freemasonry.

In practice, Díaz was not a very active Mason. As Zalce y Rodríguez states, and as the letters mentioned above corroborate, Díaz was as involved in the Mexican National Rite as he was in the Scottish Rite. Zalce y Rodríguez also states that Díaz was initiated into the Mexican National Rite and then transferred to the Scottish Rite.[236] In this way, his status as member on paper helped him to exercise a certain control over the lodges, the same ones that sought his approval and sympathy. In this regard, the Mexican historian Luis González y González (one of the few non-Masonic Mexican historians who have even touched upon the topic of Freemasonry in Mexico) argues:

> Díaz's strong personality also contributed to the Scottish
> Masons' accepting, in a way, General Díaz's leadership
> [...], the military achievements and triumphs that Díaz
> had won since 1855 (when he took over as political chief
> of Ixtlán) demonstrated that he was an indefatigable

---

235 See Antonio Lara Téllez. "*Compadrazgo Político en el Porfiriato.*" Bachelor Thesis. Department of International Relations, University of the Americas-Puebla, summer 1998.

236 *Zalce, op. cit.,* 295.

man, his own master, who knew how to use the carrot and the stick, self-sufficient, cold, diplomatic, a globe-trotter and visionary. Because of these characteristics, Díaz is mentioned as the head of the generation of the "machete," part of which was made up of himself and the group that swirled around him.[237]

González y González refers to Díaz's personality and clear and firm political strategies that assured his political success and control of institutions, Freemasonry among them. Therefore, another aspect that influenced Díaz's success with the "Scottish" was that from the beginning, despite their differences, Díaz took note of Juárez's popularity and reputation, used him as a symbol, and at the same time aspired to such a reputation, apparently intending to carry on Juárez's great work.[238] Since Juárez was a great Mason, and was considered by the Masons to be a great liberal, it was important that the people think that Díaz was following in his footsteps. Díaz also considered it important that he include some members of the Scottish Rite in his cabinet, in order to control them more closely and to exercise an institutionalized control.[239]

Another very important aspect was the politics of conciliation with the Catholic Church that Díaz cultivated during his administration. Jean Pierre Bastian notes that "this Catholic emergence caused a growing polarization in the towns where there were radical minorities, protestants, Masons and spiritualists."[240] These politics did not agree with what Juárez had achieved; but Díaz was careful at the beginning, and later very strict, so he was never openly attacked by the members of the Freemasons. This was a political strategy he employed to assure that no group had absolute power. However, Díaz was aware that Freemasonry could regain the power and influence that it once had within Mexican politics, and to keep this from happening he acceded to centralizing it under his command by contributing to the creation of a Masonic institution called the *Gran Dieta Symbólica*, as we will now see.

---

237 See Luis González y González, *La ronda de las generaciones*, México, Clío, 1997, 37.

238 Perry Laurens B. *Juárez y Díaz. Continuidad y ruptura en la política mexicana*, México, Era, 1996, 293.

239 "Una vez llegado el poder, (Díaz) adoptó una política de conciliación, librándose de hombres como Tagle y Benítez, dando acomodo a antiguos lerdistas como Manuel Romero Rubio y Felipe Berriozábal." Ibid., 273.

240 Bastian, Jean Pierre, *Protestantes, Liberales y Masones, op. cit.*, 148.

DÍAZ AND THE *GRAN DIETA SYMBÓLICA*

Before he came to power, Díaz received notable support from the Free-masons, since he was a member of the lodge Fraternidad No. 1 in the city of Oaxaca. This is clearly shown in the letter that Ignacio Pombo sent to President Díaz (33rd Degree Mason) on February 12, 1869, in which he tells him:

> The columns of this Respected "Lodge," Fraternidad No. 1 were raised, that from the month of November of 186(illegible), "V" had fallen because of political events that had overwhelmed the country [therefore, he said:] reminding you that because of your high degree, "you are Member," natural of that Respected "Lodge."[241]

The above is ratified by Porfirio Díaz himself in the letter that he sent to Ignacio Pombo on March 27, 1869, in his own handwriting (A.M.C.) in which he replied:[242]

> I have the honor to acknowledge to you receipt on February 12, 1869, expressing with special appreciation for the medal enclosed with which you honor me.

> By said plenary session I am informed with satisfaction that on August 22, 1868, of our non-Masonic calendar the columns of the Most Worshipful Grand Lodge Fraternidad No. 1, of which I have the honor to be an active member, were erected.

> Received with a fraternal embrace.[243]

This shows clearly the communication established and maintained between Porfirio Díaz and his masonic brothers since before the time he was elected. (The following letter presented here, from 1870, also shows this

---

241 A.M.C. = Alberto Ma. Carreño; Alberto Ma. Carreño, *Archivo del General Porfirio Díaz*, comp., VII, 218.

242 Ibid., 219. Note that the original letter had several masonic abbreviations related to protocol that have been omitted to avoid confusion; however, the translation provided here does not change the meaning.

243 It is important to mention that in the letter sent by Pombo to Díaz, mentioned above, he informed Díaz that a medal would be awarded as a badge to the members of the Grand Lodge Fraternity No. 1 of Veracruz. *Archivo Porfirio Díaz*. Alberto Ma. Carreño, Volume VII, 218-219.

relationship.) Díaz did this, probably with the idea that in order to achieve his objectives, it was important to have the Freemasons as allies.[244] It is also possible that the Masonic lodges were, for Díaz, the place of political preparation, which combined with the military training he had received on the battlefield. As a member of the Masonic fraternity, Díaz enjoyed a position of great privilege, since he was admired as a military man, a general famous for having won many battles—he was known as the Hero of April 2—and, later, as President of the Republic. And although it is not mentioned either in the statutes or books about the organization, it is relevant to mention that it was, and continues to be, a great Masonic tradition to invite important persons who could elevate the name of the fraternity to be members. Consequently, Porfirio Díaz never failed to take advantage of the position that the Masons gave him, at times using it for their benefit. Díaz saw the Freemasons as one means of achieving the presidency and winning many supporters within the organization. This is shown in the following letter, written by Luis Pombo to Porfirio Díaz on August 13, 1870:

> Dear sir, and fine friend:
>
> The violence of my march to this capital kept me from coming to say goodbye to you as I wanted to, but I left my brother in charge of notifying you and of relating to you the cause for my not having wished you a farewell in person.
>
> Imposed upon your desires to establish the Mexican National Rite in this city, after you arrive, I proposed to G.'. L.'s [Grand Lodge] that they authorize you to create a workshop, and my proposal was unanimously accepted, and today they turned over to me the letter of authorization, that I am not sending to you, since you are in Bristol, and it would be badly worn; but meanwhile I include here an authorized copy of the letter, by which one can begin to get an understanding of the works of the liturgies of the 1st, 2nd, and 3rd degrees, which are those I am sending today.

---

244 Porfirio Díaz, before becoming a Mason, had a good relationship with Masonic groups. There is no doubt that Díaz belonged to Freemasonry, since there are Masonic letters and documents signed in his own handwriting. In this work we are not interested in knowing when Díaz entered Freemasonry; rather, we are interested in seeing how he used it for his political purposes.

I will soon send authorizations and other things that are lacking.

Before concluding this letter, I congratulate you for having had the good fortune to have established Freemasonry in our State and for opening the doors of light with the torch of reason, as well as liberating it more than once with your sword from tyranny and from the foreign yoke.

At your most humble service. Your fond friend and avowed servant, Kiss His Hand.

Luis Pombo[245]

The above missive reaffirms that the Masons were, in fact, in contact with Díaz and that there existed a great interest in involving the great hero of Tuxtepec and the future leader of the nation. On the other hand, Díaz gave them a place in his political agenda, so as to have them on his side and to win greater fame, popularity, and support with the Masons that would help him win adherents among its ranks. It has not been proven that Díaz instituted Freemasonry in any state; what Pombo is referring to in the letter is that Porfirio Díaz contributed to the formation of some lodges. He did, however, have his eyes fixed on the future, and he saw among the members of the Masons the idea of working with him in his presidential reelection, as he revealed in a letter written in 1884 to the French Grand Orient. Thus, he was aware that leaders were cultivated and prepared within the ranks of the Masons, whom he had to identify in order to invite them to form part of his government, to keep them close by so as to keep a close eye on them. "It was said at the time," says Luis Zalce y Rodríguez, "that wherever there were tendencies toward fraternization and prolific activity, there appeared the hand of the distinguished brother General Porfirio Díaz, President of the Republic and personal friend of the Pombo family."[246]

During the years between 1860 and 1890, there was the creation and proliferation of various rites as well as the independence of some lodg-

---

245 In the historical context of 19th century Mexico, the abbreviation B.S.M. commonly refers to "Besa Su Mano" (Kiss His Hand). This expression was used as a courtesy formula in formal correspondence, especially in letters addressed to persons of high social or ecclesiastical rank. It was a respectful and deferential way of concluding or signing a letter, showing submission or respect to the addressee. Alberto Ma. Carreño, *Archivo del General Porfirio Díaz*, Tomo IX, 9-10.

246 Zalce, *op. cit.*, 322.

es. In 1869 the Ancient and Reformed Scottish Rite was created, headed by Juan de Dios Arias, and with the support of the lodges from Mexico City and Veracruz. And as a reaction against the Supreme Council of 33, Emilio G. Cantón and Ignacio Manuel Altamirano founded the Ancient and Accepted Scottish Rite of Free and Independent Masons (1878–1890). For their formation they included more than 100 workshops in different states and were recognized by the lodge in Mexico City. The correspondence from Díaz to the lodges in Paris and Washington confirms the opinions of Marco Antonio Flores and of Mateos that the creation of this rite is the genesis of the *Gran Dieta*.[247] On the other hand, in response to the control of Emilio G. Cantón of the Ancient and Accepted Scottish Rite of Free and Independent Masons, the Ancient and Reformed Scottish Rite (1892–1900) arose.[248]

The almost indiscriminate creation of rites, along with the discord and independent nature of certain lodges, had as a consequence the creation of the *Gran Dieta Simbólica Escocesa de los Estados Unidos Mexicanos* (Great Symbolic Scottish Diet of the United Mexican States) in the year 1890. At the end of 1889, the Masonic bulletin (official organ of the *Gran Dieta Simbólica*) says that the Great Orient of Mexico, with the goal of uniting all the Masonic elements of the Republic, had its Great Lodge of the Valley of Mexico No. 1 sign treaties with the Supreme Council of the 33rd Degree; by virtue of these treaties, the Great Orient was dissolved, and *the Gran Dieta Simbólica de los Estados Unidos Mexicanos* became the exclusive regimen for the Apprentice, Fellow Craft, and Master Mason degrees.

On February 15, 1890, the *Gran Dieta* was solemnly instituted, and the venerable brother Porfirio Díaz, president of the Republic of Mexico, was elected as Grand Master.[249] It is worth making clear, as was mentioned earlier, that despite being named Grand Master, he was not a very active Mason. More than anything, this was an honorific post that would later become so officially. This marriage of convenience was very important since, on the one hand, Díaz succeeded in obtaining both control of Free-

---

247 See Marco Antonio Flores Zavala, "*Los ciclos de la masonería mexicana, 1760–1936.*" Paper presented at the XI Congress of Mexican, American and Canadian historians. Institutions in the history of Mexico: forms, continuities and changes. Monterrey, Nuevo León, Mexico, October, 2003, 16. See also José María Mateos, *op. cit.,* 322-378, Zalce, *op cit.,* 293-350.

248 Ibid., 335-350.

249 Navarrete, *op. cit.,* 120.

masonry and the support of its members and, on the other, the recognition awarded the Masons by Díaz both suited and pleased them, since their mere proximity to him opened doors for the organization and gave it a certain prestige.

The founding of the *Gran Dieta Simbólica* was supported in large part because it was thought that in this way the sympathy of President Díaz could be won, as turned out to be true. The *Gran Dieta* was the ideal model to complement the strategies of the dictator. The *Gran Dieta Simbólica* served as a consultative body in what would be called Masonic dogma and had under its control more than 150 symbolic lodges.

For his part, Díaz promoted the formation of the *Gran Dieta* and saw in this union a key aspect for the control of the body of Freemasonry. In this respect, Díaz's leadership marked the transition between a mythical Masonic leadership, established by the founders, and a Freemasonry that in practice bore a close relationship to the presidential office. Díaz became the Grand Master of the Grand Lodge of the Federal District in 1883[250] and of the *Gran Dieta Simbólica de los Estados Mexicanos* in 1890.[251] The Masonic historian, Gould, provides the following story about the nomination of Díaz as Grand Master, which was corroborated in the letters of the Supreme Council of 33:

> On July 25, 1883, twelve lodges met in the capital. They established the Grand Lodge of the Federal District (or city) of Mexico, with Porfirio Díaz as its first G.M. The event was announced to the Masonic world in two circulars, the first being in Spanish—an immense document of some 180 pages! The second is in English, and its only notable characteristic is a declaration of the American system of the State Grand Lodges, each of which has an exclusive jurisdiction that has been adopted [....] As these pages go to press, I understand that the recognition of the Grand Lodge of which Porfirio Díaz was leader by the Grand Lodges of Louisiana and Florida was protested by Carlos Pacheco, Sov.G.Com.33o, and by Carlos K. Ruíz, who claimed to be a legitimate Grand Master. It seems, according to *la Gran Logia*, a bulletin published

---

250 Gould, *op. cit.*, 373.

251 Coil, *op. cit.*, 413.

by several members of the Ruíz Grand Lodge (and designated its official organ) that on the same day and at the
same time and in the same vestibule, then and there was
the Grand Lodge organized and installed.

Nevertheless there was a difference, and it is that while
Díaz's group carried out its business in the body of the
lodge, Ruíz's supporters saw themselves reduced to tend-
ing to theirs in the anteroom—the last of the original
convention having retired while it was being organized,
but without abandoning the building, in the vestibule of
which they continued to conduct their own processes.[252]

Gould's chronicle shows a certain tension during the process of forming the *Gran Dieta*, a tension that would lessen with Díaz's presence. For
several years the *Gran Dieta Simbólica* had much success and apparently
achieved unity and harmony among Mexican Masonry. Even so, by 1893,
in the *Boletín Masónico de México* (Masonic Bulletin of Mexico), we see
the creation of Grand Lodges in Mexico's states, which would have leaders who bit by bit began to desire both their independence as well as the
power to make their own decisions regarding local matters. Other things
that weakened the *Gran Dieta* were the formation of women's lodges, the
expulsion of Ignacio de la Peña from the *Gran Dieta* (who gave a certain
power to the Grand Lodges of the Mexican states), and the retirement
of President Díaz as its director. Although in reality Porfirio Díaz was
only director in name, his occupying that post cemented the connections
among many Masons.[253] Even so, Díaz established himself as supreme
boss, and the Masons were compelled to go to him to resolve problems or
to make decisions.

As mentioned earlier, it was thought that once the *Gran Dieta* was established, Díaz would be able to achieve command of the Masonic institution.[254] But in spite of the fact that Díaz had a particular interest in
the unification and control of Freemasonry, he did not spend all his time
directing what happened with the *Gran Dieta*. So, as a result of the rivalries that developed within Masonry because of the various rites and
lodges, and because of the problems they dragged along with them from

252 Gould, *op. cit.*, 373.

253 Flores, Zavala, *op. cit.*, 22.

254 Bastian, Jean Pierre, *op. cit.*, 139.

their past, the model of the *Gran Dieta* led to the decline of some lodg-es.[255] This was due also to questions regarding the recognition of national lodges by international ones, friction between some lodges and Masonic rites, and political interests. (The fraternity without brotherhood that was discussed in the preceding chapter lasted until the end of the nineteenth century.)

It can be clearly seen that Porfirio Díaz's popularity was growing in the Masonic environment of Mexico. In addition, all his control strategies were meeting with great success. Díaz was truly respected, and the mem-bers of the lodges believed in him, as his rapid climb within the *Gran Di-eta* shows. Also, in the Masonic environment on the international level, Díaz received various decorations, among those being that of Honorary Member of the Supreme Council of the 33rd Degree of the Southern Ju-risdiction of the United States of America.[256] In the same way, since the Masons supported him within their organization, they also strongly sup-ported his government, as well as his political campaigns and reelections.

If we accept the idea that Días *used* Freemasonry, then public perception of this organization should be studied and analyzed more carefully be-cause of the importance it holds for a better understanding of Mexican history. There is a great possibility, as we have said, that Díaz involved himself with Freemasonry in support of his *pax porfiriana*. The general was aware of the tensions between Masonry and the Catholic Church; in order to avoid a resurgence of that conflict, he convinced the Masons that when he became a part of Freemasonry, he would guard the secular interests of the State. It bears mentioning that Díaz's politics was success-ful since there was neither crisis nor critical tension between Freemason-ry and the Church, as had happened decades earlier, also decades later during the 1920s. Díaz's ideas were pragmatic in that they provided a de-gree of opportunity to each group, while he maintained supreme control.

Freemasonry, as we saw earlier, was one of the institutions that utilized General Díaz to extend its power, and in that way to have control of the

---

255 "This comment made more significant by the fact that Bernardo Reyes was a Mason, as was Porfirio Díaz; but during this time, Reyes considers the Nuevo León meeting to be among vulgar people and that the effort to revitalize it would be too great." Gue-rra, *op. cit.*, 171.

256 The Letter that Díaz sent to said Council on November 14, 1898, is found in the Ar-chives of the 33rd Degree Council in Washington, D.C.

political class. If one looks closely at what was happening within the ranks of the Masons, it is apparent that Díaz's idea of uniting all the Masons had its political advantages. Díaz, as Luis Zalce points out, attempted to maintain "a liberal appearance [...] to 'better connect' with those who said they were 'his new friends,' and to be able to keep a closer eye on the malcontents by bringing them together in places where the least prudent among them would reveal their most intimate feelings, safely unburdening themselves."[257]

The dynamic between Freemasonry and Porfirio Díaz was a positive one. It is seen crystallized in the strategy that he used in favor of the *pax porfiriana*. The evidence suggests that Freemasonry was employed as an instrument for the greater part of his administration—Díaz was not thoroughly convinced of his Masonic brothers' loyalty. Freemasonry's history up to that moment made him proceed with caution, because it made him consider the possibility of dissenters: "As new opposing political parties arose in the 1900s, they were quickly infiltrated as though they themselves were Masonic lodges."[258] In truth, the Masons were recruited by Díaz as part of his political base to keep them close and to avoid any type of dissent.

In spite of all these efforts, Díaz's project did not bring absolute control of the ranks of the Masons. There were lodges that never became part of the *Gran Dieta*. The majority of these lodges were critical of the authoritarianism that reigned in Mexico, and which was the flag under which Díaz governed. In this regard, Zalce y Rodríguez points out:

> Political life, which seemed to have parted from the lodg-
> es with the victory of *porfirismo* and the predominance
> of personal loyalties, in large part revives at the begin-
> ning of the twentieth century in those privileged places
> of formation and transmission of modern ideology that
> are the societies and lodges.[259]

As Díaz's regime came undone and the Mexican Revolution began, the lodges persevered, and the old accusations of conspiracy that were once

---

257 Luis Zalce, *op cit.* 321.

258 Alan Knight, *The Mexican Revolution: Porfirians, Liberals, and Peasants.* Lincoln: University of Nebraska Press, 1986 [1990], 32.

259 Ibid., 173.

forgotten returned. In 1914, when anticlericalism increased, the leaders of the Catholic Church said that what had taken place was the result of a great malevolent plan that had the support of the Masons.[260] Together with the mysticism conferred by Masonry,[261] the fact that Díaz supported both it and Catholicism (as opposed to what happened at the beginning of the nineteenth century, during and after the Guerra de Reforma [War of Reform] when such double affiliation was lessened[262]) evokes the balance that the head of state encountered with Freemasonry as a counterweight to Catholicism, and therefore as a means to maintain his credentials with both sides during the bitter confrontations between the Church and the State—which were, and perhaps still are, an important aspect of Mexican affairs. Freemasonry was useful as a supply of human resources in the services of the dictator; Díaz's wife Carmelita was the Catholic in the house that balanced the equation.[263] Freemasonry would provide the certainty that Díaz was a liberal (although he was not), in spite of the fact that to many he was pragmatic and conservative. In any case, Díaz did not view Masonry as a weapon against Catholicism as his predecessors had. What mattered to him was that it be his ally and form a harmonious part of his very successful conciliatory politics.

DÍAZ AND MASONIC FOLKLORE

There are several stories that confirm that Díaz garnered certain benefits thanks to his Masonic affiliation. One of these tells of the way that he managed to enter Mexico aboard a North American ship after his brief exile in New Orleans with the help of a brother Mason. Usually this type

---

260 Zalce, *op. cit.*, 20-26.

261 "... the nation possesses functionaries that serve as a sort of priesthood. So the schoolteacher becomes a vehicle of popular historical knowledge; the Royal Family has a highly papal role; members of the military too are professionals of ritual; even some sports uniforms play a part in the transmission of national values and glory." Ninian Smart, "Lands of Hope and Glory, *Times Higher Education Supplement*, February 2, 1990, 15.

262 The Reform War caused great discontent between both organizations, as shown by the numerous propagandas, papal bulls and other documents that criticized the other's work. See, Pastoral Letters of Herculano López; Letter about the origin of the image of Our Lady of Guadalupe of Mexico, written by D. Joaquín García Icazbalceta to the Illmo. Mr. Archbishop D. Pelagio Antonio de Labastida y Dávalos, Mexico, 1896.

263 Roger Aubert, *et al.*, *The Church in the Industrial Age*, London, Burns & Oates, 1981, 133.

of account is considered as narrative fiction, part of the many myths, legends, or fantastical stories that surround Masonry.[264] However, in the archives of the San Francisco lodge *la Parfaite Union*, which is part of the heritage of the Grand Lodge of California, there is a manuscript with a detailed description of this story; the document contains information that posits that the apparently fictitious story was in fact true. This manuscript is found under the title "A Master Mason's Word of Honor and a Brother who Refused Fifty Thousand Dollars for it, Alexander K. Coney, Preceding Remarks by the Speaker." The following is a telling of the story that shows again the support that Díaz had from the Freemasons, illustrating an episode of his life that is rarely mentioned, i.e., his return following his exile in New Orleans.[40]

In 1876, after Díaz revealed himself to be against Lerdo de Tejada, he fled to New Orleans to avoid being taken prisoner. Lerdo de Tejada offered a $50,000 reward to whoever brought in Díaz, dead or alive. During his period of exile in New Orleans, Díaz sought out other exiled politicians and his brother Masons so that they might help him. He received that help; but despite this, he was anxious to return to Mexico and by doing so to continue the fight. His ambition to become president of Mexico motivated him to attempt the return, and after several attempts, a brother Mason helped him with the plan. The brother Mason put him in touch with Alexander K. Coney, a member of the Lodge *la Parfaite Union No. 17*[265] of San Francisco, and the purser of the ship *City of Havana*, which would sail from New Orleans to various ports in Mexico. Díaz went to Coney, and when he saw him, he made a sign that only a brother Mason would understand. Díaz told the purser that there was a $50,000 price on his head. Coney promised to help him, giving him "his sacred word of Masonic honor." To avoid his charge's being detected, Coney registered Díaz under a fictitious name and hid him in a secret room aboard the steamship. When it arrived at the port of Tampico, a group of soldiers went aboard to register the ship and found nothing. The soldiers remained on the ship

---

264 There is a whole genre of these stories, some true and some of questionable origin: soldiers giving the Masonic sign about to be scalped ..., sailors raising a blue flag with the picture and compasses thus asking for help. See, e.g., Brian J. Bennett, "El Primer Masón Aborigen Australiano," *Newsletter*, Logia de Investigación CC, Irlanda, 1992, s. p.

265 The Parfaite Union Lodge was established in 1851 and had a large number of members from Mexico, Latin America and other parts of the world. Their ritual differed from other Californian lodges, and they frequently received visitors from countries as exotic as Tahiti.

during its passage from Tampico to the port of Veracruz. There, they disembarked without discovering the fugitive.

After the *City of Havana* had sailed from Veracruz, it made a stop along its way during the night to unload. Coney decided that that was the perfect opportunity for Díaz to be able to leave the ship. He gave him the dirty clothes of a seafarer so that he might go without being recognized. Díaz decided to take the even further precaution of jumping from the ship into the sea so that he might reach land swimming without being detected. The escape was a success—and months later, Díaz became president of Mexico.[266]

Once in power, President Díaz invited Coney to the *Palacio Nacional*. Coney accepted the invitation, and when he arrived, Díaz said, "Here is the man who saved my life, making it possible for me to become president of our beloved country." In gratitude, Díaz gave Coney a check for $50,000, the amount of the reward that had been offered for the capture or killing of Díaz. Faced with this gesture, Coney thanked the president and told him that at the port of New Orleans he had sworn to help him under "the word of honor of a brother Master Mason," and he therefore could not accept the money. When Porfirio Díaz saw that in this case the offering of money did not apply, he proposed that Coney become the Mexican General Consul in Paris, France. This gesture of gratitude from Díaz was agreeable to Coney, and he accepted. Later, Coney became a naturalized Mexican, and Mexican Consul in Paris; later still, he was Mexican Consul in San Francisco.[267]

---

266 Archive 17: Gran Logia de California, San Francisco. "A Master Mason's Word of Honor and a Brother who Refused Fifty Thousand Dollars for it, Alexander K. Coney, Preceding Remarks by the Speaker." See also William R. Denslow's description of the incident in *10,000 Famous Freemasons, op. cit.*, 1957, 313.

267 As stated above, before finding it in the archives of the Grand Lodge of California, San Francisco did not know if this was just one of the many legends surrounding Freemasonry. A variant of this story is also mentioned in Meyer and Sherman's book:

There is one of us whom we hope will soon occupy the Chair of the East of that Lodge—the protector and savior of a Grand Master Brother, who was a fugitive, and with a price of $50,000 on his head. He who was once a fugitive, pursued and hunted even to the very limit of death, is now at the head of all royal masonry of this country; he who has been freed through his complicity—our most adored and illustrious brother PORFIRIO DIAZ, 33rd, Grand Master Mason and President of the Mexican Republic—and the brother who protected him in his most desperate moments, the illustrious brother ALEXANDER K. CONEY, 32nd, The Prince of the Royal Secret of the Loge La Parfaite Union, No. 17, and Mexican Consul General in San Francisco ...

The foregoing clearly shows that Díaz's Masonic affiliation helped him escape persecution unscathed. In the same way, the story corroborates the idea that the principles of Masonic brotherhood (despite political rivalries) can bring an influence to bear upon individuals that at times spreads into the political arena. Perhaps this event contributed to Díaz's support for Freemasonry and to the fact that, despite his personal interests, he neither alienated the group nor destroyed it.[268]

If one were to ask why a man like Díaz would decide to affiliate himself with Freemasonry, it could not be discounted that perhaps it was because of the simple pleasure it gave him to belong to a select group and to participate in its rites and rituals. Freemasonry offers a social and dramatic space, making secret rituals accessible, making possible the attainment of degrees and decorations as well as a knowledge to which not everyone has access. It should be recognized that Freemasonry has a certain allure, as much for its secretive character as for its sociopolitical influence during the nineteenth century.

MASONRY IN THE MEXICAN REVOLUTION

In the month of March 1908, a New York magazine (Pearson's Magazine), published the declarations of Porfirio Díaz, in which he stated that the Mexican people were ready to install democracy. This interview was translated and published in the Mexican newspaper *Imparcial*. Díaz also stated that he would view with approval the creation of an opposition party, which would help to strengthen democracy, and, for his part, he would retire from political life.

Before Porfirio Díaz revealed his plans to James Creelman in this interview, the *partido Anti-reeleccionista* (Anti-reelection Party) had already taken shape, and in April of 1910 it launched Francisco I. Madero as a candidate (also a brother Mason), for which Madero was jailed in San

---

"Haut le Calice! À la hauteur du front. Vive le Loge La Parfaite Union! À moi pour la batterie! Acclamation!" Michael Meyer and William Sherman, *The Course of Mexican History*, 3a Ed. New York, Oxford University Press, 1987, 140.

268 In my next investigation I intend to delve specifically into Porfirio Díaz. It is worth mentioning that I collected material from the Porfirio Díaz Archive of the Universidad Iberoamericana in Mexico City and the Universidad de las Américas-Puebla, where I found interesting letters in which the Freemasons sent to Díaz reports of activities they carried out. Likewise, there is a special letter that is printed with symbolic writing, which I consider has valuable information that I will try to present in future research.

Luis Potosí. The election took place, and Díaz was again elected president. Madero managed to escape from prison and fled to San Antonio, Texas, and from there issued his *Plan de San Luis*.[269]

In this plan, he incited the Mexican people to rise up and take arms against the dictatorship on November 20, 1910. The Mason Rafael de los Ríos, who was possibly the *Primer Secretario de la Gran Logia del Valle de México* (First Secretary of the Grand Lodge of the Valley of Mexico), stated in a speech given on the 25th anniversary of the Mexican Revolution:

> On November 20 ... occupies, from the shadowy past, the exact vision of Social Justice and projects it in a fountain of lights onto the future [...].
>
> And it is in this vibration of claims, in these movements of rapid evolution, that Masonry—the highest exponent —takes definitive action, a manner of volition that transforms the roots of static and conservative tradition and redirects it toward the concept of a spiritual and human readjustment, into infinite mutations of justice.
>
> If there is a place that the word Revolution takes on its exact meaning, its full vigor, it is in the Lodges; where a boundless love for the imminent spirit of social justice is incubated and cultivated [...].
>
> Our Institution does not possess the specific form of a political party, because the organisms of platform informed by political promises, their narrow and fleeting mission having been completed, crumble and fall when they do not endure the usufruct of power. No, Masonry, secular paladin of justice, refuses the sad ambition to rule over men and peoples; and as it never had the political interests to bother with the comings and goings of those who govern, all this has channeled its trajectory, full of goodness and disinterest, along the white path of making men equal and free; free from all political, economic and social oppression [...]. Nevertheless, it is the members

---

269 See John M. Hart, *Revolutionary Mexico: The Coming and Process of the Mexican Revolution*, Berkeley: University of California Press, [1987] 1989, 237-275; Alan Knight, *The Mexican Revolution* Vol I-II, Lincoln: University of Nebraska Press, 1990, 15-71.

of the Masonic Society who have made revolutions.[270]

The discourse of the Revolution presented by De los Ríos shows the Masonic posture with regard to and interpretation of that rebellion. As representative of Freemasonry, the figure of Díaz the Mason, founder of the *Gran Dieta*, has been supplanted by that of another Mason, Francisco I. Madero. According to De los Ríos, it was the Masons who liberated the people, in the name of democracy and by Madero's actions, thus safeguarding a Masonic principle: freedom.[271]

The traditional Masonic posture can be seen in this narrative, in which Freemasonry is perceived as the origin of all events that define the nation. As it has developed throughout this work, my interpretation differs from that presented by De los Ríos. It is true that Masonry has been key in the historical and formative processes of the Mexican republic, for its organization and its society, and as a political party; however, it can't be given credit for all that has come to define the nation. This vision arose in the Mexican imaginary, due in large part to the attacks that Masonry withstood in Europe during the eighteenth century and because of the persecutions it suffered in New Spain. In fact, Freemasonry's enemies had held it responsible for many other revolutions and movements. In light of this, the Masons have sought out Masonic participation throughout history and given the main credit to its followers. Even so, other actors have contributed in one way or another to the process of formation and development of the history of Mexico.

What the Masonic discourses (such as those of De los Ríos) argue is that Mexican Freemasonry, beginning at the time of the Mexican Revolution up until the present day, sought to make itself into a kind of political lobby, that is, a group of individuals trying to exert certain influence on political decisions. This differs from the Masonic lodges in other parts of the world (for example, in the United States), where Masonry became a philanthropic organization, complete with social functions, and whose

---

270 Rafael de los Ríos, "La Institución Masónica y la Revolución Mexicana," Speech given on November 23, 1935, at the Hidalgo Theater in Mexico City, at the Velada organized by the Very Respectable Grand Lodge "Valle de México to commemorate the 25th anniversary of the Mexican Revolution.

271 Unfortunately, there is not a great variety of documents to provide abundant information about the revolutionary era, since due to the armed rebellion, it was not possible to maintain the archives. Many of them were lost (there is a possibility that they may have been sold) or for political reasons they have been destroyed.

members[272] see it as a social club with symbols and rituals. In Mexico's case, the Masons, despite no longer being political protagonists, do exert (or attempt to exert) political pressure toward fundamentally defending a lay and secular State. Nevertheless, Freemasonry's political influence has diminished over the years. This does not mean to say that they do not continue to be a thriving organization and that they come together on important dates to pay homage to their members in the public monuments and make it clear that they are still ready to preserve their principles and to perpetuate their history (the real as well as the imagined).

What had been political parties (the Scotties and the Yorks) during the time of Mexican independence and *la Reforma*, lost strength as political organizations during the *porfiriato*, and during the revolutionary period became political lobby and influence groups. De los Ríos comments that Masonry started and developed the Mexican Revolution. Obviously, as I have pointed out, this is the traditional Masonic position. It can be stated that to give all the credit to Freemasonry is part of what Benedict Anderson calls "imagined communities," in which many members of the Masons imagine a world in which this organization has safeguarded the nation and has protected it against the dangers that lay in wait for it. In the same way, they have breathed life into dead heroes and to many achievements they attribute as "initiated" by them. This is what Anderson calls ventriloquism, or what Katherine Verdery defines as "the political life of dead bodies."[273] Although it may be overly ambitious to state that this organization brought about the Mexican Revolution, what can be proposed is that this institution had a very active role in the movement, an example of which was the participation of Francisco I. Madero, an 18th-degree Mason[274] and a member of the lodge *Lealtad Número 15* (Loyalty Number 15).

As previously mentioned, some of the lodges that refused to join the *Gran Dieta* continually criticized the Díaz government. One of the aspects they

---

272 It should be noted that some of the members see the lodges as a space to develop professional contacts, others as a space for socialization, others as a philanthropic club.

273 See Benedict Anderson, *Imagined Communities*, 274-278; Katherine Verdery, *The Political Life of Dead Bodies: Reburial and Postsocialist Change.* New York: Columbia University Press, 1997, 1-22.

274 This can be ratified in a letter sent to John Cowels, Sovereign Grand Commander in Washington from W. B. Richardson, also a Mason, with the purpose of indicating to him who the most important Masons in Mexico have been. (I obtained both letters from the archive of the 33rd Degree Supreme Council Temple in Washington D.C.)

most frequently attacked was the control that he exerted over all matters concerning the country, as well as his numerous reelections. It was also argued that:

> In addition to the creation of the *Grand Dieta Simbólica* (centralizing organ for the majority of the Mexican lodges), of which he was Grand Master, a few lodges … refused integration and remained outside the *Gran Dieta*. If the lodges were an ambiguous space where Díaz's spies proliferated and where avowed enemies (like Filomeno Mata) or future opponents (like Librado Rivera) were found, the other societies—liberal, radical, as well as protestant and spiritualist—enjoyed a greater autonomy and independence.[275]

Francisco I. Madero was one of the Masons most critical of the system. There is no evidence that he was organizing the revolutionary movement from a Masonic lodge, but we do know that he had the strong support of the majority of his *brother* Masons. In his classic book on the Mexican Revolution, Alan Knight points out that different spaces that were considered dissident, such as the *Partido Liberal* (Liberal Party) and some of the Masonic lodges, were infiltrated by Díaz's people.[276] Other scholars also point out that some of the anti-reelection political clubs, such as the one in Pachuca, Hidalgo, joined with Masons of different rites.[277] When Madero became president of the Mexican Republic, Freemasonry again returns to the circles of power:

> The brothers Francisco and Gustavo Madero and José María Pino Suárez joined the respectable lodge *Lealtad No. 15*; they, along with Don Francisco Madero, Sr. Federico González Garza, and the Ingeniero Manuel Bonilla, who were members of the presidential cabinet, came to form part of the Supreme Council of the 33rd degree. Juan Sánchez Azcona, personal secretary to President Madero, returned to activity.[278]

---

275 Jean Pierre Bastian, *op. cit.*, 139.

276 Alan Knight, *op. cit*, 32.

277 Zalce, *op. cit.*, 43.

278 Ibid., 50.

Madero's big mistake was to allow several Masons from the cabinet of Porfirio Díaz to hold high public positions in his own administration. These "unloyal brothers," as Padilla points out[279] encouraged the opposition and the plots against the very man who had helped them and, despite being "brother Masons," they did not practice brotherhood with Francisco I. Madero. In this question, Zalce y Rodríguez states that "all the former *porfiristas* changed their look and their attitudes, although not their tendencies."[280] During this time in history, the phenomenon of "fraternity without brotherhood" returns within Freemasonry, since it was a brother Mason, Victoriano Huerta, who organized the plot to assassinate Francisco I. Madero. In light of this, it is essential to emphasize that in spite of the Masonic brotherhood, not all the lodges were under the same umbrella; in fact, many of them did not even recognize each other. As was to be expected, many Masons opposed Huerta's coup d'état, while others supported it. Faced with the coup, Venustiano Carranza's rebellion arose and was supported by many Masons, who continued backing it during all the years of his presidency and were beside him for the *Congreso Constituyente* (Constitutional Congress) of 1917.[281]

The division among the Masons as well as the armed movement diminished Masonic works in the years 1913–1917, particularly in political and military matters. It was not until 1920 that Masonry fully resumed its ritual activities.[282] I have come to this conclusion due to the scarcity of Masonic material that exists for this period; the sparse materials as do exist indicate very limited Masonic activity. There is the possibility that many lodges met without any evidence of having done so, as they have done during many armed conflicts or times of persecution, both within the Mexican territory and in other parts of the world.

One of the fruits of the Mexican Revolution was the Constitution of 1917, which crystallized the principles of the armed movement and the aspirations of society, giving them form and legal content. It is important to point out that, of the 218 representatives to the *Congreso Constituyente de 1917* from which arose the constitution that is still in effect in today's

---

279 Padilla, *op. cit.*, 71.

280 Zalce, *op. cit,* 50.

281 Ibid., 48-51. *Congreso Constituyente* was the meeting in which the current Mexican Constitution was written in 1917.

282 Flores Zavala, *El grupo masón, op. cit.,* 30.

Mexico, more than half were Masons (it should be pointed out that they were from different rites). The Masonic presence at the *Congreso Constituyente* does not guarantee that Masonic philosophy remains within the *Carta Magna*.

Nevertheless, the Masonic stance in this regard was, and continues to be, that Masonic principles were manifest in the Mexican constitution. In spite of the fact that we dismiss this stance in the current work, it cannot be denied (using Roderic Ai Camp's partiality thesis) that since there were several Masonic representatives, there were also Masonic interests or philosophy that these sought to defend, although it may not have necessarily been by means of their participation on an institutional level at this historic moment. The Masons aggressively defended the separation of Church and State and protected the principles of the Laws of Reform,[283] which were included in this constitution. Based on this, it can be safely and accurately stated that if the Masonic lodges had not had active participation in the *Constituyente* in Querétaro, or if they had not played a role, they would have been very satisfied with the document produced by that Congress.

The Masonic discourses, such as that of De los Ríos, create a fictional narrative in which the present-day consolidation of the political system is attributed to Masonry; but such narratives and public perceptions cannot be taken as fact. Nonetheless, neither can those historic moments be ignored in which Freemasonry as an institution played a preponderant role in Mexico's political life. One very clear example, as was pointed out in the second chapter, was the case of United States ambassador Poinsett, who exerted influence by means of the Masonic lodges (the York Rite, in that case) in efforts to install Vicente Guerrero as Mexico's president. Therefore, in the twentieth century, certain U.S. diplomats also exerted influence in efforts to sustain the revolutionary system and its candidates. These type situations inspired Martín Luis Guzmán to write in one of his books: "In Mexico, no political party has by itself enough power to dominate; their security and their power demand the consideration of a

---

283 The Laws of Reform (*Leyes de Reforma*) in Mexico during the 19th century was a series of liberal laws enacted between 1855 and 1863 as part of the larger effort to modernize the country, reduce the power of the Catholic Church, and establish a secular state. These reforms were central to the Liberal Reform Movement led by figures such as the most recognized Mexican Mason, Benito Juárez. They aimed to transform Mexico's political, social, and economic structures.

foreign power."[284] Both during the *porfiriato* and the years of the Mexican Revolution, attempts at unity by the Masons took place, as was the case of the *Gran Dieta Simbólica* and later, in the 1920s, with the creation of the First National Masonic Congress. These attempts at unification occurred for different reasons. In the case of the *Gran Dieta*, as we saw at the beginning of this chapter, it was developed to achieve control with regard to the creation of new rites, to have greater ability to keep an eye on them and to secure Díaz's endorsement. The Masonic Congress, on the other hand, was an attempt to establish an authority that would decide which lodges were regular and which irregular, as well as to create a national Masonic organization.

It can be seen in different stages of Mexican history that many of the historical processes of Masonry (such as the process of Masonic unification) proceed apace with several political processes of the Mexican nation (though this does not mean that the nation depends on Freemasonry). The Mexican nation, by nature historically heterogeneous, has been — both by Díaz and by the discourse of the founding fathers (to borrow a term from the United States) and the Mexican Revolution—to be homogeneous, to be a cohesive unit, so as to have greater control and to make the interests of society uniform.

Freemasonry too has a heterogeneous nature and has sought to consolidate and unify itself to achieve greater control among its ranks, to defend Masonic principles, and to keep an eye on its interests (especially the safeguarding of a secular and lay state). However, in Freemasonry's case, attempts at Masonic unity, both during the *porfiriato* and the revolutionary period, were just that: attempts. Freemasonry is not a homogeneous organization. As we have seen, efforts to create a *Gran Dieta Simbólica* to watch over Masonic unity were, and remain, unsuccessful; therefore, when one refers to Masonry, one should do so in the plural rather than in the singular. Its history, along with its elements and diverse characteristics are evidence of its heterogeneity.

---

284 Martín Luis Guzmán, *La Querrella de México*, obras completas, t. 1, 27- 28, taken from Padilla, *op cit.*, 72. Jean Meyer, *La Cristiada: El conflicto entre la Iglesia y el Estado 1926-1929*, 8a. Edición México, Siglo XXI, 1983, 174.

CHAPTER 4

THE POST-REVOLUTIONARY PERIOD, TWILIGHT AND TRANSFORMATION (1917–1994)

The new philosophy and political life that is noted on
the American Continent, especially beginning with the
revolutions at the start of this Twentieth Century, makes
intellectuals of every type, almost by natural inertia, set
about to "assess" the new governments.[285]

MASONS AND POLITICIANS IN POST-REVOLUTIONARY MEXICO

After the Mexican Revolution was over, Freemasonry became a group that exerted political influence—a lobbying group—and took charge of promoting laicism and secularization. This is supported in the Masonic magazines and daily papers of the epoch, as well as in the correspondence of the Supreme Council of 33 that I have compiled.[286] Therefore, as Beatriz Urías Horcasitas has posited, both Masonry and the political class, along with some sectors of the middle class, created an alliance that gave rise to the formation of a network of new solidarities that considerably influenced the post-revolutionary program of "social engineering."[287] Based on this, I propose that Freemasonry continued participating in political life during this period, and continued to meet and to form contingents active in politics. This was not necessarily on the institutional level of the Masonic order, but instead was the work of individuals or of a network of mutual interests that pushed government interests of promoting a new nationalism based on laicism and a secular State. This does not mean that the Masonic lodges sustained the prominence it enjoyed during the nineteenth century. More than anything, its participation changed in proportion to the transformations within Mexico; among

---

285 Gómez, Francisco, *Intelectuales y Pueblo,* Editorial DEI, San José, Costa Rica, 1987, 40.

286 See correspondence with Mexico, Supreme Council of 33, Washington, D.C., 1930–1950.

287 Beatriz Urías Horcasitas, "De moral y regeneración: El programa de "ingeniería social" posrevolucionario visto a través de las revistas masónicas mexicanas, 1930–1945. *Cuicuilco* 11 (septiembre-diciembre 2004): 87–119.

the Masonic ranks were reproduced many of the models and discourses that post-revolutionary governments began to utilize.

In the 1920s and 1930s, in the times of Álvaro Obregón and Plutarco Elías Calles, Freemasonry again took up its work toward secularization it had done in the nineteenth century; that is, the struggle to maintain the separation of Church and State, but no longer as a principal actor but instead as constant support for safeguarding laicism. This became a symbol and a bulwark of Mexican Freemasonry to such a degree that Masons lay claim to having created it.[288] During this period, the conflicts between the Church and Freemasonry were complicated by the *cristero* movement.[289] Masonry had been vigorously involved in this conflict.[290] One letter dated December 12, 1926 and sent to the Episcopate by Leopoldo Ruiz y Flores, Apostolic Delegate, declares that all Catholics were forbidden

---

288 I define the concept of secularism according to the dictionary of the Royal Spanish Academy (RAE) as "Doctrine that defends man's or society's independence, and more particularly that of the State, with regard to any organization or religious affiliation." I also use the RAE to define anticlericalism as "doctrine or procedure that is against everything related to the clergy." To delve deeper into topics related to secularism and the religious issue, see: Roberto Blancarte, *Historia de la Iglesia Católica en México*, México, El Colegio Mexiquense y Fondo de Cultura Económica, 1992; Patricia Arias, Alfonso Castillo y Cecilia López, *Radiografía de la Iglesia en México, (1970–1978)*. México: Instituto de Investigaciones Sociales de la UNAM. Cuaderno de Investigación Social núm. 5, 1981; Rodolfo Casillas, "La pluralidad religiosa en México," in Gilberto Giménez, coord. *Identidades religiosas y sociales en México*: México: IFAL, Instituto de Investigaciones Sociales UNAM, 1996, 103-144; Carlos Martínez Assad, ed, Religiosidad y política en México, México: Cuadernos de Cultura y Religión, núm. 2, Universidad Iberoamericana, 1992; Cristián Parker Gumucio, "The Sociology of Religion in Latin America: Teaching and Research," *Social Compass*, Vol. 41, # 3, September 1994, 339-364.

289 The Cristero War (1926–1929) in Mexico was a violent conflict between the fiercely anticlerical government of President Plutarco Elías Calles and Catholic insurgents, known as Cristeros. The war stemmed from the enforcement of the 1917 Mexican Constitution, which imposed severe restrictions on the Catholic Church, including limits on clergy rights, church property ownership, and religious education. Calles intensified these measures with the Calles Law (1926), sparking widespread resistance, particularly in rural areas. The Cristeros, mostly peasants and devout Catholics, took up arms under the rallying cry "¡Viva Cristo Rey!" ("Long live Christ the King!"), engaging in guerrilla warfare against federal troops. The conflict resulted in thousands of deaths and deepened social divisions. A fragile peace was brokered in 1929 with U.S. mediation, but tensions between church and state persisted in Mexico for decades. See Jean A. Meyer, *The Cristero Rebellion: The Mexican People between Church and State, 1926–1929*. Cambridge University Press, 1976.

290 See David Bailey, *¡Viva Cristo Rey!: The Cristero Rebellion and the Church State Conflict in Mexico*, Austin: University of Texas Press, 974.

from joining the Freemasons, stating that this organization was the cause of all Mexico's national misfortunes.[291]

During this period, the government took strong measures against the Catholic Church, which resulted in a rebellion to government-imposed limitations. This response on the part of the Church, led by the so-called *cristeros*, caused the government in turn to react radically, to such an extent that it closed down Catholic churches, seizing some of them. In fact, many of the confiscated churches were awarded to some of the Masonic lodges, where they continue meeting to this day. (In Puebla there are several examples of this.) Although there is no convincing evidence of the Masonic activity of Álvaro Obregón and Plutarco Elías Calles, we do know that both presidents, in addition to being members of the Masons, supported the institution; the donation of confiscated Catholic churches to the Masonic lodges is an example of this. Urías Horcasitas points out that during the Obregón and Calles administrations, "the Masonic organization emerged with a new moral power, capable of substituting for religion and of offering alternative forms of spirituality."[292] So Masonic lodges became, for some, an alternative space to religion, and for others, places for political education in the promotion primarily of a lay and secular state. For this reason, politicians regarded the lodges favorably, since the Freemasons were promoting the same liberal ideas and discourse of secularization that the government itself championed. And inside the lodges, the development and practice of political skills was taking place, such as the art of public speaking, debate, and philosophical reading, to name a few.[293]

During that time, Mexican Masonry was restructuring itself and trying to maintain the international recognition it had achieved, since it had not only friction with the Church but also internally. These internal divisions arose because of the debate among members about the political role the fraternity should play. As to this question, Luis Zalce opines that "anarchy existed among those who practiced symbolism." He suggests therefore that this was caused by the political interests of those Masons who sup-

---

291 Abascal Salvador, *Lázaro Cárdenas: Presidente Comunista*, tomo 2, Editorial Tradición, 1988, 227.

292 Beatriz Urías Horcasitas, *op. cit.*, 93.

293 See De los Reyes and Rich, "Freemasonry's Educational Role," 957-967; Urías Horcasitas, 94-95.

ported the politics of Calles in religious matters.[294] Nonetheless, such a position on the question of religion was what allowed the Masons to recover a role close to the governments of the time. These leaders turned to the Freemasons in order to garner a degree of support in the matter of the spread of the secular discourse and the formation of political cadres.

One figure who worked as a protagonist within the Freemasonry of the 1920s and 1930s was General Lázaro Cárdenas del Río. It should also be noted that Cárdenas likely saw himself in need of becoming involved in Freemasonry in order to reconcile the religious and anti-religious factions that had caused so many problems in the immediate past. In 1927, Lázaro Cárdenas founded the *Independiente y Simbólica Gran Logia Mexicana* (Independent and Symbolic Grand Lodge of Mexico), which, although not recognized and accepted by the other existing rites, achieved great popularity and did spread throughout the entire Republic. But not everyone was happy in light of these events, as was the case of Grand Commander Genaro P. García, who sent an insistent letter to the sovereign Grand Inspector General in Texas, Walter C. Temple, on October 10, 1938, in which he spoke of the irregularities occurring within Freemasonry in Mexico, and expresses further his:

> … great antipathy and anger owing to the formation of an
> irregular lodge by General Lázaro Cárdenas, who is now
> President of the Republic, when he was Governor of one
> of our States. One of the most important stated principles
> for this so-called Grand Lodge was that Masonry should
> be exclusively for this country. Since Cárdenas became
> President of Mexico, the lodges under the jurisdiction of
> his special Grand Lodge became important entities, with
> factors both political and bureaucratic. […] Some Grand
> Officials of several Grand Lodges have visited these clan-
> destine lodges and have accepted clandestine Masons in
> their own lodges.[295]

The above clearly shows the struggles taking place within Mexican Free-

---

294 Zalce y Rodriguez Luis, *Apuntes para la Historia de la Masonería Mexicana*, tomo 2, 1950, 92-95.

295 Letter sent to Mr. Walter C. Temple, Sovereign Grand Inspector General in Texas, Dallas Valley Texas from Genaro P. García, 1-2. This letter was obtained in the Temple Archives of the Supreme Council of the 33rd Degree, Washington D.C.

masonry during those times. There was competition among the different Masonic Orders or Jurisdictions to demonstrate their own respective preponderance in the matter of irregular lodges. This diversity has been disorienting to researchers unfamiliar with Freemasonry, to such an extent that they have confused some of the Masonic terms within their own works.

One of the factors that considerably influenced the rise of Cárdenas to power was incorporated by the lodges that he himself had formed, and at the request of a higher-ranking brother Mason: President Plutarco Elías Calles. Some Masonic analysts claim that during the Cárdenas presidency, Freemasonry enjoyed its heyday. The fictional narratives indicate that almost all of Mexico's important people, from the army to the government, were Masons. In many cases, that is how it was—but not in all. Therefore, both in reality and in the cultural and popular imaginary, the phrase that Fray Servando made popular was coined: *"¿Quién que es, no es masón?"* ... "Who is not a Mason?" It cannot be said with certainty that this in fact was Freemasonry's zenith; what we can be sure of is that it was one of the most active periods for Freemasonry in Mexico's politics and that there was an attempt by Cárdenas to create national Masonic lodges.

THE *CARDENISTA* LODGES

The government led by General Lázaro Cárdenas (1934–1940) was very significant to Mexico's history, as well as to the history of Mexican Masonry. It has been said that it was a time when Mexican nationalism was fortified, that it had the character of reform, although there is some disagreement that it had such a character.[296] So says Alan Knight, when he states that *"cardenismo* was a very weak vehicle for creating change."[297]

One illustrative example of this can be seen in the role that Freemasonry played during the Cárdenas presidency. During those six years, there was a close relationship between the Cárdenas and the Masons; it is no

---

296 No historian, as Knight points out, questions the importance of Cardenismo, but there are different opinions about its intentions. Alan Knight, "The Rise and Fall of Cardenismo," Leslie Bethell ed., *Mexico Since Independence*, Cambridge University Press, 1991, 245.

297 Knight, Alan, "Cardenismo; Juggernaut or Jalopy?" Working Papers of the Mexican Center, Institute of Latin American Studies, University of Texas at Austin, Paper No. 90-02, 28.

coincidence that in the years following his presidency a great number of lodges carried his name and that they recognized him as the promoter of a new and broad movement within Freemasonry. Cárdenas's connection with the institution probably confirms that he had diverse motives and interests as he reconfigured the labor movement in Mexico.[298] Additionally, his relationship with Freemasonry illustrates that Cárdenas attempted to have the final say in all decisions concerning Mexico, as Enrique Krauze points out: "The division of powers at any level was of no importance to him."[299]

Freemasonry's relationship to the Cárdenas presidency, and to the history of Mexico generally, has not been widely researched, in spite of a great number of Mexican politicians having achieved the most stratospheric and extravagant Masonic titles (Grand Pontiff, Master of the Royal Secret, among others). Particularly in the case of *cardenismo*, the activities carried out by this fraternal institution should be included in the analysis of the politics that Cárdenas implemented in his management of the farming sector, and the way he managed Freemasonry in order to control and direct certain sectors of the population (particularly the worker and the farmer).

In spite of the fact that the various Masonic degrees are not included in the discussion of Mexican political culture, the concept of fraternity has been a prominent part of the political system in that country.[300] It should be mentioned that this is not true exclusively of Freemasonry, since the guild model is also permeated with the concept of fraternity. On the other hand, research into these ritualist and secret organizations answers Henry Lefebvre's observation that "the successful investigation of a country's history is based on the examination of its secret or clandestine life."[301]

---

298 Riding, Alan, *Distant Neighbors: A Portrait of the Mexicans*, Vintage Books, New York, 1989 (1984), 55.

299 Krauze is generous in his description of Cárdenas: "His incessant return to rural areas in order to bring hope to the farmers, along with his enormous compassion. Even so, his presidency created the modern corporate state, and diminished the other branches of government down to nothing." Enrique Krauze, Mexico: Biography of Power, Harper Collins, 1997, 43-47.

300 For a discussion of the urban hierarchy see Rennie Short John, *The Urban Order: An Introduction to the Cities, Culture and Power*, Blackwell, Oxford, 1997, 36 *ff*, 113.

301 Henri Lefebvre, *Writings on Cities*, Kofman Elenore y Lebas Elizabeth eds., Oxford, Blackwell, 1996, 113.

In Mexico's case, the power that Freemasonry acquired supports the thesis that the diversity achieved across the subcultures is psychologically essential[302] and that its study provides an explanation of the long-term consequences of the Cárdenas regime in Mexico; therefore, the Masonic activity which he directed should be amply discussed. In the first place, it can be said that he was not only a notable Mason, but that he also has the creation of what is called a Masonic rite attributed to him. A rite consists of a succession of different ceremonies, such as the Scottish Rite, which has had a broad presence in Mexico and which features 33 degrees.[303] The claim that Cárdenas founded his own rite is unfounded thus far and deserves a detailed and thorough discussion. To begin such a discussion, the following is a quote from Peter Calvert that speaks erroneously of the *Rito Cardenista*:

> In addition to the generally known facts about the role of Freemasonry in the Mexican Civil War two decades after its Independence, Brandenburg has added a wealth of detail about subsequent events that indicate that it enjoyed renewed importance in 1930. [The presidents] Portes Gil, Ortiz Rubio, Rodriguez, and Cardenas were all Freemasons, the last of these being Grand Master between 1929 and 1931 of the Independent Grand Lodge of Mexico (founded in 1927) ... The importance of all this is that it confirms the active role of Freemasonry as a political force in Mexico during the 19th century as well as in our own time [20th century]. It also dispels the doubts of interpretation regarding the tendencies of the Mexican Revolution, the foreign influence that remained strong in many lodges in 1920, and its elimination, which was one of the leading causes behind the formation of the *Cardenista* Rite.[304]

---

302 Cristiano, Kevin J., *Religious Diversity and Social Change; American Cities, 1890-1906*, Cambridge University Press, Cambridge and New York, 1987, 70. Cf. Rich Paul, "Kim and the Magic House," Mulvey Roberts Marie y Ornsby-Lennon Hugh eds., AMS Press, New York, 1995, 322-338.

303 "A rite, in the modern sense, is a collection of rituals that have been, even for a considerable period of time, a group or a unit, whether because they have had a single government or that they have been associated with a series of works." Wilson Coil Henry, *Coil's Masonic Encyclopedia, op. cit.*, 526.

304 Calvert Peter, *Mexico*, Praeger Publishers, New York and Washington, 1973, 232.

In fact, Cárdenas carried out a remarkable Masonic effort with the aim of creating lodges that were loyal to him and that supported his political projects. It was in these lodges that the majority of government employees and members of groups sympathetic to Cárdenas were concentrated. It is for this reason that it is believed that Cárdenas was the creator of a new rite.

This information is contradicted in a letter sent to the Supreme Grand Commander in Washington, D.C., and dated July 10, 1940, in which the situation of the lodges supported by Cárdenas is described, and in which no rite is discussed, but instead "the *cardenista* lodges." Victoriano Anguiano Equihua notes that Cárdenas, moving away from the existing lodges, created the "Grand National Rite," which was, in Anguiano's words, a "heretic lodge" that he would have had to manage, essentially with political goals. With the title of Grand Master, he undertook the task of "Masonizing" his home state, Michoacán. According to Anguiano all of the employees, leaders, professional politicians and protégés became Masons, and lodges were organized in different parts of the state.[305] However, it should be kept in mind that the Mexican Grand National Rite had already existed since the prior century, when it was founded (in 1825) to reconcile the conflicts that existed among the Masons following Mexico's war for independence.[306] It is for this reason that one can fall into the misperception that Cárdenas created a new rite. It happened that lodges existed of all the Masonic rites with strong leanings toward the ideas proposed by Cárdenas. But at no time did this constitute a new rite (per the definition provided earlier) that would bring new elements to Masonic practice. So as to corroborate the question of lodge versus *cardenista* rite, the author had the opportunity to interview a Mason who was very close to Cardenas during his government in the state of Michoacán, Don Jesús Fraustro, who claims to have been a close friend of Cárdenas:

> For example, let's take my name, Jesús Fraustro. With all that I have done in my life, more than 70 years in the Masons, but we're not going to call it *fraustrista* Masonry! There is no *cardenista* rite, but the *cardenistas* did form a Masonic group. The idea of a *cardenista* rite was begun with General Cárdenas and General Damián Rodríguez,

---

305 Victoriano Anguiano Equihua, *Lázaro Cárdenas*, México: Editorial Eréndira, 1951, 52.

306 See Wilson Coil Henry, *op. cit.,* 419.

who were very good friends. General Rodríguez was a Great Light of the Mexican Masonic Rite [Mexican National Rite]. You could say that because of Masonry he got very popular [...] At least to me, all the groups constructed in the time of General Damián were *cardenista* groups [...] People had great esteem for General Cárdenas. I'm one of them. Rodríguez Triana, who was a very close friend of Cárdenas, thanks to him, I spoke with General Cárdenas in San Pedro de las Colonias, where Triana was governor. Cárdenas came to congratulate Triana each year on his birthday. In that way I came to know Cárdenas very well [...] The *cardenista* group organized in the majority of the states of the Republic [eventually] joined the Scottish Rite of Masonry, or the lodge that was the most powerful according to the state.[307]

This is why in the present day, when a lodge claims to be a *cardenista* lodge, it is primarily because of the political tendencies or ideas and not for the way it carries out its rituals. Some authors state that the Cárdenas period was not as completely pleasant for Mexico's farmers and workers as the official discourse has made us think.[308] Therefore, it is important to ask if Freemasonry comprised a part of the political debates among these sectors.

Without a doubt, Freemasonry has traditionally been used for political purposes. Cárdenas recognized this dynamic and, through his association with the organization, engaged with an institution that has been highly controversial in Mexican history. In this context, my aim is to highlight the influence of Freemasonry on the national imagination, public perception, and the formation or self-definition of networks of exchange. Letters sent to Washington, D.C., between 1930 and 1950 reveal both a desire for prominence and a lack of unity among Freemasons, which ultimately weakened them. Although *cardenista* lodges held a presence due to Cárdenas's influence, they did not play a central role in decision-making. Instead, they functioned as networks leveraged to achieve political objectives within the ruling party and other political or semi-political organizations.

---

307 Interview, by the author and Yased Ramírez with Jesús Fraustro, August 21, 1998.

308 Viviane Brachet-Maruez, *The Dynamics of Domination: State, Class and Social Reform in Mexico, 1910–1990*, Pittsburgh: University of Pittsburgh Press, 1994, 73.

Another characteristic in the development of Freemasonry in Mexico is that the majority of its members came from among the predominantly urban[309] elite and the middle class. We find an explanation of this fact in the enormous government centralization in the urban zones, in the broad growth of the cities, and in the relative prosperity that the urban centers enjoy. The lack of opportunities for development in rural areas has precipitated urban growth and is evidenced by the concentration of Masonic lodges in the cities. Finally, this high density of the most important Masonic precincts in urban zones is due to the simple fact that the jewelry and vestments necessary for carrying out their rituals are out of reach of the salaries of workers and farmers.

In this respect, Cárdenas moved to establish a new type of Masonic lodge that stood as an exception to the typical Mexican Masonry founded on the elite.[310] Despite his critics, Cardenas was profoundly interested in the social development of Mexico's farmers and workers, among whom this type of organization was scarce and of little impact. He therefore brought Freemasonry to these segments so that they might have influence within the Mexican political system. Cárdenas may have been ahead of his time in recognizing the importance non-governmental organizations have in the process of democratization; or the reverse could also be argued—that he did it to win supporters and sympathizers among an organization that owed him a debt of loyalty. Said another way, he set up clientelism. He supported the creation of lodges especially for Mexico's farmer and worker classes, which would have been a unique decision in the sense that it would break with the tradition of the Masonic institution that, in practice, was meant only for the middle and upper classes.

A question arises in light of this action: What was Cárdenas's true objective in attempting to introduce Masonry to the farming and working sectors? A definitive answer is not to be had, since there are no documents to support one. But by analyzing his legacy, it can be safely said that Cárdenas sought to carry Masonry to the popular sectors and that he tried to reaffirm Mexican nationalism within this organization. In other words,

---

309 However, the Mexican population at this time was predominantly rural. Short, 42-43.

310 A rite generally includes a certain number of degrees in which the initiate takes part. The fact of making some "cosmetic" changes in the performance of rituals does not imply the creation of a new Masonic rite. An example of these changes is the noted instance of replacing the Bible with the Mexican Constitution when initiates take their oath in the blue lodges that grant the first three degrees.

Cárdenas attempted to put Mexican Freemasonry's European and U.S. past behind it, so that it might be seen as an essentially Mexican organization. It can be said, then, that the Mexicanization of Freemasonry is more evident during this period than in others. This does not mean that there weren't efforts to Mexicanize Freemasonry, dating back to the nineteenth century. In fact, some Rites began to use the Mexican constitution in their ceremonies, rather than the Bible as is required by international masonic manuals. The Mexican National Rite arose due to this very reason—although in practice it did not achieve that aim.

As we have mentioned in other examples throughout this book, the socialization and the apprenticeship within the lodges made up the final phase of education in oratory and leadership for some Mexican politicians. In rural Mexico, there were no courses in leadership to satisfy such an educative need; in contrast, in the Masonic lodges the young could acquire experience in politics and oratory. In light of this, the fact that Cárdenas was interested in the possibility of carrying out an organizational effort for this sector through Freemasonry is not surprising at all.

Thus, by observing Mexico's history, Lázaro Cárdenas saw that Freemasonry utilized the image of the country's founding fathers, who were also members of that fraternity, in order to build its own prestige. Juárez is a clear example, having been Grand Master of the Grand Lodge of the Mexican National Rite. Seen in this way, the idea of utilizing Freemasonry as a vehicle to achieve political ends was not as eccentric as it might seem to us today.[311]

On the other hand, very rarely is altruism a presidential virtue. The question is whether Freemasonry is merely another example of Cárdenas establishing or reconfiguring organizations so they might give him greater political support, as was the case with the workers' movement, the *Unión General de Obreros y Campesinos* (General Union of Workers and Farmers), the *Comité Nacional de Defensa Proletaria* (National Committee of

---

311 Jean Pierre Bastian in his work *Los Disidentes: Sociedades Protestantes y Revolución en México, 1872–1911* points out that: "Masonic lodges, for their part, although at the beginning they could rely on the participation of many priests, gradually became anti-Catholic, due as much to the tense relationship between the Church and the Liberal State (after 1859) as to the constant attacks on Masonry by the Popes throughout the nineteenth century; and for that reason they created other privileged spaces, particularly in rural areas, in order to propagate liberal civic faith, often with the participation of protestant religious leaders and teachers as featured orators."

Proletarian Defense), and the *Confederación de Trabajadores de México* (Confederation of Mexican Workers).[312] It was in this context that Cárdenas, a politician with strong convictions and a deep commitment to the agricultural sector, actively promoted Freemasonry in rural areas. He saw this as a way to counteract religious fanaticism, which he believed hindered the growth and development of the rural sector. As a result, it is my judgment that Cárdenas did not create a new rite but instead promoted a variety of Masonic groups that contributed to fomenting nationalism and to educating a specific sector of the population in order to support his political causes. There exists no convincing evidence that Cárdenas created "The Grand National Rite." As stated earlier, the "Mexican National Rite" already existed, created in the nineteenth century, of which rite there exists an institution that claims to be a descendant.

RURAL FREEMASONRY

The support Cárdenas bestowed upon Masonry caused an increase in the number of lodges, but the majority of these new lodges were "irregular."[313] For this reason, this new type of *cardenista* lodge did not enjoy the support of other Masonic groups. The new lodges fulfilled Cárdenas's purpose: to promote nationalism in the rural sector with the aim of supporting his political goals, above all when there was the belief that the *Rito Escocés Antiguo y Aceptado* and the York Rite were under foreign control. In this way we see that, for example, the *Gran Logia del Valle de México* (Grand Lodge of the Valley of Mexico) lost some of its members, who found themselves drawn to the new Masonic movement headed by Cárdenas. This migration of various members of the Masons toward Cárdenas is similar to that during the times of Benito Juárez or Porfirio Díaz, in which there was great interest in being close to the president. Finally, some members in these different governmental moments created two lodges with great political influence. The first of these, in Mexico City, was called *Tierra y Libertad* (Land and Liberty); the second, *Unificación Campesina* (Farmer Unification), was located in Tlanepantla, in the State of Mexico.[314]

---

312 Alba Victor, The Mexicans: The making of a Nation, New York: Praeger, 1967, 179-181. Cf. Knight, "The Rise and Fall of Cardenismo," 252, 277.

313 An irregular lodge is one that does not enjoy the recognition of the older grand lodges and those of other countries.

314 Ibid., 148.

The lodges found themselves deeply enmeshed in the country's political affairs. One convincing bit of evidence of this is that the President of the Republic became the supreme chief of the Masons and that the ministers of property, agriculture, and of the Agrarian Department were Masons. In addition, the lodges that Cárdenas created had the objective of incorporating the farmer into the Masonic rite; this is probably the closest thing one can find to what might be called the farmer Mason. The mistake that Cárdenas made was to attempt to enlist the farming sector into the moral principles and foundations of such initiation by means of the lodge *Tierra y Libertad*, imposing the rituals and liturgies of the middle- and upper-class lodges without making any modifications to these rituals, so that the farmers could neither understand nor interpret their meaning. As stated earlier, Freemasonry's important and influential members regarded Cárdenas's Masonic activities with suspicion.[315] However, the lodges that had *cardenista* influence seem not to have had any profound long-term social impact.

As we saw earlier, Freemasonry in Mexico has remained the province of the middle and upper urban classes. In addition, although there have been many Masonic groups, none has successfully incorporated the rural sectors. As Urías Horcasitas points out, "The average Mason belongs to the 'ideal type' of citizen, that the program of 'social engineering' attempted to forge. The greater part of the lodges' regular members were professionals of the middle class, since Freemasonry refused admission to the illiterate or the destitute, despite the fact that it promoted beneficent works and assistance programs for the needy.[316] The degrees awarded by the Scottish Rite have leaned significantly toward majestic performances, requiring a large investment on the part of the candidate for the instruments and the attire to be used. At the same time, each member must satisfy a quota for each of the degrees that he advances. Freemasonry had greater growth in the cities and among the well-to-do classes.

But this does not mean that Freemasonry was (or is) completely absent in the rural regions. In fact, there are some lodges in rural towns, though these practice only the first three ethnographic degrees. This is important since the study of rural lodges could represent an enormous opportuni-

---

315 Cockcroft's view is that in 1981, 26 of the 31 governors and 8 members of the cabinet were members of Freemasonry. *México: Class Formation, Capital Accumulation, and the State*, Monthly Review Press, ed. rev., 1990 (1983), fn. 22.

316 Beatriz Urías Horcasitas, *op. cit.,* 94.

ty for ethnographic/symbolic studies, to discover the blue lodge's huge value toward the investigation of rural sociology.[317] Unfortunately, this analysis could only be conducted on more recently established Masonic lodges, as they lack historical archives that would enable a broader historical perspective. The study of the several types of Masonries that have developed in the various regions of Mexico is vitally important for the analysis of how civil society has developed there. Also, in Mexico, the relationship between these secret associations and the broader rural sector has indeed been very weak. Cárdenas tried to nationalize Freemasonry as he did with oil; in other words, his conceived Masonic project can also be seen reflected in other areas of his politics. He tried, therefore, to enlist the farmers in order to provide them with more opportunities. The *cardenista* lodges contributed to the president's project by helping him establish social and political networks that facilitated the formation of political cadres, ensuring support for his policies. Contrary to claims made by some Masonic authors, Freemasonry did not inspire the political ideas that Cárdenas developed. Rather, his ideas found a platform within Freemasonry, which helped promote them and garner support from certain sectors of society.

As the presidency of Lázaro Cárdenas del Río ended, attempts to incorporate the rural sector into Freemasonry ended too. Cárdenas's attempt to create special lodges for the rural sector did not meet with the success he had hoped for. He was only able to inspire a high level of lodge activity during his time in power. Apart from that, the only thing he succeeded in doing was to increase the degree of confusion that exists in the Freemasonry of Mexico. Finally, it should be made clear that Masonry was not—and perhaps still is not—prepared to incorporate the country's rural sectors, even despite the unconditional support of General Cárdenas that it enjoyed.

THE POST-CÁRDENAS EPOCH

When the Cárdenas presidency ended, the long-awaited succession gave rise to various political tensions. Ambition for power caused groups that

---

317 For examples of rural Freemasonry see Kay Vaughan Mary, *Cultural Politics in Revolution: Teachers, Peasants, and schools in Mexico, 1930–1940,* The University of Arizona Press, 1997, 90, 111, 120, 135. Also consider Van Young Eric, "Introduction: Are Regions Good to Think?" Van Young Eric editor, *Mexico's Regions: Comparative History and Development,* Center for U.S.-Mexican Studies, UCSD, 1992, 1-38.

had been united for extended periods to separate. Even Freemasonry was unable to halt these differences, and there repeatedly arose new disputes among "brother Masons" within Freemasonry itself. Beginning at that time, this organization that had once been so powerful entered into a low period. Manuel Ávila Camacho became president of Mexico,[318] supported by President Cárdenas as well as by the conservative sector within Freemasonry. The Masons threw their support behind Ávila Camacho more as a gesture of loyalty to Cárdenas than due to any fondness for the candidate himself. Ávila Camacho had not demonstrated any particular anticlerical thought and sentiment, which was a sign that the Masons looked for in a candidate as a guarantee of respect for the idea of separation of Church and State. With the rise of General Manuel Ávila Camacho to power (which process was begun within Freemasonry, according to Luis Zalce y Rodríguez), and with Miguel Alemán and Adolfo López Mateos behind him, positive actions were taken that favored the Masonic institution.

The affiliation of Mexican presidents and other political leaders have lent the organization a certain degree of projection. When some Masons take public office, they apparently support their lodges and their brother Masons. As we have stated here, several Mexican politicians have staffed their cabinets with Masons, as was the case with Victoria, Díaz, Cárdenas, and others. This situation has contributed to the perception that Freemasonry has been (or is) an institution that has played (or does play) a prominent role in the history of Mexico. It should be noted that I said *perception*; nonetheless, as several studies have argued, oftentimes perception has a greater impact than reality.[319]

Miguel Alemán's government was the last instance in which it can be shown that there was a Mason as president of Mexico. During that administration there was a great relationship with Masonry in the United States, since Mexican President Alemán had a close relationship with U.S. President Truman and Senator Tom Connally. This relationship was chiefly for the purpose of creating networks of mutual support in the business sector. I obtained what information there is available about this question from several letters and memoranda from various Mexican lodges and

318 See Needler Martin C., *Mexican Politics: The Containment of Conflict,* 2nd edition, Praeger, 1992, 7.

319 See Paul Rich, *Creating the Arabian Gulf: The British Raj and the Invasions of the Gulf,* Lexington, 2009.

from some Masons in the U.S. These documents point out that the organization in Mexico continued to have the same problems with the regular/irregular distinction that it had had in prior decades, but they gave credit to President Alemán for succeeding in rechanneling Freemasonry into its original apolitical course. (This was a requirement that foreign lodges requested of Mexican Freemasonry.) It should be made clear that many lodges did in fact comply, but others preferred to maintain their irregular status so as not to alter the status quo.

In the case of Miguel Alemán, the Masonic lodges close to him inducted businessmen and other members of the middle class who benefited from their Masonic affiliation in that it helped them to establish relationships with Masons in the United States who made up part of the private sector. Correspondence from that period also indicates that the Catholic Church continued to give "many, many headaches to Mexican Freemasonry."[320] In these letters is described the political situation in the United States, reporting that among the Masons in this country there are as many Republicans as there are Democrats and that their vote is independent of their Masonic affiliation. On the other hand, the Mason who wrote the letter tells its recipient in confidence that he does not agree with Truman's politics as regards the civil rights of citizens, among other points. In all these letters, Alemán and his politics are spoken of with marvel, and he is invited to visit Houston and Washington.[321] The friendliness toward Alemán was due to his interest in developing the private sector for the purpose of establishing commercial relationships, as well as for his eagerness to make the Masonic lodges regular.

After these administrations, especially with the subsequent presidents of Mexico, Masonry did not have the same visibility. Although one portrait titled *Perfil Político de los Candidatos Oficiales a la Presidencia de la República* (Political Profile of Official Candidates for the Presidency of the Republic), published by the newspaper *El Nacional*, did state that all the Mexican presidents up to José López Portillo were Masons and that with Miguel de la Madrid this continuity was broken. It is of less consequence that this statement be true; what is of great importance is that the public image of Freemasonry surpasses reality, and the general perception is that

---

320 Correspondence Mexico, President Miguel Alemán, 1950 Supreme Council of 33, Washington, D.C.

321 Correspondence Mexico, President Miguel Alemán, 1950.

all Mexican presidents were Masons. In fact, this does not seem implausible at all; to the contrary, it seems quite logical, since if one analyzes the number of traditions that persist, one six-year term after another, and if every one of the presidents continues with the project of the men behind the Reform and the Mexican Revolution, then it seems that Freemasonry had some part in it. With no other source than what was published in *El Nacional* and the interview of several Masons, I believe that Miguel de la Madrid did break the tradition. This does not seem unlikely, since according to the speeches published in Masonic magazines, there is no evidence of the organization's having any particular closeness to Miguel de la Madrid; and if the Masons did approach him, there is no evidence that there was reciprocity. Another hypothesis is that perhaps he was not interested in being a part of Freemasonry, perhaps because of not wanting to enter into a secret society, or perhaps because his technocratic ideas didn't have anything in common with Masonic ideas and interests of the time. Unfortunately, one can reach no definitive conclusion in the matter; what we can state is that the impression of Freemasonry as a powerful institution continues to the present day.

In the second half of the twentieth century, an event of great transcendence took place in Mexican Freemasonry. The Masons of Mexico came together and made clear to the president of Mexico, in this case, José López Portillo, that Freemasonry as an institution would fight for its members to be part of the solution to Mexico's biggest problems. This Masonic event was entitled *First National Encounter of Mexican Masonry,* and it was held on July 18, 1981.

From the content of these speeches, it can be inferred that Freemasonry was attempting a return to political participation. More than seeking a direct involvement in the political arena, Mexican Masons (uniformly across the Rites, Jurisdictions, and Orders), wanted the organization to be considered as an important element in the making of decisions. What they really wanted of the Executive Federal Branch was that they be integrated in a vital and dynamic way in the task of "making a better Mexico."[322] This does not mean that they have achieved anything in particular in this regard; in fact, it cannot be concluded that from that moment they had any more or less participation in politics. What can be said is that this attempt at unity and determination on the part of this association con-

---

322 Remberto Padilla, *Historia de la Política Mexicana,* EDAMEX, México, D.F., 1993, 78.

tributed to its cohesion and in its being considered as a politically active group ready to safeguard its interests at any cost.

On this topic, in an interview with the Mexican president, the representative of the Scottish Rite said:

> We are not going to be passive spectators of our own historic moment; instead, we have decided to actively collaborate with the men who guide our country in the solution of the great problems that afflict us, fundamentally with all the might of our National Organization.[323]

The National Mexican Rite had this to say on the subject:

> We consider politics to be a social science that allows us the instruments to give the most concrete and accurate solution to the most concrete problem of Mexico; we consider that the *Reforma Política* is the solution to the problems that the Government of the Republic and our people have today.[324]

The above passages show the interest on the part of the Freemasons in demonstrating that the organization was still alive and that its unity would give it more power to fight for its interests. The president of the National Confederation of Liberal Organizations (the majority of which are Masonic groups) confirmed this when he said that "throughout universal history the Masons have flaunted their participation, shaping reality, making culture, and participating in the activity of the human being." Thus, he praises the fact that the Masons have, in an unalterable and current way, preserved the principles of the Masonic institution. This was carried out in a framework in which a great number of Masons were present, celebrating the organization's history and proposing a better future. There, as an invited guest to the event, was the Secretary of the Interior, Jesús Reyes Heroles. In the opening speech, they thanked him for being there, and said, "We extend to you the combative and critical solidarity of Mexican Freemasonry [...] because we consider you as one of our own." (There is no evidence that Reyes Heroles was ever a Mason.) To this, the Secretary of the Interior replied:

---

323 *Acción de la Masonería*, EDIMAS, 1978, 6. Véase Padilla, 78.

324 Ctr. Ibid., 78.

> It is for me a real honor to accept these things in this
> house in which so many Masons have officed. In this
> house of government in which so many distinguished
> Masons have served Mexico.[325]

Certainly, the speech by a Mexican politician solidified the perception
that Freemasonry had not died; in addition, it reaffirms Freemasonry's
historic participation and proves the perception held of this association as
political agent. However, if a comparative analysis were made of the Freemasonry of this time and that of other historic periods, it can be concluded that in that moment the organization was not living its heyday. Even
so, the congress was a demonstration of its members' interest in snapping
back out of it and returning to more active political participation.

In the past, Freemasonry was a constructive force in Mexico; it fought a
thousand battles simultaneously on many different fronts and was able
to bring its influence to bear in the struggle for the freedom of religion,
free speech, freedom of expression. In addition, it contributed to the establishment of a secular-lay society; one sees over the years that many of
its members have used the association's historic weight to support their
quest for the Masonic organization to regain the place it once occupied in
Mexico's political life.

Freemasons in Mexico live inspired and motivated by what once was
brotherhood. Despite the fact that a great majority of them claim that
Freemasonry is not a political institution, present-day Masonic thought is
closely tied to the organization's past political accomplishments. It should
be noted that many nonmembers of this institution share this thought.
One example of the idealized vision between Freemasonry and politics
can be seen in the following speech excerpt:

> Mexico's greatness of yesterday and today are linked by
> the secular struggles of Mexican Masonry that heated it
> up, toughened it, and allowed it to give without receiving
> [...]
>
> Freemasonry achieved its greatness in Mexican politics.
> To scorn politics in Freemasonry is to cut oneself off from
> eighty percent of what Freemasonry should mean to life
> in this country [Mexico]. Politics is the supreme reality

---

325 Ibid.

of the human being. With Politics, reality is shaped. With
Politics, culture is made. I believe that your decision to
return—following the great Masons of our History—to
return to Politics, is a decision to Mexico's benefit as well
as that of all Mexicans who see it as full of valor and hope
for the future.[326]

The above passage is an example of the idealization of the relationship between Freemasonry and politics; in addition, the passage shows the positive perception that Masons and their sympathizers alike hold regarding
the institution's achievements. As a counterbalance, there has always existed the negative perception which, despite its not being very flattering, cor-
responds to Freemasonry's proximity to the seats of power. As I have emphasized at various points previously, these perceptions combine to make
up the fictional narratives about Masonry that impact public perception.

However, it is important to mention that 1994 was perhaps a key year for
Freemasonry as a lobby group, as well as marking the beginning of its decline, its twilight and its transformation. During that time, there was less
heard that compared the institution with the Freemasonry of its earlier
years. Even so, due to the political transformation that Mexico was supposedly undergoing, Freemasonry began to manifest a greater presence
beginning in 1992, and it consolidated that presence in 1994.

By means of a *Cartilla* (Primer), the position of the group of Mexican
liberals was made public,[327] who expressed that they were very concerned
by the difficult moment that Mexico was enduring. The Mexican Masonic
Organization, through the *Organización de Grandes Logias Liberales de la
República* (Organization of Liberal and Grand Lodges of the Republic)
signaled their purpose in this way:

> To serve our country, to be part of the tireless search for
> solutions to our national problems, active participation

---

326 Ctr. Ibid., 79-80.

327 Masons are also referred to in this way. In my opinion this is the title they use to be
able to intervene in politics. This is because by definition and principles, Freemasonry
is apolitical and should not act or have any relationship or influence with it. However,
in practice it happens. Then the members of Freemasonry, in order to have greater
influence and participation in politics, use the title of Liberals of Mexico in order to
purify the name of Freemasonry. In the same way, to avoid direct attacks from the
association's historical enemies.

in nationalist, revolutionary and patriotic political action, in the fortification of our economy as well as our
political and social institutions.

With finishing this "*Cartilla,*" says one Masonic authority, "the Mexican
Masons will contribute, alongside all Mexican patriots, to the progress of
Mexico, to the resilience of our institutions, and the solution of problems
that affect our country."[328] The Grand Master of the Lodge of the Valley of
Mexico, inspired by the "*Cartilla,*" declared:

> Our institution considers the system of maintaining the
> country as the best, and that in its construction—it is
> important to emphasize—to which many of our broth-
> ers gave their ideas and their lives, distinguishing them-
> selves from the independence movement, even that of
> 1910, by enacting our laws and setting the arguments for
> the Mexican Revolution.

The Grand Master goes on to say that the democratic system was produced in the Masonic workshops and that Masonry has allowed the development and survival of the human being. Therefore, states the Grand
Master, it has been supported so that it may perfect itself and be a permanent reality and may continue the struggle as it did in the past, so that
the election and selection of its directors take place through a response
linked to the rights and duties that citizens should exercise by their vote.
The Grand Master also says that the use of democratic mechanisms is vital for "the best men, the most capable, the most representative, the most
honest and nationalist, so that credibility is rescued and the forces unified to achieve a more just, free, and happy society."[329] According to these
statements, in which the clear bias of the Grand Master is observed, Freemasonry is the organization charged with safeguarding the State and for
achieving social justice.

However, it is almost impossible to find a Masonic publication that is not
an apology for the institution. It should be mentioned that these statements bear testament that Freemasonry at the end of the twentieth century had not been extinguished and that it continued to count among its
ranks Masons, both men and women, who fought to promote that organi-

---

328 *El Excélsior* newspaper, 17-03-82; See Padilla, 80-81.

329 *El Revolucionario*, 4-VI- 1982, Padilla, 82.

zation. In Mexico there is a significant number of women Masons, which is a topic not undertaken in this book. While other scholars and I have written various scholarly works about it, this topic that deserves further research.[330]

The Freemasons of the 1990s, nostalgic for a glorious past and political influence, tried to bring the organization's influence to bear on politics as a lobby group, by being observers of elections, and by attempting to involve themselves in public events; as well as by inviting presidential cabinet members to their events and continuing their public adulation of Mexico's national heroes, particularly Benito Juárez on the anniversary of his birth at the monuments in his honor. However, during that time, Freemasonry enjoyed no grand social transcendence, due to the fact that it had eroded internally, and publicly it had been discredited by its enemies as well as by some supporters who did not care to follow the order's principles or preserve its prestige. Despite it all, its critics are not as severe as they once were.

One authority on the organization says this about Freemasonry in the 1990s:

> In spite of its small problems, the Masonic institution continues to live; it is shaking itself awake from its lethargy; it is working in its workshops, practicing its fundamental objective; because Freemasonry is a science, a philosophy, a system of doctrines that is taught in a particular way using allegories and symbols.[331]

Freemasonry did not give up. During this period the organization continued recruiting, forming cadres, and seeking to achieve significant social participation. In this regard, Remberto Padilla states that "with the Masonic fraternity's recent decision to once again actively participate in politics, all the rites in their respective lodges are preparing their cadres, so that from these may arise leaders and standard-bearers."[332] Padilla's affirmation summarizes the objective that many lodge members hoped would come to pass with their organization. Without taking into account the rite, the benefit of the political role the Masonic order has played within

---

330 See, Guillermo de los Reyes, *Female Emancipation and Masonic Membership: An Essential Combination.* Washington, D.C., Westphalia Press, 2023.

331 R.W. Mackey, *El Simbolismo Francmasónico*, Diana, 1981, 6a. edición, México, D.F., 2.

332 Ibid., 82.

Mexican society is a theme that should be undertaken thoroughly. There are those who believe that Freemasonry in Mexican history has been "a symbol and a great instrument for the creation of a 'neutral' modern society, a society in which statutes fixed in the medieval world moved to the needs of a changing and dynamic socioeconomic structure, in which artificial and dysfunctional distinctions of the group are ignored, and the individual is judged for what he has achieved instead of having a prescribed status."[333] There are others who disagree completely with such a statement and who blame Freemasonry for Mexico's political chaos. I do not seek to take any particular stance in this regard; but I will say that these discours es surrounding Freemasonry are very relevant for the impact they have had on Mexico's political and cultural imaginary, to such a degree that it is no longer as relevant whether this leader or that one was or is a Mason, or if the Masonic lodges were key to the War of Reform (1857–1861)[334]; the important thing is to know that there exists a perception that to be a part of the political class, one should belong to the Masonic order.

TWILIGHT AND THE TRANSFORMATION OF MASONRY

During the 1990s, Freemasonry had an amiable relationship with the governments of Carlos Salinas and Ernesto Zedillo (it is not known if these men were Masons; the only information I was able to gather by means of interviews with Masons in Mexico City is that both were invited to be members) as well as with the *Partido Revolucionario Institucional* (PRI). In this segment I will focus primarily on the period during which Carlos Salinas de Gortari governed. Traditionally, Freemasonry has always kept up-to-date in the matter of governmental activities and official ceremonies, assemblies, and other events. Politics never escapes them. The in-

---

333 William A. Muraskin, *Middle- Class Blacks in a White Society: Prince Hall Freemasonry in America*, University of California Press, Berkeley, 1975, 22, citing Jacob Katz, *Jews and Freemasons in Europe, 1723–1939*, Cambridge (Massachusetts), 1970, 210, 214.

334 The War of Reform (*Guerra de Reforma*) in Mexico occurred between 1857 and 1861. This was a civil war fought between liberals, who sought to establish a secular state and reduce the power of the Catholic Church and the military, and conservatives, who wanted to maintain traditional institutions and privileges. The conflict was triggered by enacting the 1857 Constitution, which introduced liberal reforms. The war ended in 1861 with a liberal victory, led by Benito Juárez, who then assumed the presidency. However, political instability continued, leading to the French Intervention (1862–1867) and the establishment of the short-lived Second Mexican Empire under Maximilian of Habsburg.

formation gathered about this time period will be presented here; it was compiled by visiting several Masonic lodges throughout Mexico. These included: The Grand Lodge of the Valley of Mexico, the Grand Lodge of Mérida, the Grand Lodge of Puebla, and the Grand Lodge of Tamaulipas.

Among the most relevant of this information is the report from the period 1993 to 1994 from the Grand Lodge of the Valley of Mexico, published in the magazine *Acción del Saber*, which is the official magazine of the Grand Lodge of the Valley of Mexico.[335] One of the most important events was the speech given by the then-Grand Master of the Lodge of the Valley of Mexico, Salvador Ordaz Montes de Oca, on the *CXXI Aniversario Luctuoso* (CXXI Sorrowful Anniversary) of the death of Mason and Mexican hero, Benito Juárez García, on July 18, 1993.

Firstly, it is important to mention that the words introducing the speech were directed to the "Lic. Carlos Salinas de Gartari, to the distinguished representatives of the legislative and judicial powers, and liberal friends."[336] Afterward, following an eloquent introduction, he stated:

> We present to you Juárez and *juarismo*, bastions that for 121 years have signified all the strength, all the nationalist integrity of the member of the cooperative, of the worker, of the student, of the government employee, of the housewife, of the soldier—in general, of all Mexicans.

According to Ordaz Montes de Oca, Benito Juárez is a "bastion of the Mexicans." This speech contains language that makes tacit reference to the Masons and particularly utilizes the myth of Juárez as an icon of Masonry and of the lay and secular project in Mexico. In the same way, it is interesting to note that the Grand Master makes no mention of his Masonic brothers. Might this be because it is a public ceremony and the Masons do not wish to sacrifice their characteristic privacy? Or because they prefer not to mention the term "Mason" at events related to politics (or politicians)? Or is it perhaps a strategy for creating greater interest? In another part of the speech, he says, "Juárez, the best of us, who forged his republican conviction." It is obvious that the phrase "the best of us" refers to the best of the

---

335 All the fragments of the G.M. Salvador Ordaz discourse were taken from the Revista Acción del Saber, No1, March 1993/1994, published by the Grand Lodge of the Valley of Mexico, 2, 29-30.

336 In my research I have verified that "liberal friends" is the term given to Freemasons in political jargon.

Masons; however, again neither the word "Mason" nor "Masonic" is explicitly stated. This rhetorical strategy has to do with a discreet but powerful style that occasionally can be more effective than if it were said outright. Later, continuing with this strategy of discretion, he notes that "with a clear vision and a deep dedication to upholding the law, he understood that the bitter social problems of the people were rooted in the Babel of incipient national unity, in the nature of a system that made working slaves of men, that legalized the privilege of a minority; that implacably practiced tolerance [of this], that enriched the few and impoverished the many." This is an open criticism of the country's situation. We cannot be certain if he was criticizing Mexico's president directly; what should be noted is that Carlos Salinas de Gortari's decision to amend the Mexican constitution's Article 130 (which again bestowed juridical character upon the Church, which had been denied it in the constitutions of 1857 and of 1917), has not been very popular among the Masonic ranks. To the Masons, this was an assault on the legacy of Juárez. It is not ridiculous to think that the Grand Master was attempting to convincingly remind the government that it was important to respect the achievements of Juárez; and that if this were not done, then Freemasonry would let its unhappiness be known.

One interesting part of the speech that reveals a subtle criticism[337] of the Salinas government is its closing, particularly when Ordaz Montes de Oca says:

> Today, we all commit to each other. A time of risk, a time of definitions; the times of President Salinas are like those of President Juárez: times in which the liberals of Mexico are witness to a renewed republican act, in which there is no room for letting things be, for letting things pass.

In the speech, he also makes use of the occasion to respectfully but firmly express his view to the Mexican president that the Masons are totally against the union of Church and State, as Benito Juárez always preached. However, while it is clear this point belongs to them through the repercussions of history, there are other matters that also worry them, as we see here:

---

337 It must be remembered that until this time, no institution publicly criticized the president (the Great Tlatoani), therefore, despite the discontent, we do not have a severe criticism of the government of the time, despite the great discontent that it caused them.

> We Mexican liberals [...] want to continue contributing to the building of tomorrow. To this end, soon we will extend to every corner of the Republic the basis for constituting a National Liberal Movement, in which—regardless of political party, creed, or social condition of its members—it will be our duty to unite, to always renew those principles in which Juárez believed, those for which Juárez fought, those grown in Mexico.

According to this passage, the Mexican liberals—in other words, the Mexican Masons—wished to regain the strength they had in Mexico's past by carrying the banner of the liberal principles of Benito Juárez and the other distinguished men who contributed to bringing about the War of Reform.

On the other hand, one can appreciate Freemasonry's openness toward Mexican society. Although they do not identify themselves as Masons, they do identify themselves as Mexican liberals. In this speech, as in many others, there is latent hope—perhaps nostalgia? —of recovering the political power Freemasonry had in the nineteenth century. The bases for the liberal movement that Grand Master Ordaz speaks of "will stand beside our institutions." One interpretation of this might be that Masonry will reclaim as its own certain institutions, such as the Mexican Constitution of 1917, or even the presidency of Mexico. It would then perhaps be by means of them or together with them that the liberal movement will continue to evolve, according to Ordaz. On the other hand, during that time there was a strong relationship between the members of Freemasonry and the PRI, so perhaps he is referring to this. During this period, the call that Masonic speeches make for lay and secular ideals to be respected predominates, since the Masons of the time felt that Carlos Salinas de Gortari had broken with the tradition many Mexican presidents had managed to protect. However, despite the Masons' discontent, they did not organize acts of civil disobedience; everything stayed within the discursive points or in discreet complaints. Perhaps this was because of their closeness to the PRI and, at the same time, because of being part of a system in which the ultimate authority is not questioned—in this case, the president of Mexico.

In the magazine *Acción del Saber*, another speech by the Grand Master Salvador Ordaz Montes de Oca, which he made at the meeting of Mexican liberals on the terrace of the PRI with the then-president of that party—and later candidate for the Mexican presidency—Luis Donaldo Colosio, on the occasion of the 188th anniversary of the birth of Benito Juárez.[338] He begins this speech by recalling the *Benemérito de las Américas*, Juárez. Again, in this speech he uses neither the word "Mason" nor "Masonry"; although in the first part of it he does make reference to Masons like Valentín Gómez Farías, Guillermo Prieto, Ignacio Manuel Altamirano and Juan A. Mateos. In my opinion, here too is demonstrated the desire to continue with the same privacy, discretion or secrecy that characterizes Freemasonry, or he is being careful to keep the relationship between Freemasonry and politics out of the speech so as to avoid the problems of the past. In the body of his speech, Ordaz expresses the wishes of Freemasonry for Mexico: "Democracy. We feel that it is an indispensable requirement for modernity and the development of our nation. We demand it, yes, more complete, much more perfected, but never, ever again [...] bloody."[339] The rhetoric about democracy is a commonplace in speeches; in fact, during that period, it was the common denominator to many of them, since Mexico was attempting to become a democratic and developed country. The words that stand out are those that speak of a democracy "never, ever again [...] bloody," since not long after this speech was delivered these words echo with irony with the assassination of Luis Donaldo Colosio, an event that both interrupted and literally bloodied Mexico's march toward democracy.

These words spoken by one of the ultimate authorities on Masonry reveal the great interest that the members of the organization have in becoming a political action group:

> Juárez lives, but he will live more if the next president of the United States of Mexico and the men of these times build a team with a true ethos of service, similar to that led by the Indian of the Blue Mountain, so that its army manifests, in a real way, palpable: fewer Mexicans unemployed, with a greener, more productive and flourishing green in our fields, a bigger and better educational level in our classrooms [...]

338 The fragments of Salvador Ordaz's speech presented below were taken from the Revista Acción del Saber, Ibid., 3-5.

339 Ibid.

The above excerpt is a definitive test in which one gets a glimpse of Freemasonry as a lobbying group; Ordaz tacitly says to Colosio, "You, who are an official candidate, if you want our vote as an institution, you must treat our requests accordingly." Thus, he suggests, "with a good team (perhaps the Masons), you must safeguard the glorious past and modernize the country." On the other hand, the Masonic principle of forming youth cadres by following the example of Mexico's national heroes comes to light in this speech. Obviously, he said all this because, judging from prior experience and the prior victories of PRI candidates, Colosio would be the next president of Mexico. In his speech, he communicates to the candidate for president the interests of Masonry and the conditions the organization desires in order to continue to support the presidential candidate of the then-official party, particularly during the time in which the PRI needed to rally its supporters, since in the prior election the *Partido de la Revolución Democrática* (Party of the Democratic Revolution, PRD) had won many sympathizers.

In the final segment of his speech, Ordaz expresses his policy of "never to allow the interference of the high clergy in government politics." This is perhaps because there existed a certain fear among the Masonic ranks that the Church would again cast the long shadow it did in the past as an element of real power. This fear was not unfounded, since both during the Salinas administration and that of Vicente Fox (2000–2006), and that of Felipe Calderón Hinojosa, the Church has been better positioned than in prior decades.

The speech finally concludes with, "History awaits you, friend Colosio. The decision is yours!" Here Ordaz gives us the impression by the use of the word "friend" that its true translation would be "brother," forming the analogy "liberal is to Masonry as friend is to brother." This supposition becomes perhaps somewhat subjective with the quest to relate everything in the speech to Freemasonry. The way the speech is managed and the symbolic and cabalistic portrayal of Freemasonry, makes one think that behind the simple words there are many symbols and clues that prove the interests Freemasonry still has in Mexican political life. It is also clear that its members recall with nostalgia a past in which their organization had great political power. In 1994, Freemasonry in Mexico continued to be an influential group, or an elite close to the official party and the seats of government. The organization continued recruiting young people and others who aspired to politics by keeping the tradition of forming liberal cadres to protect the secularization of the Mexican State.

In the various political speeches that define this strong interest in continuing to be a part of the circles of power within the Mexican government:

> We remain attentive, always moving, for the next appearance of the bases to shape the National Liberal Movement in every corner of the country. It is this effort, with full respect to our personal situation and to our political, religious, or any other preferences we may have in this beloved land, a land of full freedom, a refuge for the weak and those persecuted because of their steadfast belief in justice, an altar to the empire of the Law, and an indestructible bulwark, to defend the actions to achieve a time that man ceases to be a beast of a man.[340]

In this speech the desire to create a national liberal movement is noted, a movement that is nothing more than a group for political preparation within the government. The phrase "together with President Carlos Salinas de Gortari" can be found on repeated occasions in different speeches given by members of Freemasonry. Two speeches delivered to Salinas, one on July 18, 1993, and the other given before the Liberal Union on July 3 of the same year, make use of certain phrases that reflect that Freemasonry's desire is to work alongside the president of Mexico. In spite of there not being enough information about whether Salinas made particular use of the Masonic institution, it comes as no surprise that the meetings and closeness with them was an attempt to keep them pacified as to the changes to the Mexican constitution that Salinas was making. Another hypothesis might be that Carlos Salinas de Gortari, perhaps inspired by Porfirio Díaz, made use of Freemasonry for the benefit of his government. As we said previously, despite the fact that the Masons were in total disagreement with the decision on the part of Salinas to grant legal status to the Church, they did not register a severe criticism of the president's decision.

---

340 Speech by MRGM Salvador Ordaz Montes de Oca, on July 3, 1993, at the Fiesta Americana Reforma Hotel, at the "Liberal Unit" breakfast. With the representatives of the different Masonic groups, as well as with the representative of the Secretary of National Defense, Division General, Ángel Barrón and Lic. Mario Ruíz de Chávez, Municipal President of Naucalpan, Ibid., 14-17.

MASONIC RECRUITMENT AND POLISHING SCHOOL

One of the methods the Freemasons deploy to politicize their numbers is oratory, in that they organize preparatory courses and workshops for their membership, especially for the young Masons (those who belong to the AJEF lodges, which stands for *Asociación de Jóvenes Esperanza de la Fraternidad*) with the purpose of teaching them public speaking. These forums become de facto centers for political training. I noted in various interviews and personal exchanges as well as in Masonic publications that the Masons have a great interest in cultivating orators, the aim of which is purely political. In the magazine *Acción del saber* of March 21, 1994, it was stated that "the Grand Oratory will meet with the Orators from all workshops within the jurisdiction to initiate the work plan in which there will be proposed, among others, courses of oratory, the very detailed study of our laws, the *Constitución del Valle de México* [Constitution of the Valley of Mexico] as well as the Electoral Law and the Penal Law, so that our orators know how to defend their people, since we imagine that an Orator who does not know will not correctly defend his brothers; or vice versa, an orator that does not know his rights and obligations will abuse his post ... and we will expect that every workshop be strictly put into practice, because this will also permit our symbolic works to be supported."[341]

The dynamic of these speakers' competitions follows a prescribed sequence. The first round is open to "profane individuals" (people who are not Freemasons). Subsequently, the tournament is carried out in the same way as any other contest of its type. The topics for the speeches are usually related to the history of Mexico, national and international events concerning that country, or of problems that affect society in general, for example, drug addiction, human rights, etc. These contests may be carried out in a room at the lodge itself or in some other appropriate place for them. In the case of the *Gran Logia de Tamaulipas* [Grand Lodge of Tamaulipas], the oratory contests have been held in the room where the town council of Tamaulipas convenes. Finally, the awarding of prizes takes place in the Masonic temple in one of the workshops, in what is called a *tenida blanca* [Open Lodge], a Masonic ceremony which the "profane" public may attend, in the presence of the Grand Master, who normally delivers a speech similar to those often made by public officials. The above

---

341 Interview with Ramón Sifiri Jiménez, who holds the position of Grand Speaker of the Grand Lodge of the Valley of Mexico by *Acción del Saber* Magazine, 19.

information comes from first-hand observation, since years ago I had the opportunity to participate in many such contests.[342]

Of the events in which I personally participated, two important things should be pointed out: 1) In the majority of these speaking contests sponsored by the Masonic lodges, the organizers were members not only of the Masons but of the political party PRI. That is to say, there was a strong connection between these two institutions; and 2) These tournaments are for the purpose of recruiting young people, of inviting them to participate in the world of Freemasonry.[343] It should be noted that no one is ever forced to join the Masons; although the organization does attempt to recruit from among Mexico's youth, no one is obligated to enroll. With the benefit of these experiences, I came to realize that at the local level, as I saw in Tamaulipas, Freemasonry is closely linked to politics; the relationship between the organization and local government is clear and evident. This is in no way peculiar to Tamaulipas, since this connection is also seen at the national level.

In an interview conducted by the Masonic magazine *Acción del saber*, Ramón Safiri stated that "Masonry is not political; Masonry creates Masons, and these serve as agents of transformation ...." The following questions arise from this statement: What type of Masons actually form Freemasonry? Are they politicians? Revolutionaries? Businessmen? Philanthropists? Also, to what "transformation" does he refer? Is it perhaps political, economic, or cultural?—after all, they are all related. As we have also seen in this chapter, Freemasonry has not disappeared from the public

---

342　All of this is related as based on personal experience, which I will expand upon below for a better understanding. In Tampico and Ciudad Madero, Tamaulipas, each year the Grand Lodge of Tamaulipas holds oratory and speech contests, which are open to the entire public. The way I found out about these contests was that on one occasion, in 1986, I participated representing my high school in a contest organized by the school district. After I had won, a person from the public invited me to a contest organized by the Masonic lodge. Because of my great interest in oratory and speech contests, I chose to participate in the event. The dynamics of the contest were as I explained previously. It is interesting to mention that the awards ceremony shows a little of what the Freemasons do, and I was personally invited to enter Freemasonry for young people. In fact, this was not the only contest organized by a Masonic lodge in which I participated. For several years I competed in various oratory and speech competitions.

343　On one occasion one of the organizers of the contest asked me – How old are you? – and I answered, 18; then he told me – "It's a shame you still have three years left to be able to belong to Freemasonry, and you are such a good speaker."

eye. In fact, until 1994 it underwent a certain level of activity, particularly with the modifications that Carlos Salinas de Gortari made to the 130th constitutional article.[344] These changes caused members of the Masons to establish civil associations of free thinkers with the aim of bringing about political pressure and continuing the struggle in the image of Juárez. We can also see in this chapter the very important work done within Freemasonry by Cárdenas, who tried to nationalize it just as he had done with the petroleum industry. To this aim he made a futile attempt to involve the country folk and farmers in the Masonic ranks, without stopping to understand the great quantity of study necessary for initiation into the Masons, achieving the Masonic degrees, and practicing their rituals. The effort was fruitless since those of the rural population were often illiterate.

In this chapter we again saw Freemasonry as a sort of preparatory school for politics and government. The Masonic lodges provide spaces for the young, many of whom do join AJEF lodges (*Asociación de Jóvenes Esperanza de la Fraternidad*) which is a Masonic youth organization in Mexico (and other parts of Latin America) designed for young people from 14 to 21 years of age as a preparatory step to Freemasonry. It focuses on leadership, civic responsibility, ethics, and intellectual development, operating under the guidance of Masonic Grand Lodges, whose motto is "*esperanza de la fraternidad*" (the brotherhood's hope).[345] These lodges help young men prepare themselves to help continue the development of the Masonic institution, the same as Guadalupe Victoria, Vicente Guerrero, Lorenzo de Zavala, José Marí Luis Mora, Benito Juárez, Porfirio Díaz, Bernardo Reyes, Francisco I. Madero, Lázaro Cárdenas, Miguel Alemán, and many others whose names today cover the walls of Masonic temples and government palaces throughout the Mexican republic. These storied Masons provide much grist for conversation as well as for the many fictional narratives that have arisen about this controversial institution.

---

344 This article is a continuation of Mexico's anti-clerical policies that originated in the Reform Laws (1855–1861) and were reinforced during the Constitution of 1917, following the Mexican Revolution. These laws were particularly significant in limiting the power of the Catholic Church, which had historically been very influential in Mexico. Separation of Church and State: The state remains secular and does not recognize any official religion.

345 There is no exact equivalent in the U.S.; similar Masonic youth organizations include DeMolay International (for young men), Job's Daughters International, and The International Order of the Rainbow for Girls (for young women). Unlike DeMolay, which is broader in scope, AJEF lodges are deeply rooted in Spanish-speaking heritage and emphasize civic activism and national identity.

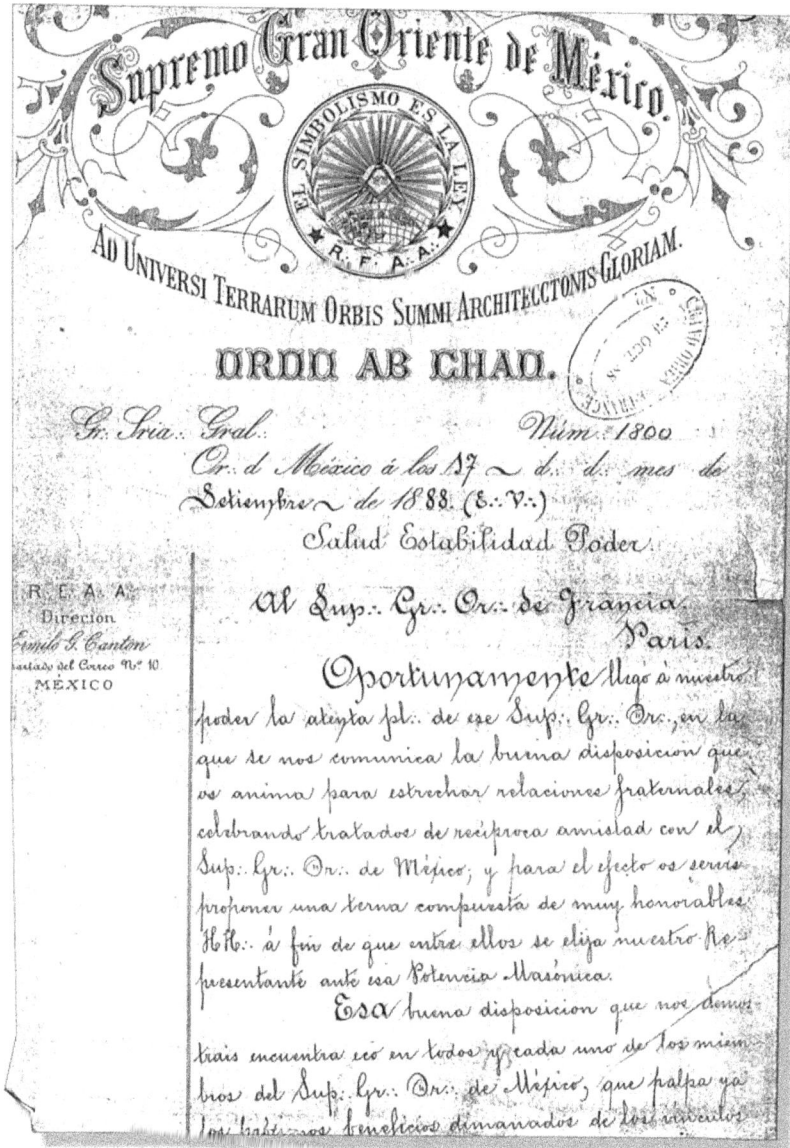

Letter from the Supreme Grand Orient of Mexico dated September 17, 1888.
In this correspondence with the Grand Orient of France, the aim was to establish relations between the two bodies and obtain mutual recognition. The Grand Orient of France had a significant impact on Mexican Freemasonry at the end of the 19th century.

Correspondence from the Grand Symbolic Diet of the United Mexican States with the Grand Orient of France, signed by Grand Master Porfirio Díaz on May 15, 1894. It refers to the friendly ties between both groups and formalizes the relationship between these two Masonic Orients.

Diploma received by the author in a declamation contest organized by the AJEF lodge Rubén Márquez Romo, in which he won first place. The event was held in Tampico, Tamaulipas, on May 19, 1990. The author participated in several oratory and declamation competitions o rganized by various Masonic lodges and AJEF lodges in his home state of Tamaulipas, Mexico.

Lithograph of a Masonic initiation published in *Mauricio el ajusticiado o una persecución masónica* (1864), a novel by Lorenzo Elizaga that criticized and sought to reveal Masonic secrets.

Lithograph of the Third Degree of the symbolic lodge published in *Mauricio el ajusticiado* by Lorenzo Elizaga. During that period, there were several attempts to discredit Freemasonry.

MENPHIS ORGANO DE LABOR MASONICA

V∴ H∴ Lic. Miguel Alemán Valdez
Presidente Constitucional de la República

Que con su labor excelsa ha imbuído en el ánimo de todos los mexicanos el deseo de engrandecimiento de nuestra Patria, practicando el grandioso lema de la Orden Masónica TRABAJO.

NUMERO 6

Junio de 1947.   Precio: $ 0.20.

Miguel Alemán Valdés (1903–1983) was one of the most active presidents in Freemasonry during the 20th century. Here he appears on the cover of *Revista Menphis*, June 1947 edition.

EPILOGUE

FROM EQUINOX TO SOLSTICE

You may conclude from this that the Masonic institution,
subject as it must be to the natural influence of the customs
and tendencies of the times we live in, cannot survive with an
aristocratic and irresponsible directorate.[346]

This epigraph encapsulates two extremely important aspects that merit reflection. The first has to do with Masonry and the historical context in which it has evolved ("the natural influence of the customs and tendencies of the times"), and the second refers to those of the institution's leadership. Regarding the first point, it seems to me very important that we remember that Freemasonry over the centuries developed within many and varied contexts, influenced by the history's events and by varied traditions, which have all contributed to its construction. In like fahion, it has passed through these various epochs redefining, even reinventing, itself. The Freemasonry of early nineteenth-century Mexico is very different from that during the time of the Cárdenas regime or that at the end of the twentieth century. As a consequence, when one thinks of Masonry in Mexico, one should think of a heterogeneous Masonry. Perhaps, as I mentioned in the final portion of the third chapter, one should speak of Masonries—in the plural rather than in the singular. Therefore, in future studies, I will refer to Masonries in the plural sense, and I recommend that scholars of the topic consider the suggestion to do the same.

As far as the Masonic leadership is concerned, the author of the above epigraph was quite worried about Masonry's relationship with politics, and by the situation in which the organization found itself in the nineteenth century. He therefore emphasizes that Masonry "cannot survive with an aristocratic and irresponsible directorate," referring to certain Masonic bodies that were very involved in politics unrelated to the institution's symbolic aspects. In the same way, I feel that he is alluding to irregular lodges and/or the expansion that took place among certain Masonic groups. This situation intensified up until the present century, since there have been conflicts within the Masonic organization regard-

---

346 José María Mateos, *Historia de la masonería en México, op. cit.,* 302.

ing questions of regularity or irregularity of the lodges—in other words, aspects of international recognition.

This reflection, inspired by Mateos's words, can help us to better understand what is discussed in these pages, as well as the crossroads where those of us who study Freemasonry now find ourselves due to the topic's complexities. Despite the difficulty and controversial nature of the task, it is important to propose conclusions, even though they be partial, which I hope will promote further studies of Freemasonry at an academic level. I further hope that this introductory investigation may serve as a basis for more and closer study of the topic.

Arriving at the home stretch of this book, we can conclude that Masonry has played a significant role in Mexican politics from its inception through the 1990s. (This is not to suggest that its role diminished entirely after this period, but rather that the scope of this study concludes in 1994.) The extent of Masonry's involvement varied over time: at certain moments, such as in the early nineteenth century, its presence was particularly pronounced; at others, especially from the second half of the twentieth century, its participation was more discreet. Nevertheless, Masonry's imprint on Mexico's political landscape has remained consistent throughout the country's history.

Importantly, this dynamic was not unidirectional. The evidence shows that political figures and institutions not only engaged with Masonry but also sought to shape, appropriate, or even manipulate it for their own purposes. Some leaders attempted to steer the organization to align with their political agendas. As examples, Díaz leveraged Masonry to reinforce his image as an all-powerful ruler, while Cárdenas sought to nationalize and adapt the organization to fit his broader project of Mexicanization; in other words, he attempted to Mexicanize and nationalize Masonry.

It can be fairly stated that Freemasonry is a transnational ideological-political combination that has enjoyed great success in different parts of the world, even where it has been prohibited. Freemasonry is an institution that has global impact. There are masonic lodges in many countries of the Globe.

Throughout this investigation, I have emphasized the great importance of studying Masonry as a means of gaining better insight into Mexico's history. This book is only an introduction to Freemasonry's history in that country, from the organization's founding up until 1994. The book has probably raised more questions than it has answered; nevertheless, I hope that it has aroused the reader's curiosity to learn more about this fascinating subject. I invite the new generations of students of Freemasonry, and of Mexican history in general, to continue this research.

As we demonstrated in Chapters 1 and 2, there was a great potential within the Masonic ranks that the group's members used either to contribute to an organized political movement or simply to exercise a particular influence in certain areas of society and politics.[347] Such potential was realized at the moment the Masonic lodges became political parties, and later, with the transformation they underwent as they continued to achieve places of power, both within the political sphere and in society in general (each with its own orientation and particular characteristics).[348]

On the other hand, many scholars of Mexican history, in an effort to make sense of a complex political landscape, have tended to portray Freemasonry exclusively as a liberal and anticlerical force. While it is true that the Masonic organization played a key role in Mexico's secularization process and the development of liberal thought, I believe it is essential to approach its history from multiple perspectives—an approach I have tried to employ in this book. Naturally, this work does not exhaust the many possible avenues of study on the subject. For example, it has not addressed the role of women within Mexican Freemasonry, a topic that may prove crucial for understanding alternative social spaces for women beyond the spheres of the Church and formal education.

Furthermore, women's participation in Freemasonry is a phenomenon that distinguishes Latin America from other regions of the hemisphere. In the United States and Canada, women have historically been excluded from regular Masonic lodges; instead, they participate in affiliated organizations known as co-Masonic groups, which require the presence of men for ritual activities. In contrast to that of its northern neighbors, the involvement of women in Mexico's Freemasonry developed independently, as it had within continental Europe.

---

347 Bastian, Jean Pierre, *op.cit.*, 153.

348 At the beginning of the Mexican Republic, Freemasonry served as a political party. Later it became a pressure and influence group. This can be seen in the political campaigns for the presidency of the Republic in 1988 and 1994 wherein the Freemasons were observers of the elections. Other Masonic groups, such as the Liberals of Mexico, have also participated in many civic and political events.

Despite the great degree of power Freemasonry has wielded in certain epochs, it is impossible to say with certainty that it is the cause of all liberal movements and all political practices. There have been occasions over the course of Mexican history when Freemasonry has been presented as much more relevant than it actually was. Masons have had to support the idea that the organization is the great protector of the Republic, the guardians of the Revolution, and/or a continuing source of democratic values.[349] The apologetic discourses initiated as a reaction to the Church's paranoia against Freemasonry, and which were reinforced at the ends of the nineteenth and twentieth centuries, should be read less literally and instead be studied in context. Therefore, the myths and legends that assure that Masonry has been responsible for all the ills that Mexico has suffered, as many critics have averred, should be analyzed fully and framed appropriately.[350]

However, the idea in Mexico and elsewhere that *for one to be president, one must be a Mason* is a product of a discourse of auto-propaganda aimed at attracting initiates.[351] The impact of these discourses on the national imaginary is significant. While it is true that a large number of Mexico's presidents have been Masons, it has been by no means a requirement for one aspiring to the highest post in the land. Neither can it be ruled out that those very same Presidents of the Republic have been compelled to don Masonic aprons "just in case," in their efforts to achieve their goals. It can be added here that, as the public sees it, during the post-revolutionary governments up through that of Miguel de la Madrid, if one wished to have any hope in politics it was considered necessary to be initiated as a Mason. This idea persists in the present day, even though with less impact than it had at the end of the last century.[352]

---

349 See Alan Riding, *Distant Neighbors: A Portrait of the Mexicans*, Vintage/Random House, 1989 [1984], 20-24.

350 Many of the texts against Freemasonry, particularly the inquisitorial processes and those of the 19th century, contain very valuable information about Freemasonry and are sometimes the only primary source available.

351 On a visit to the Masonic mausoleum in honor of George Washington in Alexandria, Virginia, during a tour of the facilities by a lodge guide, passing by one of the rooms where they have photographs of several Mexican presidents (Benito Juárez, Porfirio Díaz, Francisco I. Madero, Miguel Alemán, among others), the guide told us: "In Mexico, all presidents have to be Masons, according to the Mexican Constitution." Obviously, this information is erroneous; however, it is a great example of the strength that these myths and legends have about Freemasonry and politics in Mexico.

352 Since I began my studies of Freemasonry, more than a decade ago, until now, I have

Another aspect that should be mentioned is that success in public relations is very notable among the ranks of the Masons. The organization's presence can be seen at many public events and in issuing opinions on candidates aspiring to public office. Freemasonry has served as a political formation school, in which young persons with hopes of entering government life (especially during the nineteenth and twentieth centuries) could practice for that life and develop their oratory skills, as well as establish personal relationships that might carry them to success, as we saw in Chapter 4.

One example that helps us to see this idea more clearly is an event that took place at the end of the XIV *Conferencia de Supremos Consejos del Mundo* (14th Conference of Supreme Councils of the World), in which all the members of Freemasonry, from every country, unanimously recognized Mexico's heroes—especially the men who fought for Independence, in the War of Reform, and in the Mexican Revolution, as has been discussed throughout this book. With this, national Masonic figures became transnational heroes. This is the case with Benito Juárez and Miguel Alemán, whose busts and portraits are found in many Masonic temples throughout the world. Conversely, in Mexico one may find images and statues of José Martí, Simón Bolívar, George Washington, among others. The universal Masonic fraternity has moved beyond boundaries, creating a transnational Masonic culture that greatly respects Masonic heroes from the world over.

As we have emphasized, Freemasonry was present not only in the years prior to Mexico's independence but even more so in the immediate years immediately surrounding it. In that time, Mexico's Masons took their English, French, and United States American brothers as their models, bringing many of their ideas to Mexico, implementing the liberal thought that contributed to Mexican political life during that time. Such ideas were introduced by Mexicans in exile as well as foreign politicians, or they arrived by way of books brought into Mexico as contraband, as we saw in

collected countless fantastical stories about the association. For example, some of the people I interviewed in Mexico think that Freemasonry practices rituals similar to black magic or that they use tarot. Some will attest that Freemasonry has links with the devil. A former student feared that her son would become involved in a college fraternity out of concern that it had ties to Freemasonry. These perceptions and urban legends have been increasingly developed, in recent years, by publications and films that touch on the subject of Freemasonry.

Chapter 2. It should be noted that Freemasonry's ideas are not the only ones responsible for these movements coming to pass. It should not be overlooked that during that period other institutions, such as a part of the Catholic Church and other para-Masonic societies, had a big impact on the move toward Mexican independence.

One excellent example very much worth underscoring regarding Freemasonry's influence in politics in Mexico could be seen at the time of the election of Mexico's second president, Vicent Guerrero. Guerrero, a York Mason, came to power with the help of another Mason, also of the York Rite, the United States American Joel Poinsett. Along with this episode there are many others, such as Benito Juárez, Porfirio Díaz, Lázaro Cárdenas, among others, whom we have discussed throughout this book and who clearly demonstrate Freemasonry's impact on the political world.

As noted earlier, from the moment a group begins to impact the politics, education or economy of a country, the group may be considered politically influential. Such is the case with Freemasonry, which from the time of its origins in Mexico began to wield a degree of power and to have a great impact over the many years. In the same way, it could be appreciated that Freemasonry, at some historical moments, has become a cadre of the elite, as Gramsci and Pareto point out. Thus, the group has passed through different historical cycles, each of which has had an impact on its cultural and social development. In fact, as noted at the beginning of this book, it was in accordance with Gramsci's idea of these historical cycles that this study of Freemasonry in Mexico was divided into such cycles or stages. I can state that the subject thus divided was easier to research. I hope this division has helped the reader to better understand the historical development of the group and that it has both provided a methodological base for further study and promoted such study. This division has allowed us to observe that the Masonic institution during certain periods had greater political power and participation than it did during others, as well as demonstrating its transformations. It had great power in the nineteenth century (the creation of political parties emanating from Masonry, as an example); it later receded at the beginning of the twentieth (due to the chaos caused by the Mexican Revolution); it underwent a resurgence with the presidencies of Lázaro Cárdenas and Miguel Alemán; and following that its power was again reduced as Miguel de la Madrid came to power, and it continued this trajectory with President Carlos Salinas de Gortari. The reforms to Article 130 of the Mexican Constitution, as explained in Chapter 4 of this book, that President Salinas promoted contributed to Masonry's organizing and reacting against such a significant change to the constitution. For the Masons, this was a step backward to the Laws of the Reform and to the tireless struggle of Juárez and other liberals for the separation of Church and State.

The Masons in Mexico appear far from being any democratic movement, since they are directed autocratically by leaders who are not elected democratically, their proceedings are never publicly discussed, and their membership derives from a portion of the Mexican population that is not representative of the Mexican population as a whole. In addition, they have been closely identified with the PRI, the official political party, and with the office of Mexico's presidency.[353]

I agree with the idea that the Freemasons are present at society's changes; they themselves state that they contribute in the form of their democratic principles of equality, brotherhood, and freedom. Nevertheless, I doubt that the Masons, within the sanctum of their own organization, are as democratic as they boast of being. For example, while they claim it to be a democratic organization, its structure is extremely hierarchical, with lofty titles such as "Grand Master" or "Supreme Grand Commander," which do not fit exactly the democratic mold. Even so, as a group, exerting political pressure, observing elections, and contributing to the public debate, they have a collaborative role in the development of civil society. Despite the hierarchy within its own ranks, its interest in maintaining the separation of Church and State in Mexico, and its eagerness to be a politically influ-

---

353 A danger of discussing Freemasonry is that there are people who see a conspiracy behind every tree, and the mere mention of Freemasonry excites conspiracy-theory lovers. As Roberto Wernick proposes: "The Jesuits are just one in a long line of veiled and vicious organizations that have been controlling the levers of destiny in Conspiracy Theory over the years. They were preceded by the Knights Templar and were followed by the Freemasons, the British Intelligence Service, the 'Elders' of Zion, the Mafia, the Comintern, the Trilateral Commission, the CIA, the Masters of the Lost Continent of Mu (the mythical stronghold of the Pacific of some proto-Polynesian peoples). Some of these are more related to real life than others and have all sorts of real-life conspiracies, big and small, within their merits. They are a very diverse group, but in the livid dream world of the Conspiracy Theory they are all exactly the same. They are huge, faceless, malevolent and ubiquitous, and above all, they are supra-naturally efficient." Robert Wernick, "Don't Look Now—But All Those Conspirators May Be Hiding Under Your Bed,'" *Smithsonian*, Vol. 24 No.12, March 1994, 113.

ential organization have allowed the Masons to contribute, one way or another, to the country's discourse of democratization.[354]

It can also be noted that Freemasonry, as a social-philosophical organization, has a close relationship to society beyond its relationship to politics. The former of these was conceived as a form of conscience and of the development of thought, in which relationships within the community and in the groups or classes that arise within it are reflected.[355] Certain Masonic lodges have historically been closely related to politics due to their origins as political parties, such as the *Yorkinos* and the *Escoceses*, as I discussed in Chapter 2; because of the events in which they have been involved throughout history; because of their social conscience; and, as a famous Mason once said, "because it means the failure of a historical destiny."[356] Freemasonry continues to be a controversial force, active and strong, within Mexico.

Finally, I return to the question posed at the beginning of this book: Did Freemasonry influence the movements toward political and spiritual independence from Spain? Did it influence the War of Reform, the Mexican Revolution, the *Cristero* War? My impression is that it indeed had an impact on these events in Mexico, and that it also gained power, both real and perceived, within society. Thus, it is important that we conclude that it is not the real influence that Freemasonry had, or exactly what historical documents tell us about the political efforts of this institution, or the presidents that can be proven to have been members, that should be mentioned. In my opinion, it is extremely important to consider the work done by the Masons in the promotion of a secular state and, conversely, its impact on the cultural imaginary that it has fueled, from its origins down to our times. Society's perception of Freemasonry should be considered as part of such imagined influence, since this has formed part of this institution's cultural history and, indirectly, that of Mexico.

While my book examines the development and influence of Freemason-

---

354 A topic that should be studied more closely is altruism in the activities of Freemasonry, particularly in the Mexican case. Another interesting topic to explore would be the question of Masonic philosophical precepts and their relationship to democratic ideas.

355 Salvador Gámiz Fernández, "Conferencia en el XIV Congreso Masónico de Morelia," *Supremo Consejo* 1 (Primavera 1994): 27.

356 Ibid.

ry in Mexico through 1994, the period from 1994 through 2025 marks a complex phase in the institution's trajectory—one characterized by diminished public visibility, internal fragmentation, and the challenges posed by a rapidly changing political and cultural landscape, the post-PRI transition era, the rise of neoliberalism, and the democratization process left Freemasonry increasingly disconnected from national political life, unlike in earlier decades when it had been closely tied to elite networks and educational reform. Internally, Mexican Masonry experienced a proliferation of competing obediences and ideological divisions, weakening its cohesion and public voice. Yet during this time, some lodges and leaders sought to reclaim Freemasonry's moral and civic mission, engaging in educational and cultural projects, albeit with limited impact. The institution struggled to resonate with younger generations, particularly in a context marked by religious resurgence, social inequality, and shifting values. Thus, this period reflects a transition from influence to introspection and sets the stage for new questions about the relevance and reinvention of Mexican Freemasonry in the 21st century. These dynamics, along with their implications for civil society and national identity, will be the focus of my next work.

Freemasonry's role in history and in the cultural imaginary is undeniable. The facts demonstrate that this organization has been and continues to be a ritualistic society that participates in public life as a political pressure group and that seeks to leave its mark on the history of the Mexican nation. I hope that today, in this age of technological revolution, some sectors of Masonry will open their doors to researchers and give them access to their historical archives so that the puzzle of its history can be completed with pieces that were not available at the inception of this book. In any case, I hope that these first steps in the study of Freemasonry in Mexico help achieve an approach to a deep analysis of this most singular institution.

BIBLIOGRAPHY

Primary Sources

Archives of the Supreme Council of the Ancient and Accepted Scottish Rite, Southeastern Jurisdiction of the United States of America.

"Impartial Notes for the History of Mexican Freemasonry by an Old Mason Who Has Followed Its Progress Almost Since the Establishment of the Ancient and Accepted Scottish Rite in the Republic." Velazco, A. Supreme Council of the 33rd Degree, Correspondence Between the Temple and Mexican Lodges, 1885.

Archive of the Parafite Union Lodge, available at the Library of the Grand Lodge of California, San Francisco, CA.

Pastoral Letters of Herculano López.

Letter Sent to Mr. Walter C. Temple, Sovereign Grand Inspector General in Texas, Valley of Dallas, from Genaro P. García, fols. 1–2, Archives of the Temple of the Supreme Council, 33rd Degree, Washington, D.C.

Letter Regarding the Origin of the Image of Our Lady of Guadalupe of Mexico, written by Joaquín García Icazbalceta to Archbishop Pelagio Antonio de Labastida y Dávalos, Mexico, 1896.

Porfirio Díaz Collection, available in the Porfirio Díaz Room at the Universidad de las Américas Puebla.

Correspondence with the Grand Orient of France, 1876–1900, Emilio G. Cantón, Secretary General. Archives of the Grand Orient of France, Paris.

Correspondence with Mexico, Supreme Council of the 33rd Degree, Washington, D.C., 1930–1950.

Pennsylvania Historical Society, Collection No. 227 B, Lea & Febiger, Carey Papers, Vol. 1, Folder 279, Catalog Card Under William D. Robinson.

Rangel, Nicolás. *The Ideological Precursors of the War of Independence: Freemasonry in Mexico, 18th Century*, Vol. II. Mexico: Publications of the National Archives, Vol. XXI, *Freemasonry in 18th-Century Mexico*, National Graphic Workshops, Mexico, 1932.

Speech Delivered by Rafael de los Ríos. *The Masonic Institution and the Mexican Revolution,* Grand Lodge of the Valley of Mexico, Mexico City, November 1935.

Fernández de Lizardi, J. *Defense of the Freemasons,* 1822.

_____. *Second Defense of the Freemasons,* 1822.

Mier, Fray Servando Teresa de. *Memoirs of Fray Servando Teresa de Mier,* compiled by Alfonso Reyes. Mexico: National Institute of Historical Studies of the Mexican Revolution, 1985.

National Archives (Archivo General de la Nación). Legal Proceedings, Inquisition Section, Pedro Burdales case.

PERIODICALS AND MASONIC JOURNALS/MAGAZINES

Boletín de la Biblioteca Nacional de México – Articles on historical archives and Freemasonry-related materials

Boletín de la Sociedad Mexicana de Geografía y Estadística – Contributions discussing Mexican historical, geographical, and social developments

El Bibliotecario Mexicano – Early 20th-century articles documenting libraries and archival sources

El Centenario – Periodical reflecting political and social commentary in Mexico

El Economista Mexicano – Economic and social analysis relevant to 19th-century Mexico

El Sol de Puebla – Regional newspaper featuring political and cultural reporting

El Universal – National Mexican newspaper, various articles on political and social issues

El Universal Ilustrado – Illustrated supplement of *El Universal,* focusing on cultural and social life

La Ilustración Española y Americana – Spanish-language illustrated magazine featuring transatlantic cultural topics

La Sombra de Arteaga – Political and cultural publication from Querétaro

Memorias de la Academia Mexicana de la Lengua – Academic publication documenting linguistic and cultural scholarship

Revista de la Biblioteca Nacional – Articles on archival and bibliographic research in Mexico

Revista de Revistas – Illustrated cultural magazine

Revista Mexicana de Cultura – Periodical focused on Mexican arts, literature, and cultural life

Revista Masónica de México – Masonic periodical reporting on lodge activities and Freemasonry in Mexico

Supremo Consejo --- Masonic periodical the activities of the Grand Lodge of Valle de Mexico

The New Age Magazine – Official publication of the Scottish Rite of Freemasonry, Southern Jurisdiction, U.S.A.

The Builder Magazine – American Masonic research publication

The Cabletow – Freemasonry periodical from the Philippines

The Master Mason – Masonic magazine addressing ritual, history, and philosophy

The Philalethes – Journal of Masonic research and education

BOOKS

Ambelain, Robert *El secreto masónico* Mexico City: Ediciones Roca, 1987

Anderson, Benedict *Imagined Communities: Reflections on the Origin and Spread of Nationalism* London; Verso, 1991

Aragón Juárez, Rogelio. "Contra la Iglesia y el Estado: Masonería e Inquisición en Nueva España, 17601820." *REHMLAC+ Revista de Estudios Históricos de la Masonería Latinoamericana y Caribeña plus* 3, no. 1 (May–Nov 2011): 197–202. University of Costa Rica, San José.

Ávila, Alfredo "Las primeras elecciones del México independiente" *Política y Cultura* 11 (1998–99): 29–60

Ayala Ponce, Jaime *Introducción a la francmasonería* Mexico City: Recca, 1983

Banfield, Edward C *Political Influence* Glencoe, IL: Free Press, 1971

Bastian, Jean Pierre, ed *Protestantes liberales y francmasones: Sociedades y modernidad en América Latina, siglo XIX* Mexico City: Fondo de Cultura Económica, 1990

Benjamin, Walter "The Task of the Translator" In *Theories of Translation: An Anthology of Essays from Dryden to Derrida*, edited by Rainer Schulte and John Biguenet, 71–82 Chicago: University of Chicago Press, 1992

Berger, Martín *Historia de la Logia Masónica P-2* Buenos Aires: El Cid Editor, Fundación para la Democracia en Argentina, 1983

Bhabha, Homi, ed *Nation and Narration* New York: Routledge, 1990

———. *The Location of Culture* New York: Routledge, 1994

Bullock, Steven C *Revolutionary Brotherhood: Freemasonry and the Transformation of the American Social Order, 1730–1840* Chapel Hill: University of North Carolina Press, 1996

Bussy, R Kenneth *Two Hundred Years Publishing: A History of the Oldest Publishing Company in the United States, Lea & Febiger 1785–1985* Philadelphia: Lea & Febiger, 1985

Camp, Roderic Ai *Intelectuales y política en México* Oxford: Oxford University Press, 1996

Carnes, Mark C *Secret Ritual and Manhood in Victorian America* New Haven: Yale University Press, 1989

Caro, José María *El misterio de la masonería* Santiago de Chile: Imprenta Chile, 1926

Carreño, Alberto María, prologue and notes *Archivo del General Porfirio Díaz Tomos V–IX–X* Mexico City: Editorial ELEDE, 1951

Clawson, Mary Ann *Constructing Brotherhood: Class, Gender, and Fraternalism* Princeton: Princeton University Press, 1989

Coil, Henry *Coil's Masonic Encyclopedia* Edited by William Mosely Brown et al Richmond, VA: Macoy Publishing & Masonic Supply Company, 1961

De los Reyes, Guillermo, "La rehabilitación del mito en las masonerías mexicana y estadounidense," *Cultura masónica: Revista temática de francmasonería*, Vol. XIV, Issue 49, April 2022: 190-200.

────── ed. *Female Emancipation and Masonic Membership: An Essential Collection*. Library of Freemasonry & Ritualism. Westphalia Press, 2023.

──────. "Freemasonry and Folklore in Mexican Presidentialism" *Journal of American Culture* 21, no 2 (1998): 61–74

──────. "The Cross and the Compass: The Influence of the Catholic Religion and Masonry in the Formation of the Mexican Political Thought" In *Recovering Hispanic Religious Thought and Practice of the United States*, edited by Nicolás Kanellos, 8–24 Cambridge: Cambridge Scholars Publishing, 2007

──────. "Translating, Smuggling, and Recovering Books in Nineteenth-Century Mexico: Thomas Smith Webb's *El monitor de los masones libres: ó, ilustraciones sobre la masonería*" In *The Critical Importance of Region: Recovering the U S Hispanic Literary Heritage Project Vol VI*, edited by Antonia Castañeda and Gabriel Meléndez, 143–58 Houston: Arte Público Press, 2006

De los Reyes, Guillermo and Paul Rich "Freemasonry's Educational Role" *American Behavioral Scientist* 40 (June/July 1997): 957–67

──────. "Policy Making and the Control of the Nongovernmental Sector: Porfirio Díaz and the Grand Diet" *Review of Policy Research* 22, no 5 (September 2005): 721–25

Domínguez Michael, Christopher *Vida de Fray Servando* Mexico City: Ediciones Era, 2004

──────. "Fray Servando y los francmasones en Cádiz" *Letras Libres* (March 2005)

Espinar de la Fuente, Francisco *Esquema filosófico de la masonería* Madrid, 1981

Estep, Raymundo *Lorenzo de Zavala (Profeta del liberalismo mexicano)*

Mexico City: s.e., 1971

Fels, Anthony D "The Square and Compass: San Francisco's Freemasons and American Religion, 1870–1900" PhD diss., Stanford University, 1985

Fernández, Alonso *La francmasonería en la independencia hispanoamericana* Ediciones América Una, 1988

Ferrer Benimeli, José A *La masonería española en el siglo XVIII* Madrid: Siglo XXI de España Editores, 1974

————. *Los archivos secretos vaticanos y la masonería* Caracas: Universidad Católica Andrés Bello, 1976

————. *Masonería española contemporánea, Vol I, 1800–1868* Madrid: Siglo XXI de España Editores, 1980

————, coord *Masonería, política y sociedad: III Simposium de metodología aplicada a la historia de la masonería española* Zaragoza: Centro de Estudios Históricos de la Masonería Española, 1987

————, coord *Masonería española y América* Zaragoza: Centro de Estudios Históricos de la Masonería Española, 1993

————. *Masonería e Inquisición de Latinoamérica durante el siglo XVIII* Caracas: Universidad Católica Andrés Bello, 1973

Flores Zavala, Marco Antonio *El grupo masón en la política zacatecana, 1880–1914* Zacatecas: Asociación de Investigaciones Filosóficas "Francisco García Salinas", 2002

————. "La masonería en la República Federal: Apuntes sobre las logias mexicanas (1821–1840)" In *Raíces del federalismo mexicano*, edited by Manuel Miño Grijalva et al, 125–36 Zacatecas: Universidad Autónoma de Zacatecas, Secretaría de Educación y Cultura del Estado de Zacatecas, 2005

————. "Los ciclos de la masonería mexicana. Siglos XVIII–XIX" In *La masonería en Madrid y en España del siglo XVII al XXI*, coordinated by José Ferrer Benimeli, vol 1, 489–501 Zaragoza: Gobierno de Aragón, 2004

Foucault, Michel *The Archaeology of Knowledge and the Discourse of Lan-*

guage Translated by A M Sheridan Smith New York: Pantheon Books, 1972

Franco B, Francisco *Masonería* Madrid: Fundación Nacional Francisco Franco, 1982

Fuentes, José *Poinsett: Historia de una intriga* Mexico City: Editorial Jus, 1951

García Robles, Marco Antonio. *Arte, prensa y poder: Masones y masonerías en Aguascalientes, siglo XIX.* Mexico City: Palabra de Clío, 2022. 393 pp.

Gómez, Francisco *Intelectuales y pueblo* San José, Costa Rica: Editorial DEI, 1987

González y González, Luis *La ronda de las generaciones* Mexico City: Clío, 1997

González Stephan, Beatriz *La historiografía literaria del liberalismo hispanoamericano del siglo XIX* Havana: Casa de las Américas, 1987

Gould, Robert *History of Freemasonry, Vol 1* New York: Charles Scribners' Sons, 1936

Gramsci, Antonio *Antología* Edited and translated by Manuel Sacristán Mexico City: Siglo XXI, 1988

———. *Letters from Prison* Edited by Frank Rosengarten, translated by Raymond Rosenthal New York: Columbia University Press, 1994

———. *Prison Notebooks* Edited and translated by Quintin Hoare and Geoffrey Nowell Smith New York: Columbia University Press, 1992

Green, James *Mathew Carey: Publisher and Patriot* Philadelphia: Library Company of Philadelphia, 1985

Guedea, Virginia "Las sociedades secretas durante el movimiento de independencia" In *The Independence of Mexico and the Creation of the New Nation*, edited by Jaime Rodríguez Los Angeles: UCLA Latin American Center Publications, 1989

Hart, John M *Revolutionary Mexico: The Coming and Process of the Mexican Revolution* Berkeley: University of California Press, 1989 [1987]

Hobsbawm, Eric *Nations and Nationalism since 1780: Programme, Myth,*

Reality Cambridge: Cambridge University Press, 1990

Home, Alex *Sources of Masonic Symbolism* Richmond, VA: Macoy Publishing & Masonic Supply, 1981

Jacob, Margaret *The Radical Enlightenment: Pantheists, Freemasons and Republicans* Lafayette: Cornerstone, 1981

———. *Living the Enlightenment: Freemasonry and Politics in Eighteenth-Century Europe* Oxford: Oxford University Press, 1991

———. *The Origins of Freemasonry: Facts and Fiction* Philadelphia: University of Pennsylvania Press, 2006

Jacob, Margaret C., and María Eugenia Vázquez Semadeni. *Freemasonry and Civil Society: Europe and the Americas (North and South)*. New York: Peter Lang, 2023. 154 pp

Jakobson, Roman "On Linguistic Aspects of Translation" In *Theories of Translation: An Anthology of Essays from Dryden to Derrida*, edited by Rainer Schulte and John Biguenet, 144–51 Chicago: University of Chicago Press, 1992

Kanellos, Nicolás "The Hispanic Exile Press in the United States" *Indiana Journal of Hispanic Literatures* 12 (Spring 1998): 59–84

———. "La expresión cultural de los inmigrantes mexicanos en los Estados Unidos desde el Porfiriato hasta la Depresión" Unpublished manuscript

Knight, Alan *The Mexican Revolution Vol I–II* Lincoln: University of Nebraska Press, 1990

Kürti, László "People vs The State: Political Rituals in Contemporary Hungary" *Anthropology Today* 6, no 2 (April 1990)

La Masonería es... Monografía publicada por la Coordinación de Estudios Especiales de la Gran Logia del Valle de México Mexico City, 1990

Laurens B, Perry *Juárez y Díaz: Continuidad y ruptura en la política mexicana* Mexico City: Ediciones Era, 1996

Leyland, Hebert T *Thomas Smith Webb: Freemason, Musician, Entrepreneur* Daytona: The Otterbein Press, 1965

Linker, Susan "A Collision of Rationalism and Spiritualism in *El hombre de la rosa* of Manuel Rojas: Decoding the Secret Signals" *Hispanic Review* 68 (2000): 21–36

López, Mario Justo *Introducción a los estudios políticos Vol 1* Buenos Aires: Ediciones de Palma, 1983

Mackey, R W *El simbolismo francmasónico* Mexico City: Diana, 1981

Martínez, Ramón *La masonería en Hispanoamérica* Mexico City: B Costa-AMIC, 1965

Martínez Esquivel, Ricardo, coord. *Historia mínima de la masonería en México*. Zacatecas: Texere Editores, 2021. 331 pp.

Mateos, José María *Historia de la masonería en México de 1806 a 1884* Mexico City: La Tolerancia, 1884

Meyer, Michael C and William L Sherman *The Course of Mexican History* Oxford: Oxford University Press, 1991

Monsiváis, Carlos *Herencias ocultas de la Reforma liberal del siglo XIX* Mexico City: Random House Mandadori, 2006

Navarrete, Félix *Masonería en la historia y en las leyes de Méjico* Mexico City: Editorial Jus, 1957

Nossack, Hans Erich "Translating and Being Translated" In *Theories of Translation: An Anthology of Essays from Dryden to Derrida*, edited by Rainer Schulte and John Biguenet, 228–34 Chicago: University of Chicago Press, 1992

Padilla, Remberto *Historia de la política mexicana* Mexico City: EDA-MEX, 1993

Palou, Joan *La franc-masonería* Buenos Aires: Dedalo, 1979

Pareto, Vilfredo *The Rise and the Fall of Elites* New Brunswick, NJ: Transaction Publishers, 1991

Paz, Octavio *El laberinto de la soledad* Mexico City: Fondo de Cultura Económica, 1985

Preston, William *Illustrations of Masonry* Facsimile of the 1775 second edition with a preface by Walter M Callaway Jr Bloomington: Masonic

Book Club, 1973

Rich, Paul *Elixir of Empire* London: Regency Press, 1993

———. *Chains of Empire* London and New York: Regency Press, 1991

———. "Researching Grandfather's Secrets" *Journal of American Culture* 20, no 2 (Summer 1997): 139–46

———. "Kim and the Magic House: Freemasonry and Kipling" In *Secret Texts: The Literature of Secret Societies*, edited by Marie M Roberts and Hugh Ormsby-Lennon, 322–38 New York: AMS Press, 1995

Rich, Paul and Guillermo De los Reyes "Ritual in the Service of the State" *Papers in International Studies*, Hoover Institution—Stanford University, I-98

———. "Reappraising Scottish Rite Freemasonry in Latin America" *Heredom* 4 (1995)

Rich, Paul, Guillermo De los Reyes, and Antonio Lara "Smuggling Masonic Books to Mexico" In *Freemasonry in Context: History, Ritual and Controversy*, 249–53 New York: Lexington Books, 2003

Rich, Paul and Antonio Lara "The Mystery of Matthew Carey: Continuing Adventures in Masonic Bibliography" In *Freemasonry in Context: History, Ritual and Controversy*, 255–58 New York: Lexington Books, 2003

Rius, *Cada quien su Dios (Mormones, Opus Dei, Masones)* Mexico City: Editorial Posada, 1992

Roberts, Allen E *Freemasonry in American History* Richmond: Macoy, 1985

Roberts, Marfie Mulvey "Masonic, Metaphor and Misogyny: A Discourse of Marginality?" In *Languages and Jargons: Contributions to a Social History of Language* Cambridge: Polity Press, 1995

Roel, Santiago, ed *Memorias de Fray Servando. Escritas por él mismo en las cárceles de la Inquisición de la ciudad de México, el año de 1819* Monterrey: Impresora Monterrey, 1946

Stevenson, David *The Origins of Freemasonry: Scotland's Century 1590–1710* Cambridge: Cambridge University Press, 1988

Stitt, Susan, ed *Guide to the Manuscript Collections of the Historical Society of Pennsylvania* Philadelphia: Historical Society of Pennsylvania, 1991

Solis Vicarte, Ruth *Las sociedades secretas en el primer gobierno republicano (1824–1828)* Mexico City: ASBE, 1997

Thompson, John B "Symbolic Violence: Language and Power in the Writings of Pierre Bourdieu" *Studies in the Theory of Ideology* New York: Polity Press, 1985 [1984]

Torres Puga, Gabriel "Centinela mexicano contra francmasones. Un enredo detectivesco del licenciado Borunda en las causas criminales contra franceses de 1794" *Estudios de Historia Moderna y Contemporánea* 33 (2005): 57–94

Trueba Lara, José Luis *Masones en México: Historia del poder oculto* Mexico City: Grijalbo, 2007

Turner, Victor *The Ritual Process: Structure and Anti-Structure* New Brunswick, NJ: Aldine Transaction, 1995 [1969]

———. *From Ritual to Theatre: The Human Seriousness of Play* New York: PAJ Publications, 1982

———. *Liminality, Kabbalah, and the Media* New York: Academic Press, 1985

Umbert, Luis *Alma masónica* Mexico City: Editorial Pax, 1990

———. *Cartilla del francmasón* Mexico City: Editorial Pax, 1990

———. *Cincuenta lecciones de cultura masónica* Mexico City: Editorial Pax, 1985

Vázquez Leos, Jesús E *Liberalismo y masonería en San Luis Potosí* Mexico City: s.e., 1996

Vázquez Mantecón, María del Carmen *La palabra del poder: Vida pública de José María Tornel (1795–1853)* Mexico City: UNAM/IIH, 1997

Vázquez Semadeni, María Eugenia. *La formación de una cultura política republicana: El debate público sobre la masonería, México, 18211830.* Serie *Historia Moderna y Contemporánea,* núm. 54. Mexico City: Universidad Nacional Autónoma de México / El Colegio de Michoacán, 2010.

————. "La interacción entre el debate público sobre la masonería y la cultura política, 1761–1830" PhD diss., El Colegio de Michoacán, 2008

————. "La masonería mexicana en el debate público, 1808–1830" In *La masonería española en la época de Sagasta*, coordinated by José Antonio Ferrer Benimeli, vol 2, 861–82 Zaragoza: Gobierno de Aragón/ CEHME, 2007

Venuti, Lawrence *The Translator's Invisibility: A History of Translation* New York: Routledge, 1995

Verdery, Katherine *The Political Life of Dead Bodies: Reburial and Postsocialist Change* New York: Columbia University Press, 1997

Walgren, Kent "A Bibliography of Pre-1851 American Scottish Rite Imprints (non-Louisiana)" *Heredom* 3 (1994): 55–120

————. "A Bibliography of Pre-Louisiana Scottish Rite Imprints" *Heredom* 4 (1995): 189–206

Webb, Thomas Smith *The Freemason's Monitor; or, Illustrations of Masonry* Albany: Fry and Southwick for Spencer and Webb, 1797

————. *The Freemason's Monitor; or, Illustrations of Masonry: In Two Parts* New York: Southwick and Crooker, 1802

————. *The Freemason's Monitor; or, Illustrations of Masonry: In Two Parts* Salem: Cushing and Appleton, 1821

————. *El monitor de los masones libres: ó ilustraciones sobre la masonería* Philadelphia: H C Carey & I Lea, 1822

————. *Monitor ó guía de los franc-mazones* New York: Joseph Desnoues, 1822

Zahar Vergara, Juana *Historia de las librerías de la Ciudad de México* Mexico City: Plaza y Valdés, 1995

Zalce, Luis J *Apuntes para la historia de la masonería en México, Vol 1–2* Mexico City, 1950

Zavala, Iris M *Masones, comuneros y carbonarios* Madrid: Siglo XXI de España Editores, 1971

Dr. Guillermo de los Reyes Heredia is Associate Professor and Chair of the Department of Hispanic Studies at the University of Houston. His research focuses on Freemasonry in Mexico and the United States and Colonial Latin American discourse with particular attention to the intersections of gender, sexuality, race, and class in the cultural and legal texts of the colonial period. He is the author of *Herencias Secretas: Masonería y Sociedad en México* (BUAP, México, 2009). He has edited several important works such as, *Female Emancipation and Masonic Membership: An Essential Collection* (Westphalia Press 2023) and *L'Enfant and the Freemasons: H. Paul Caemmer's The Life of Pierre Charles L'Enfant* (Westphalia Press, 2023) and *President John Quincy Adams's Quarrel With The Freemasons: John Quincy Adams's Letters And Opinions Of The Masonic Institution* (Westphalia Press, 2023). Additionally, Dr. De Los Reyes has authored over two dozen journal articles and book chapters on topics including gender, sexuality, Freemasonry, secret societies, and related subjects. He is the Editor in Chief of *Sexuality, Gender & Policy* (Wiley) and Fellow of the American Folklore Society.

Bradley L. Drew began his studies of the Spanish language as a high-school student 50 years ago, ultimately earning a master's degree in the language from the then-Department of Modern and Classical Languages at the University of Houston. His translations include Rodolfo Usigli's novel *Ensayo de un crimen/Rehearsal for a Crime*, and Leticia Álvarez-Recio's scholarly work *Rameras de Babilonia/Fighting the Antichrist*, as well as numerous collaborations with De Los Reyes and others that extend back to 2007. Brad and his wife travel the world and reside in Houston.

Related Titles from Westphalia Press

Ancient Mysteries and Modern Masonry: The Collected Writings of Jewel P. Lightfoot, Edited by Billy J. Hamilton Jr.

Jewel P. Lightfoot. Former Attorney General of the State of Texas. Past Grand Master of the Masonic Grand Lodge of Texas. From humble beginnings in rural Arkansas, he worked to become an educated man who excelled in law and Freemasonry. He was a gentleman of his time, well-known as a scholar, public speaker, and Masonic philosopher.

Essay on The Mysteries and the True Object of The Brotherhood of Freemasons
by Jason Williams

This isn't a reprint of a classic. It's a new rendition with new life breathed into it, to be enjoyed both by the layperson trying to understand the Craft and Masonic scholars taking a deeper dive into the fraternity's golden years—when the concepts of liberty and equality were still fresh.

Female Emancipation and Masonic Membership:
An Essential Collection
By Guillermo De Los Reyes Heredia

Female Emancipation and Masonic Membership: An Essential Combination is a collection of essays on Freemasonry and gender that promotes a transatlantic discussion of the study of the history of women and Freemasonry and their contribution in different countries.

Freemasonry, Heir to the Enlightenment
by Cécile Révauger

Modern Freemasonry may have mythical roots in Solomon's time but is really the heir to the Enlightenment. Ever since the early eighteenth century freemasons have endeavored to convey the values of the Enlightenment in the cultural, political and religious fields, in Europe, the American colonies and the emerging United States.

Freemasonry: A French View
by Roger Dachez and Alain Bauer

Perhaps one should speak not of Freemasonry but of Freemasonries in the plural. In each country Masonic historiography has developed uniqueness. Two of the best known French Masonic scholars present their own view of the worldwide evolution and challenging mysteries of the fraternity over the centuries.

Worlds of Print: The Moral Imagination of an Informed Citizenry, 1734 to 1839
by John Slifko

John Slifko argues that freemasonry was representative and played an important role in a larger cultural transformation of literacy and helped articulate the moral imagination of an informed democratic citizenry via fast emerging worlds of print.

Why Thirty-Three?: Searching for Masonic Origins
by S. Brent Morris, PhD

What "high degrees" were in the United States before 1830? What were the activities of the Order of the Royal Secret, the precursor of the Scottish Rite? A complex organization with a lengthy pedigree like Freemasonry has many basic foundational questions waiting to be answered, and that's what this book does: answers questions.

The Great Transformation: Scottish Freemasonry 1725-1810
by Dr. Mark C. Wallace

This book examines Scottish Freemasonry in its wider British and European contexts between the years 1725 and 1810. The Enlightenment effectively crafted the modern mason and propelled Freemasonry into a new era marked by growing membership and the creation of the Grand Lodge of Scotland.

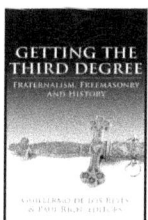

Getting the Third Degree: Fraternalism, Freemasonry and History
Edited by Guillermo De Los Reyes and Paul Rich

As this engaging collection demonstrates, the doors being opened on the subject range from art history to political science to anthropology, as well as gender studies, sociology and more. The organizations discussed may insist on secrecy, but the research into them belies that.

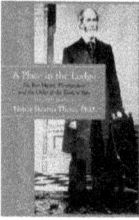

A Place in the Lodge: Dr. Rob Morris, Freemasonry and the Order of the Eastern Star
by Nancy Stearns Theiss, PhD

Ridiculed as "petticoat masonry," critics of the Order of the Eastern Star did not deter Rob Morris' goal to establish a Masonic organization that included women as members. Morris carried the ideals of Freemasonry through a despairing time of American history.

Brought to Light: The Mysterious George Washington Masonic Cave
by Jason Williams MD

The George Washington Masonic Cave near Charles Town, West Virginia, contains a signature carving of George Washington dated 1748. This book painstakingly pieces together the chronicled events and real estate archives related to the cavern in order to sort out fact from fiction.

Dudley Wright: Writer, Truthseeker & Freemason
by John Belton

Dudley Wright (1868-1950) was an Englishman and professional journalist who took a universalist approach to the various great Truths of Life. He travelled though many religions in his life and wrote about them all, but was probably most at home with Islam.

History of the Grand Orient of Italy
Emanuela Locci, Editor

No book in Masonic literature upon the history of Italian Freemasonry has been edited in English up to now. This work consists of eight studies, covering a span from the Eighteenth Century to the end of the WWII, tracing through the story, the events and pursuits related to the Grand Orient of Italy.

westphaliapress.org

Policy Studies Organization

The Policy Studies Organization (PSO) is a publisher of academic journals and book series, sponsor of conferences, and producer of programs.

Policy Studies Organization publishes dozens of journals on a range of topics, such as European Policy Analysis, Journal of Elder Studies, Indian Politics & Polity, Journal of Critical Infrastructure Policy, and Popular Culture Review.

Additionally, Policy Studies Organization hosts numerous conferences. These conferences include the Middle East Dialogue, Space Education and Strategic Applications Conference, International Criminology Conference, Dupont Summit on Science, Technology and Environmental Policy, World Conference on Fraternalism, Freemasonry and History, and the Internet Policy & Politics Conference.

For more information on these projects, access videos of past events, and upcoming events, please visit us at:

www.ipsonet.org

www.ingramcontent.com/pod-product-compliance
Lightning Source LLC
Chambersburg PA
CBHW070803280326
41934CB00012B/3029